Framed

COMMUNICATION
STRATEGY
AND POLITICS

Media and the Coverage of Race in Canadian Politics
THIERRY GIASSON AND ALEX MARLAND, SERIES EDITORS

Communication, Strategy, and Politics is a groundbreaking series from UBC Press that examines elite decision making and political communication in today's hyper-mediated and highly competitive environment. Publications in this series look at the intricate relations between marketing strategy, the media, and political actors and explain how this affects Canadian democracy. They also investigate such interconnected themes as strategic communication, mediatization, opinion research, electioneering, political management, public policy, and e-politics in a Canadian context and in comparison to other countries. Designed as a coherent and consolidated space for diffusion of research about Canadian political communication, the series promotes an interdisciplinary, multi-method, and theoretically pluralistic approach.

Other books in the series are:

Political Marketing in Canada, edited by Alex Marland, Thierry Giasson, and Jennifer Lees-Marshment
Political Communication in Canada, edited by Alex Marland, Thierry Giasson, and Tamara A. Small

Framed

Media and the Coverage of Race in Canadian Politics

...... Erin Tolley

UBCPress · Vancouver · Toronto

25 24 23 22 21 20 19 18 17 16   5 4 3 2 1

Printed in Canada on FSC-certified ancient-forest-free paper
(100% post-consumer recycled) that is processed chlorine- and acid-free.

Library and Archives Canada Cataloguing in Publication

Tolley, Erin, author
    Framed : media and the coverage of race in Canadian politics / Erin Tolley.

(Communication, strategy, and politics)
Includes bibliographical references and index.
Issued in print and electronic formats.
ISBN 978-0-7748-3123-9 (bound). – ISBN 978-0-7748-3125-3 (pdf). –
ISBN 978-0-7748-3126-0 (epub)

    1. Minorities in mass media – Canada. 2. Minorities – Press coverage – Canada. 3. Mass media – Political aspects – Canada. 4. Race – Political aspects – Canada. 5. Canada – Politics and government – Press coverage. I. Title. II. Series: Communication, strategy, and politics

P94.5.M552C3 2016	302.2308	C2015-905252-1
		C2015-905253-X

Canada

UBC Press gratefully acknowledges the financial support for our publishing program of the Government of Canada (through the Canada Book Fund), the Canada Council for the Arts, and the British Columbia Arts Council.

This book has been published with the help of a grant from the Canadian Federation for the Humanities and Social Sciences, through the Awards to Scholarly Publications Program, using funds provided by the Social Sciences and Humanities Research Council of Canada.

UBC Press
The University of British Columbia
2029 West Mall
Vancouver, BC V6T 1Z2
www.ubcpress.ca

Contents

Tables and Figures

Acknowledgments

Writing is often a solitary task, but had I been left entirely to my own devices, this book would not have seen the light of day. Elizabeth Goodyear-Grant and Keith Banting have been there from when this was just a kernel of an idea. Keith's skepticism and tough but fair questioning forced me to hone my arguments and improve on conceptual weaknesses. Elizabeth's commitment to rigorous research gave me an amazing example to emulate, while her confidence in my work propelled me forward. She is both a mentor and a friend.

We sometimes forget that political science is about people, not just about data, processes, and institutions. I am thankful to the parliamentarians, candidates, staffers, and journalists who agreed to be interviewed for this project. Their stories give life to this research and allow us a glimpse into the lives of those who navigate this minefield every day.

A number of scholars have given freely of their wisdom and experience. I'm especially indebted to Scott Matthews, who provided advice in the early stages of the project and suggested a number of ways to improve on the research design. My internal examiners, Jonathan Rose, Margaret Little, and Fiona Kay, were keen and insightful. Linda Trimble, the external examiner, is the author of much of the literature on gendered mediation that served as a springboard for my own research, and she has been generous with her analysis and ideas. Marc-André Bodet shared his data on riding competitiveness with me, and this was used to measure candidate viability in Chapter 4. Farnaz Behrooz, Laura Carlson, and Cory Leblanc undertook the coding for the media study in Chapter 2, while Adelina Petit-Vouriot provided research assistance with Chapter 5.

UBC Press's two anonymous reviewers and the series editors, Thierry Giasson and Alex Marland, provided a careful reading of the manuscript and offered a number of excellent suggestions for improving it. Shannon

Sampert – a political scientist and working journalist – read through the entire manuscript and responded with enthusiasm, as did journalist and writer Michael Valpy. Daniel Lessard, an erstwhile CBC journalist turned novelist, generously shared his time, wisdom, and contacts with me. He reminded me that writing – even the academic kind – should be interesting, although I was unable to inject the narrative arc (namely a sex scene or violence) that he suggested to spice up my discussion of research methods.

My colleagues at the University of Toronto pushed me in all the right directions. I have been blessed to land at an institution that is fiercely supportive of its researchers and willing to provide the means necessary to produce excellent scholarship. Ed Schatz and Graham White have been especially helpful, and I am grateful for their advice and encouragement. The seeds for this research were first planted when I was a policy researcher in the federal government, and I was fortuitously placed in a cubicle next to John Biles, with whom I co-authored my first academic publication. My cohort at Queen's University graciously overlooked my penchant for business casual and helped me reintegrate into academic life. They and a number of others have kept things interesting, whether in the corridor, at the cocktail party, over cards, or via cat photos; thanks in particular to Amanda Clarke, Jonathan Craft, Rémi Leger, J.P. Lewis, Edward Koning, Shauna Labman, Emmett Macfarlane, Laura Madokoro, Mary-Lee Mulholland, Sara Pavan, Lucia Salazar, Beesan Sarrouh, and Melanee Thomas. A special shout-out to Megan Gaucher, with whom I share several research interests, but most importantly an appreciation for pints and reality TV.

From the first time that I discussed this project with Emily Andrew at UBC Press, she has been onside. She couples keen instincts with a ready laugh and has an uncanny ability to make you feel like yours is the most important project on the planet. Working with her is a joy. The production and promotion teams at UBC Press – especially Megan Brand, Laraine Coates, and Kerry Kilmartin – have been efficient and supportive, while Sarah Wight successfully removed nearly all traces of my bad writing habits from the manuscript.

My parents, Daryl and Lorna, cultivated my interest in reading and writing and fostered a general curiosity about the world around us. Their insistence on the importance of education is probably the reason that I have spent nearly three-quarters of my life in a classroom. My siblings, Jay, Lisa, and Cara, taught me how to argue and now, as adults, remind me to keep it real. My (crazy Acadian) in-laws have contributed a bottomless reserve of optimism and encouragement of which I have been the happy beneficiary. My friends in Ottawa, Toronto, Saskatchewan, and beyond have offered needed respite and strengthened my work by asking questions that forced me to consider what my research means to people outside the insular world of academia. Special thanks to all the kind souls who carefully proofread the pages that follow.

Midway through my research for this book, my son, Raphael, was born; his babbling can be heard in the background of some of my research interviews, and very early on he seemed to instinctively know that he needed to sleep through the night so that I could continue to plow forward. Two years later, Seraphine arrived, waiting patiently to make her appearance until the day after I had submitted the draft of this manuscript for review. These two little people have taught me so much about balance, perspective, and patience, and they remind me every day that the world is full of wonder if you just take a moment to look around.

Above all, my thanks go to René, who took the gendered division of labour and turned it on its head. While I have read, written, and researched, my husband has cooked, cared for our children, and just generally kept the joint running. He has proofread these pages, clipped out relevant news articles, and offered a sounding board whenever I've been stuck. He has smiled, sacrificed, and supported my dreams as though they were his own, and I'm not sure he will ever fully realize just what a gift that is.

Framed . . . .

Introduction

> "Race is there, and it is a constant. You're tired of hearing about it? Imagine how f---ing exhausting it is living it."
>
> – Jon Stewart, *The Daily Show*

In the summer of 2014, a white police officer in the city of Ferguson, Missouri, shot and killed an unarmed black teenager named Michael Brown. The incident set off a series of protests and brought into stark relief long-standing racial tensions in the United States. Although early news stories ran a photo of Brown in a cap and gown at his graduation ceremony, a number of outlets later switched to an image of the teenager in a basketball jersey making what some thought was a gang-related gesture. Americans took to Twitter using the hashtag #IfTheyGunnedMeDown to ask whether in a similar situation the media would depict them as thugs and criminals or as parents, military personnel, and college graduates. Although some Canadians watched the news from Ferguson in solidarity, many overlooked that this country also has a complicated history with racial diversity. Writing for *Maclean's* about attitudes towards Aboriginal peoples, Scott Gilmore (2015) notes that Canada does have a race problem that, while we do not admit it, is much worse than the situation in the United States. He places the blame squarely on Canadians "for not paying attention. For believing our own hype about inclusion. For looking down our noses at America and ignorantly thinking, 'That would never happen here.' For not acknowledging Canada has a race problem."

Yes, we celebrate multicultural festivals, the fusion of "Canadian" and "ethnic" cuisine, and the success of recording artists like Drake and K'naan. Nonetheless, Canadians with racial minority backgrounds earn 81.4 cents for every dollar earned by a white Canadian (Block and Galabuzi 2011), and a 2014 list of Canada's ten greatest heroes, determined through a poll of twelve thousand Canadians, included just one person of colour: David Suzuki (Beeby 2014). Not even our canine friends are immune, with an episode of CBC's *The Current* suggesting that black dogs are much less likely to be adopted from shelters than their lighter-hued counterparts. And until recently, an Alberta fertility clinic prohibited clients from selecting a sperm donor with a racial background different from their own because, in the words of the clinic's executive director, these "rainbow families" would deny children a "cultural connection" with their parents (Barrett 2014).

Lawrence Hill, a Canadian author whose father was black and mother was white, "dissects the interrogation process" that individuals with apparently non-white backgrounds often face:

> Imagine me at a party, sipping mineral water. A stranger walks up.
>
> *Stranger:* "Do you mind me asking where you're from?" [This is code for "What is your race?"]
>
> *Me:* "Canada." [This is code for "Screw off."]
>
> *Stranger:* "Yes, but you know, where are you really from?" [This is code for "You know what I mean, so why are trying to make me come out and say it?"]
>
> *Me:* "I come from the foreign and distant metropolis of Newmarket. That's Newmarket, Ontario, my place of birth." [Code for "I'm not letting you off the hook, buster."]
>
> *Stranger:* "But your place of origin? Your parents? What are your parents?" [Code for, "I want to know your race, but this is making me feel very uncomfortable because somehow I'm not supposed to ask that question."] (quoted in Khoo 2007)

As Hill points out, Canadians do not openly discuss race, but they nonetheless continue to see it. Race, race-based difference, and racial prejudice persist, often in pernicious and subtle ways, but are there all the same. If one message emerges in the pages that follow, it is that race still matters.

Thinking Racially

Those who study racial prejudice argue that its structure and form have changed over time. Today's racism has been characterized as "discrimination without prejudice" in that it is based on racially grounded assumptions about what is normal or acceptable rather than on systematic, institutionalized propaganda aimed at shaping citizens' behaviour and views of one race as superior to others (Fleras 2011, 134). This racism tends to manifest itself simultaneously as the *tolerance* of racial minorities – not their acceptance or inclusion – in concert with a denial of the continued significance of race (Perigoe and Eid 2014). This form of racial prejudice has been variously called "everyday racism," "incognizant racism," and "modern racism." These terms are more or less synonymous, but I have opted to use "modern racism."

Theories of modern racism suggest that citizens, institutions, and organizational cultures are conditioned by racial views, norms, and beliefs that are so deeply entrenched as to be invisible, implicit, and encoded (Campbell 1995; Citrin, Green, and Sears 1990; Fleras 2011; Fleras and Kunz 2001; Henry and Tator 2002). To understand modern racism, it is useful to consider the distinction between *acting racistly* and *thinking racially*. Traditionally, people have considered blatantly prejudicial acts as evidence of racism. As societies have grown attuned to the idea that racism is wrong, however, these sorts of blatant acts have declined or at least become less evident, with citizens much less likely to act overtly on racist impulses. This does not mean that people do not notice or think about race, but merely that they rarely behave in openly racist ways.

The persistence of racial thinking is the cornerstone of modern racism. Those with racially prejudiced beliefs may not act overtly on these beliefs but may still harbour an antipathy towards minorities or avoid those whom they deem to be culturally different (Fleras and Kunz 2001). Modern racism is not the ethnic slurs and racist jokes of the past, but is instead manifest in subtle actions, such as a reluctance to hire an employee with a "foreign" accent, discomfort sitting next to a black man on a bus, or a belief that Asian Canadians are naturally hard workers. Modern racists tend not to recognize systemic biases, but instead prefer explanations that centre on the individual (Fleras 2012; Son Hing 2013). The discourse around "hard work" instead of "handouts" is illustrative of this tendency because it indicts individuals who live in poverty rather than probing the institutional and societal factors that may have contributed to this condition. The blame is laid at the feet of purportedly lazy welfare recipients, while all but ignoring the impact of mental illness, economic conditions, disability, race, and gender. Modern racism is subtle, not always clearly or specifically articulated in racial terms, and often so ingrained in institutional practices and discourses as to be virtually imperceptible, and even appear as common sense.

Many resist the idea that societies continue to harbour racist sentiments, perhaps because this is not consistent with practices and policies that have been adopted to address inequalities. Even the word itself – "racism" – engenders defensiveness. These skeptics point to the Charter of Rights and Freedoms, Canada's reputation as a peaceful, multicultural country, and our history of immigration. That Canada has an official story of inclusion and is committed to democracy, quality, and fairness does not mean that its citizens do not also have negative feelings about racial diversity or engage in racial thinking (Henry and Tator 2002). Indeed, Canada's pride in its multiculturalism and racial tolerance actually obscures the extent and influence of racial thinking. As Entman and Rojecki (2000, 1) put it, "The public face of race is now cloaked in a chameleon-like form, an ever-changing camouflage that obscures its force."

In this book, I draw a distinction between racism – blatant and overt acts premised on a feeling of racial superiority – and the more implicit and often unconscious acts of racialization and race differentiation. Some will disagree with this distinction, arguing that the explicit and implicit acts both constitute racism. Certainly their effects are often the same, whether intended or not. However, because the research compiled for this study does not allow me to impute motive, I set intent aside. I look instead at how racialization is embedded and articulated in media coverage and explore the implications of this race differentiation.

Race Matters

I engage in a study of race even though scholars have largely rejected the idea that race has a scientific basis. Racial classification is arbitrary, fluid, and has often been used to nefarious ends. That race is socially constructed does not diminish its power, however. Racial differentiation is real and persistent. I follow Robert Entman and Andrew Rojecki (2000, 242n211), who argue, "We can develop critique and understanding with the simultaneous knowledge that sorting people into 'races' based on skin colour is neither scientifically real nor morally desirable." We cannot erase the salience of race by simply referring to its imagined quality, nor should the acknowledgment of that social construction stop us from examining it. Race and racial discourse structure institutions, perceptions, and human interactions.

For those labelled visible minorities, the salience of race is abundantly clear. Canada's census and the Employment Equity Act define visible minorities as individuals "who are non-Caucasian in race or non-white in colour" excluding Aboriginal peoples (Statistics Canada 2007). Visible minority groups thus include Canadians with Chinese, South Asian, black, Filipino, Latin American, Southeast Asian, Arab, West Asian, Korean, and Japanese origins. The term "visible minority" has been criticized not only because it uses whiteness as the standard against which to judge other races (United Nations 2007), but also because it reifies racial distinctions and classifications. I employ the terms "visible minority" and "racial minority" with some reservation but do so because these are the labels most commonly used by the media, public institutions, and in the collection of official data.

Conversely, I use the term "white" to describe those who are not visible minorities or Aboriginal peoples. Within this category, I include individuals with non-British and non-French European origins, such as Ukrainian or Italian, who are often referred to as "ethnic minorities." A former director of the Canadian Institute of Ukrainian Studies, Manoly Lupul (1983), distinguishes ethnic minorities from visible minorities, labeling the latter the "real minorities." He notes that because ethnic minorities are "undistinguishable in external appearance and therefore socially invisible, [their main concern] is language and cultural retention and development; the main concern of the real minorities, the socially visible peoples, is to shield themselves from the worst ravages of racism" (104). Although ethnic minorities have historically faced discrimination, the gap between them and other Canadians was arguably always smaller than that between white and non-white Canadians and, moreover, it has narrowed over time. Because of their lighter skin, ethnic minorities are more easily able to blend in and may facilitate this process by altering their surnames, adopting so-called Canadian traditions, or concealing their accents. It is thus race, not ethnicity, that marks some of the most significant disparities among Canadians.

Determining who is a visible minority and who is not is admittedly fraught terrain. The categories that I employ are based on perceived racial identities, which I have ascribed using cues such as a candidate's skin colour, in much the same way that voters determine who is a racial minority and who is not. This is a strategy that scholars have rightly critiqued. Indeed, orienting this study around an externally imposed definition of racial minority status has the effect of "giving the power of racial definition to the observer and objectifying the racial subject" (Thompson 2008, 537).

Paradoxically, then, while taking issue with racialization in the media, this study simultaneously legitimizes the very racialized categories that under-pin that portrayal. This study also presents racial status as dichotomous – one is either visible minority or white – and thus does not engage with the complexity of these labels nor explore mixed-race identities (Mahtani 2014). Critical race scholars are doing important discursive work that chal-lenges this approach (Dhamoon 2009; Razack, Smith, and Thobani 2010; Thobani 2007), but this book's strategy is somewhat different. I begin with the premise that while racial ascription and categorization are problematic, individuals and institutions routinely engage in it. Instead of ignoring this activity, I confront it. By describing, quantifying, and theorizing the ways in which media coverage of visible minorities differs from that of their white counterparts, I work to provide an empirical rebuttal to those who say that race does not matter. The visible minority/white binary is simplistic, to be sure, but its strategic deployment brings into stark relief the racial differentia-tion that persists in the media and in politics. This book provides persuasive evidence of the durability, significance, and effects of racial differentiation.

One thing this study does not examine is the media's coverage of Ab-original people in politics, a choice that merits some explanation. Given the economic, social, and political disparities faced by Aboriginal people, many might assume that their experiences would be included in a book about race, the media, and politics in Canada. However, while Aboriginals and vis-ible minorities may collectively possess a "minority" identity, their separate histories, cultural heritage, political aspirations, and claims on the state are all very different. Many Aboriginal people would balk at being included in a study of visible minorities, because they do not see their place in Canada's political system – nor their experiences of racism – as at all analogous. While the media's coverage of Aboriginal people in politics deserves examination, a point to which I return in the concluding chapter, it is inappropriate to lump all this diversity into a single study. As a result, I focus here on visible minorities.

Racial Diversity in Canadian Politics

In Canada, questions about social pluralism and identity have historically been oriented around issues of language, ethnicity, culture, and class, with territorially based claims and concerns about Quebec nationalism having primacy (Nath 2011; Wilson 1993). This orientation is a reflection of the country's federalism, a mechanism that grants rights on the basis of geography, as well as the constitutional recognition of two founding nations. For this reason, Seymour Wilson (1993, 648) refers to Canada not as a mosaic, but as a "smelting pot" with "English and French both assuming totemic significance in subsuming all the other cultural and racial groupings." Even the adoption of multiculturalism – the showpiece of Canadian diversity policy – was more about the protection of linguistic and cultural rights than about racial pluralism. The federal government is said to have pushed in the 1960s for bilingualism within a multicultural framework in an effort to dilute the claims of Quebec nationalists while appeasing ethnic minorities – primarily those of Eastern European origin – who were unhappy about the dualistic assumptions that underpinned initiatives to strengthen Quebec's place in the federation (Haque 2012; Kymlicka 2012; Lupul 1983).

These foci are reproduced in the political science literature, which has been relatively silent on questions of race (Thompson 2008; Wilson 1993). This silence is not simply a reflection of societal preferences, but also a disciplinary lag; sociologists and historians have devoted comparatively more attention to racial pluralism than have their counterparts in political science (Thompson 2008). The lack of attention to race can be observed in the American and British political science literature as well as in Canada, suggesting there is something particular to the discipline over and above cross-national differences in history, social demography, and institutional configurations (Thompson 2014; Wilson and Frasure 2007). The explanation can be found, in part, in the liberal tradition that underpins Western political thought, which assumes a neutral state interacting with homogenous political subjects (read: white, able-bodied, heterosexual, and male) (Vickers 2002). Nonetheless, Nisha Nath (2011) notes that the American and British traditions have vibrant race studies and race relations programs, in contrast to the Canadian field, where race has been deactivated or decoded as "ethnicity" or "culture." In other words, the lack of attention to race is particularly acute in Canadian political science.

This erasure is partly a function of Canada's deracialized founding narrative – centring as it does on our white English and French forefathers – and the related tendency towards institutional theories of political development, which downplay the significance of other interests or social groupings (Nath 2011). In her examination of the relative sidelining of race in Canadian political science, Debra Thompson (2008) suggests that not only is race a conceptually difficult variable to measure, but it is typically overlooked in studies that focus on formal political involvement and elite-driven explanations of politics because racially marginalized actors have historically been excluded from formal political arenas. This book marries these two challenges in that it focuses explicitly on race – not ethnicity or culture – and examines the impact of race on elites in an electoral context. Some will argue that I do not fully overcome the conceptual and measurement challenges inherent in such an endeavour, but this orientation nonetheless contributes a new race-based dimension to our understanding of the media and electoral politics in Canada.

Given that Canada's political arena has been dominated by able-bodied, middle-aged, white men, it is somewhat surprising that scholars have not looked more closely at how race affects political behaviour. Although women, minorities, and other traditionally marginalized Canadians are beginning to gain an electoral foothold, a scan of the House of Commons during question period or a quick glance at the official photograph of a newly sworn-in cabinet suggests that those who occupy the corridors of power do not fully mirror those who occupy our coffee shops, our street corners, and our supermarkets. Following the 2011 federal election, 9.4 percent of members of Parliament were visible minorities, an uptick from the 7 percent who held office following the 2008 federal election, but still well below the 19.1 percent of visible minorities who make up the Canadian population. To achieve a Parliament that roughly mirrors the country's racial diversity, Canadians would need to elect about twice as many visible minority candidates.

There are a number of explanations for this numerical underrepresentation. One explanation relates to candidate supply, including visible minorities' willingness to run for public office, their qualifications and credentials, and the networks and financial resources available to facilitate their run for office. Although Canadians with visible minority backgrounds are less likely than others to vote (Jedwab 2006; Reitz and Banerjee 2007),[1] they nonetheless demonstrate levels of political interest and knowledge that are equivalent to or even higher than those of other Canadians (Gidengil et al. 2004). This suggests that some untapped political potential may exist within the visible minority population. It also raises questions about why this apparent political efficacy has not fully translated into political engagement.

Given that visible minorities express an interest in, and some knowledge about, Canadian politics, it is simplistic to conclude that they are not elected to office because they are unwilling to run. In recent years, the proportion of visible minorities who run in federal elections has hovered between 9.0 and 10.1 percent of all candidacies (Black 2013). These candidates tend to be as qualified as – if not more so than – their white counterparts, with many holding impressive educational and occupational credentials, as well as substantial records of service to their communities (Andrew et al. 2008). That said, while visible minority Canadians can be found across all employment categories, they are underrepresented in corporate leadership positions, the legal profession, and in the judiciary (Cukier et al. 2014), all of which are "feeder occupations" for the political arena. We thus need to give some thought to other sorts of barriers that may limit the supply of visible minority candidates. These include conflicting priorities, such as busy careers or a need to work multiple jobs, limited access to the financial resources required to contest public office, or difficulty building the networks that underpin success in the electoral arena. Because many visible minorities are also recent immigrants to Canada, some of these barriers may be a function of this migration experience. However, we should not simply assume that the gap in political representation will close as visible minorities become more comfortable in their adopted home. Some research in fact suggests that it is second-generation visible minorities – those who have been born and raised in Canada – who express the greatest sense of exclusion (Reitz et al. 2009).

We must also consider the demand for visible minority candidates, including parties' recruitment strategies, the openness of nomination contests, the willingness of party elites to run visible minority candidates in competitive ridings, and the extent to which voters are comfortable voting for visible minorities. These barriers to electoral office may have lowered in recent years, as parties recognize the value of putting forward diverse candidate slates (Marwah, Triadafilopoulos, and White 2013; Tolley 2013). That said, efforts to nominate visible minorities have been inconsistent across parties and over elections, and there is some evidence that visible minorities tend to be placed on the ballot in ridings in which the party is less competitive (Black 2013). Parties also tend to confine visible minority candidacies to the most diverse ridings – those where the visible minority population exceeds 30 percent – which places a ceiling on the number of diverse candidates vying for election at any given time (Black and Hicks 2006).

Evidence of voter bias against visible minority candidates comes to some mixed conclusions, depending on how researchers have examined the question. Those who have looked at actual electoral outcomes have found that, all other factors being equal, Canadians show little reluctance to vote for minority candidates (Black and Erickson 2006; Tossutti and Najem 2002). This is not necessarily because of an absence of racial prejudice, but simply because other factors, like party affiliation or preference for a particular leader, tend to override considerations related to a candidate's race (or gender, for that matter). However, the potential shortcoming of an observational approach – one that looks simply at the surface relationship between candidate race and electoral outcome – is summarized by the authors of one such study, who note that because they looked only at aggregate results, they cannot "necessarily rule out discrimination on the part of voters" (Black and Erickson 2006, 549). When researchers have probed voters' actual feelings about visible minority candidates, the conclusions are more mixed.

In one public opinion survey, 79 percent of Canadians said they would be less likely to vote for a party if its leader were black, 78 percent would less likely if the leader were Jewish, 71 percent if the leader were Aboriginal, and 63 percent if the leader were Muslim; 71 percent said they would be less likely to vote for a party led by a woman (CRIC 2004). That a majority of Canadians admit that a leader's race or gender could decrease their support for a political party shows that such characteristics continue to matter. Other researchers have used experimental methods to understand the calculus behind vote choice. These studies have similarly shown a connection between candidate race and voter preference, with most voters tending to prefer candidates whose ethnocultural background mirrors their own (Bird 2011; Tolley and Goodyear-Grant 2014). Canadians' apparent preference for politicians like themselves could be a function of racial prejudice, or it could be grounded in less nefarious assumptions about the extent to which politicians with characteristics similar to our own will listen to us, understand our issues, and advocate on our behalf.

That said, parties have made a number of efforts to engage so-called ethnic Canadians in the political process. Strategies to shore up the support and participation of immigrant and minority voters have been particularly evident within the Conservative Party of Canada, although other parties – both federally and provincially – have pursued similar strategies (Black and Hicks 2008; Harell 2013; Palmer 2013; Tolley 2013). Efforts include targeted policy measures, attendance at ethnic events and festivals, and outreach through the so-called ethnic press. Although some have decried these initiatives as cynical narrowcasting, these strategies have nonetheless increased the attention given to immigrant and visible minority voters and, if nothing else, fostered the perception that these voters are important political players. The media have been instrumental in this regard, penning numerous articles that draw attention to the "wooing of the ethnic vote" (Canadian Press 2011; Ditchburn 2006; Ibbitson and Friesen 2010; Leblanc 2007; MacCharles 2008). These stories provide a frame of reference for understanding diversity in a political context.

Connecting, Shaping, Mirroring: The Role of the News Media

This book positions the media as a vital link in the citizen-politics relationship. We can think of the media as having at least three roles in this relationship. Here, I draw attention to the media as a connector, a shaper, and a mirror.

MEDIA AS A CONNECTOR

Apart from our family and friends, the media are one of our primary sources of information about politics (Gidengil et al. 2004). It is from the media that we learn about political issues, actors, and events. The media help to connect us to political life and play a key role in educating us about the world around us. Nonetheless, Augie Fleras and Jean Kunz (2001, 53) argue that "mainstream media do not exist to inform or entertain or even to persuade ... Mainstream media are first and foremost business ventures whose devotion to the bottom line is geared towards bolstering advertising revenues by attracting audiences and securing ratings." While media do play an important informational and educative role, this function is sustained through advertising, even at public broadcasters such as the CBC. Audiences are drawn in by the unexpected, the shocking, the titillating, and the novel, and media organizations structure their content to attract market share and advertising revenues. Conflict, drama, social impact, novelty, magnitude, proximity, timeliness, brevity, and visual attractiveness are all considered when deciding what constitutes news (Johnson-Cartee 2005). The outcome of these decisions influences the issues, events, and actors to which news consumers will be connected.

This of course raises questions about who is doing the connecting, in that the characteristics of those who oversee media outlets may influence judgment on what matters. In this respect, the leadership cadre of Canada's media organizations provides a fairly stark profile of homogeneity. For example, a 2010 study of media organizations in the Greater Toronto Area found that visible minorities are underrepresented on boards of directors, occupying just 6.1 percent of all seats even though they make up approximately 40 percent of the GTA's population (Cukier et al. 2010). Looking nationally, Postmedia Network owns ten of the country's largest daily newspapers, including the *National Post, Montreal Gazette, Ottawa Citizen, Vancouver Sun,* and *Vancouver Province.* On its board of directors are eight men and two women, all white (Postmedia 2014). The *Globe and Mail,* Canada's English-language newspaper of record, is controlled by the Woodbridge Company, the investment vehicle of David and Peter Thomson, who are multi-billionaires and members of Canada's richest family (Heaven 2009). Meanwhile, Rogers Media is controlled by the estate of Ted Rogers and owns *Maclean's, L'actualité, Chatelaine,* and *Canadian Business,* as well as fifty-six radio stations, seven CityTV stations, and a number of specialty channels (Rogers Media 2015a). Its board of directors consists of five women and eleven men, none of whom are visible minorities (Rogers Media 2015b). Rogers's thirteen-person executive team is entirely male, but does include two visible minorities (Rogers Media 2015c). Finally, Quebecor Media, which is controlled by the Péladeau family, owns forty-three daily newspapers and 250 community newsweeklies, in addition to TVA and Vidéotron, respectively Quebec's most profitable television network and its largest cable company (Lange 2008; Quebecor 2012). Quebecor's eight-person board of directors includes two women, one of whom serves as the chairperson; all members are white (Quebecor 2015a). The members of its ten-person management committee are all white, although half are women (Quebecor 2015b).

The homogeneity observed at the media's corporate level is similarly reproduced at the working level of reporters and editors.[2] Women occupy about just one-third of editorial positions in Canadian print newsrooms, and more than three-quarters of English-language national columnists are men (Smith 2015). In one of the largest demographic profiles of the Canadian newspaper, television, and radio sector ever conducted, David Pritchard and Florian Sauvageau (1999) found that just 3 percent of journalists had minority racial backgrounds. Although this number may have increased somewhat in the ensuing years, several more recent case studies suggest that any improvements have been marginal. For example, in the Greater Toronto Area, Cukier et al.'s (2010) study revealed that just 5.9 percent of newsroom editors and producers were visible minorities; among senior management, the proportion dropped to 3.6 percent. A 2005 study of Canadian television news directors found that 90 percent were white, while in 2006 just 6 percent of the CBC's employees were visible minorities (Barber and Rauhala 2005; MediaSmarts 2012b). Meanwhile, John Miller and Caron Court's (2004) cross-Canada survey of daily newspapers found that visible minorities and Aboriginal people represent just 3.4 percent of news staff in Canada.[3]

On *The National*'s "Media Watch" panel, commentator Jeet Heer, himself a visible minority, noted, "The media in North America is ridiculously white – it's whiter than snow, it's whiter than cocaine – and that creates a certain set of biases or assumptions as to what's relevant" (January 20, 2015). In her interviews with female journalists in Canada, Vivian Smith (2015) highlights their status as outsiders, a situation that diminishes attention to issues like social justice, poverty, and health, and which prompts a number to in fact leave the profession. While newsroom diversity may not *on its own* lead to more inclusive coverage, it does send a message about the importance of including diverse perspectives and connecting Canadians to a wide range of beliefs and voices (Pease, Smith, and Subervi 2001). The media are not passive facilitators but instead help shape how we see the world around us.

Media as a Shaper

The media play an active role in determining which stories are covered, how subjects are portrayed, and the standards by which events, issues, and personalities are understood and evaluated. In connecting us to the world, the media are thus gatekeepers that funnel the political universe into a limited selection of stories. This selection of stories is framed by a particular – often narrow – set of interpretative lenses. Gatekeeping theory suggests that the media determine which information citizens will receive and how it will be conveyed (Donohue, Olien, and Tichenor 1989; Donohue, Tichenor, and Olien 1972; Shoemaker and Vos 2009). The genesis of this literature was a study by David Manning White (1950) that followed the work of "Mr. Gates," a newspaper wire editor, over a one-week period in 1949. White compared the wire stores that Gates received to those that actually appeared in the newspaper; he coupled this with Gates's written explanations as to why a story was published or discarded. White found that the decision to run a story is in fact "highly subjective" (386). Gates's personal evaluation of a story – particularly his assessment of its truthfulness – was the reason for one-third of the rejections; space constraints or the inclusion of other similar stories were the reasons for rejecting the rest of the stories. White notes that nearly 90 percent of the wire stories that Gates received never appeared in the paper, suggesting that media choices are not inconsequential. They help to determine the issues, events, and actors about which citizens will learn.

Since the publication of White's pioneering study, others have expanded on and revised it, adding the work of multiple gatekeepers, categorizing types of gatekeepers, and examining structural considerations (Bass 1969; Folarin 2002; Gieber 1956). I adopt a dual individual-institutional conceptualization of gatekeeping, which is in line with Steve Chibnall's (1977, 6) observation that "the reporter does not go out gathering news, picking up stories as if they were fallen apples, [s]he creates news stories by selecting fragments of information from the mass of raw data [s]he receives and organizing them in a conventional journalistic format." This conceptualization underscores the media's role not simply as a reflector, which I discuss below, but just as importantly as a shaper. Media choices determine not just what constitutes a story, but also how this story will be told. As Lydia Miljan and Barry Cooper (2003, ix) note, "Stories are told from perspectives: that is not an accident or effect, but the essence of stories." In short, the media set the agenda and prime Canadians to think about particular issues, actors, or events in certain ways.

Research on media effects has evolved, with scholars debating the relative strength of effects – whether powerful or minimal – as well as the conditions under which these effects will take hold (Neuman and Guggenheim 2011). Early studies focused on propaganda and persuasion, and tried to establish a direct causal link between media messages and citizen behaviour (Lasswell 1930). This model often depicted the media as a hypodermic needle, with messages being directly and powerfully "injected" into consumers. Over time, researchers began to look for more nuanced accounts of media effects. Many of these frameworks suggested that the media have limited effects on audiences because citizens select the media they consume, choose the messages they retain, and opt to interpret them in any number of ways (Klapper 1960). According to minimal effects models, personal and social characteristics circumscribe the media's effect on consumers. As media saturation grew, however, researchers began to argue that selective exposure was no longer possible.

The third stage of research returns to the idea that the media can have powerful effects and tries to demonstrate these using new methodological tools and better measurement (Neuman and Guggenheim 2011). Many of these accounts look at the cumulative effects of the media, and argue that media messages have the potential to focus attention on certain issues, alter public opinion, influence behaviour and emotions, or legitimize particular responses or directions (McQuail 1994; Soroka 2003; Werder 2009). The effects can be significant when the messages are ubiquitous, uniform, and repeated over time (Noelle-Neumann 1973). While under some conditions, there will be no effects or the effects will not be absolute, media coverage matters overall because it has the potential to affect how citizens view the world, the criteria they use to evaluate issues, and the decisions at which they ultimately arrive (McCombs and Shaw 1972; Patterson 1993). The media influence which issues are on the agenda, how the public will judge those issues, and the schema through which we will understand the world around us. These theoretical frameworks are referred to as agenda-setting, priming, and framing.

Writing about the media's agenda-setting role, Robert Hackett (2001, 199) argues, "Through their ability to focus public attention on some events and issues, and away from others, the media influence public perceptions of what exists, what is important, what is good and valuable, what is bad and threatening, and what is related to what." The agenda-setting literature hypothesizes that when an item is accorded more prominence or space, audiences will give it more significance or importance when they make decisions (Cohen 1963; Lippmann 1922; McCombs and Shaw 1972). Although agenda-setting studies often focus on the ways in which *issues* are made salient, a new body of work examining the salience of *attributes* is emerging. Each issue, event, or actor has a number of features or qualities, and the media make choices about which attributes to highlight. In turn, this attribute agenda influences voters' evaluations of the subjects in question.

Even if the intent is benign or subconscious, the ways that the media present subjects and the attributes on which they choose to focus have an impact on how citizens view those subjects. As Maxwell McCombs, Esteban Lopez-Escobar, and Juan Pablo Llamas (2000, 78) point out, "Both the selection by journalists of objects for attention and the selection of attributes for detailing the pictures of these objects are powerful agenda-setting roles." In their research, they found a strong positive relationship between the attributes highlighted by the media when presenting political candidates and those mentioned by voters when describing those candidates. Similarly, results from an experimental study by Catherine Lemarier-Saulnier and Thierry Giasson (2015) suggest that when voters read a news article with a gendered frame, they are more likely to evaluate it using gendered criteria or descriptors. In other words, how the media choose to frame candidates – the language that they use, the qualities that they highlight, and the features that they leave out – does influence how voters think about those candidates. This influence is sometimes referred to as priming. This body of research argues that by highlighting certain attributes, the media make those criteria more accessible and may prime citizens to consider them more seriously when making their decisions (Iyengar and Kinder 1987).

The issues and attributes that are made salient through agenda-setting and priming can be thought of as the story's frame. A frame is the angle, schema, or narrative arc that journalists use to highlight one or more aspects of an event, issue, or actor (Nelson, Oxley, and Clawson 1997). Frames refer to the elements that are included, excluded, emphasized, or downplayed when a story is reported on (Gitlin 1980). They are a way of simplifying and organizing information in a manner that helps citizens understand the features, characteristics, or attributes that are most important. We can distinguish between substantive frames, which focus on policy issues, problems, and possible solutions, on the one hand, and procedural frames, which evaluate "political actors' legitimacy based on their technique, success, and representativeness" on the other (Entman 2004, 5–6). The most recognizable frame used in political news coverage is the game frame, which focuses on tactics, strategy, and the horse race. Stories about who is leading, or slumping, in the polls fall squarely within the game frame. Substantive frames are much less common, with the media routinely devoting less attention to policy discussion than to the "battle" (Farnsworth et al. 2007).

Frames are necessary if we are to understand the complex and unfamiliar world around us. Nonetheless, they alter the weight and relevance that is accorded to a given consideration or angle and thus "promote a particular problem definition, causal interpretation, moral evaluation and/or treatment recommendation" (Entman 1993, 52). In the next chapter, I will discuss some of the frames that the media use when reporting on candidates in electoral politics. The key point here is that in choosing what to cover and how to cover it, the media help to shape our understanding of the world. This understanding is, of course, grounded in the real world, which brings us to the media's third role, that of a mirror.

MEDIA AS A MIRROR
The media have been said to hold up a "mirror to society," reflecting the events and issues of the day (Gans 1979; McQuail 2010). Although the image has been popular among journalists because it carries the implication of

fair and accurate reporting, others have suggested that news is in fact a reflection of the interplay between journalists and the subjects that they cover. In this way, the media are a "distorted mirror" (Taras 1990). This is not to say that the news is a work of fiction, but rather that it is a construction or interpretation of reality (Schudson 1989). How the news is told – and indeed what constitutes news itself – is determined by the media. This process is influenced by an understanding of the narratives that will resonate with the public. As Robert Hackett (2001, 202) argues: "The news draws from, and contributes to, the values and assumptions of its surrounding culture." These assumptions are premised on a positioning of media audiences as consumers, not citizens. Consumers are differentiated by their purchasing power and are thus not equal; this distinction imbues inequality into the media system (Hackett 2001).

A recognition of systemic inequality runs headlong into the notion of journalistic objectivity. Objectivity requires journalists to adopt a position of neutrality or independence, to report on facts, to present stories fairly and accurately, and to strive for balance in the representation of issues and subjects (Donsbach and Klett 1993). Although objectivity figures prominently in discussions about journalistic responsibility, the concept is itself contested. Robert Hackett and Yuezhi Zhao (1998, 87) argue that "objectivity disguises and denies how the culturally conditioned gaze of the observer helps to construct that which is observed." When we describe the media as "objective," we ignore journalists' situatedness in society, as well as the evaluation and interpretation in which they must routinely engage. While objectivity serves as a "normative ideal," a perfect reflection is not attainable (Hackett and Zhao 1998, 83). The twin realities of inequality and imperfection determine the image that is eventually reflected by the media mirror.

Day-to-day pressures and practicalities of newsmaking also influence how the news is fashioned. Journalists face deadlines and space limitations that can affect which stories get told, which ones are set aside, who is asked to provide background or opinion, how detailed an item is, and even the page on which it will appear. Time constraints can limit the depth of reporting, and stories may as a result be oversimplified or only partially explored. Editors may encourage this tendency by narrowing the angle or removing complicated details (Randall 2000). Stereotypes, symbols, caricatures, and other rhetorical devices may be employed as shortcuts or for added "colour" (Campbell 1995). The sources on whom journalists rely may be limited by time pressures, familiarity, or challenges building connections with new interlocutors; these limits can constrain the range of voices and perspectives that inform a news article or report (Randall 2000; Taras 1990).

Stories that are deemed newsworthy are the ones most likely to be told, which means that most news items include an element of the unexpected. That which is "commonplace" rarely appears in the media precisely because it is not striking, significant, or surprising enough. Reality is thus framed through a media-centric perspective about which stories are worth telling (Fleras 2011). This perspective is in part influenced by news judgment, journalistic routines, and organizational behaviour, but also by what the media predict citizens will believe, tune into, and accept. In this way, the framing of news stories reflects, reinforces, and refashions reality. According to Augie Fleras (2011, 36), "Mainstream media are neither neutral nor value-free. Rather, they are so loaded with deeply embedded ideas and ideals about what is normal and acceptable with respect to race, gender, and class that media representations of diversities and difference are invariably raced, gendered, Eurocentric, and classed." Such representations are not a function of wilful racism, sexism, or classism on the part of the media, but rather a function of the racialized, gendered, and classed society of which the media are a part.

While the mirror that the media hold up may be somewhat distorted or partial, the images they are reflecting are nonetheless images that we have created and condoned. It is for this reason that understanding the media's portrayal of race is so important: not only does it tell us something about the media but also something about ourselves.

Framing the Argument

This book provides the first extended study of the media's coverage of race in Canadian politics. It explores the racialized frames that emerge in political news coverage and looks at the extent to which these mirror and manufacture reality. It examines the contextual nature of racialized coverage by looking at a number of factors, including candidate gender, political party affiliation, and the diversity of the ridings in which candidates run. It investigates candidates' own views on media coverage and race in politics. It sheds light on the work that journalists do, the constraints that they face, and how they think about covering stories about diversity. Finally, it raises questions about the media's role in shaping views about race, inclusion, and democratic politics.

Motivating this study is a desire to understand the extent to which the media's coverage of Canadian politics is differentiated by the race of its subjects. Are visible minority candidates covered differently from their white counterparts? Is their coverage less frequent, more negative, or less prominent? How does a candidate's race influence the portrayal of their qualifications, policy interests, and socio-demographic background? And do candidates' gender, party affiliation, or political experience affect the racialization of their media coverage in any way? These questions are probed in Chapters 2 and 3, which are based on an examination of more than 1,380 news stories in two periods: during the 2008 federal election, and a longitudinal analysis extending from 1993 to 2013. I find that candidate race influences both the *form* and the *focus* of media coverage.

Visible minority candidates' coverage is systematically and substantively different from that of white candidates. This is particularly so for non-incumbent visible minority candidates; these candidates must, in effect, prove themselves as electoral contenders before being taken as seriously as their white counterparts. Female candidates face a similar barrier to entry, which raises questions about how intersecting identities affect media coverage. How do the media portray candidates when they possess race and gender identities that are often marginalized in the political arena? What frames characterize the coverage of visible minority women? Are these frames different from those that have been identified in the coverage of white women? What gendered and racialized narratives are apparent?

To complement the aggregate, quantitative media study presented in Chapter 2, I also use an intersectional and discursive approach to examine the media's coverage of visible minority women in politics. Chapter 3 thus shows the more implicit ways in which media coverage can be both gendered and racialized. By analyzing the language, imagery, and rhetorical strategies used in the political news coverage of visible minority women, this approach breaks down silos that have emerged in research on gender and race in Canadian politics. Although women have made some cracks in the proverbial glass ceiling, I argue that the gendered and racialized discourses that characterize the media's coverage of visible minority women in politics indicate the durability of what I call the "stained glass ceiling." To fully understand the experiences of these women, we must go beyond "whitestream" accounts, which are often silent on the impact of race and other markers of diversity.

Integral to this study is the development of a new theoretical framework for understanding the media's coverage of race in politics. This book advances a theory of racial mediation: rather than being neutral reflectors of the political sphere, journalists act as mediators, making choices about story selection, presentation, and framing. I argue that while a number of factors influence these choices, the race of electoral candidates is among them. Race provides a cue or angle around which stories are oriented, which results in coverage that is racially differentiated. Situating my discussion of racial mediation within the literatures on political communication and race studies – and drawing on existing studies of gendered mediation – I introduce the frames through which information about candidates' socio-demographic background, political viability, and policy interests are communicated, often in racialized ways.

The book moves beyond media outputs, however, to look at the inputs that result in the coverage that we see. Chapter 4, in particular, is a response to the assertion – raised anecdotally as well as in the literature – that to the extent that media coverage is racialized, this is largely a reflection of how candidates present themselves. This claim has some basis: candidates provide the raw ingredients for the framing of their backgrounds, political qualifications, and policy interests. However, media portrayals are not purely a function of self-presentation. Based on my interviews with members of Parliament, former candidates, and political staffers, I argue that while all public figures engage in some degree of strategic self-presentation, their media portrayals are not a perfect reflection of the images that they project. Rather, mediation is occurring, and candidate race is one factor in the relationship between self-presentation and media portrayal. When a story involves a visible minority candidate, media coverage will often emphasize the diversity angle, through a focus on socio-demographics, minority issues, novelty, unexpectedness, or unlikelihood. The media are not passive reflectors; race and racialized assumptions affect media coverage.

Why is that so? Do assumptions about race influence news judgment, story selection, and framing? Are media institutions and practices inherently racialized? And what guidelines or training do journalists receive to help them cover stories about race? Chapter 5 delves into these questions. I discuss the institutionalization of whiteness and argue that the media are embedded in cultural norms that privilege – often implicitly – majority and mainstream representations, practices, and beliefs. Media choices are not isolated. Rather, they occur within a broader societal context that is fore-grounded by an assumption of whiteness as standard. The media are not solely responsible, but nor are their choices neutral. In representing diversity as exotic and newsworthy, the media help to shape perceptions and attitudes about race. These choices are at the heart of racial mediation.

A series of interviews with journalists, discussed in Chapter 5, provides rich insights into the factors that affect story selection and framing, the complexities and nuance of news judgment, and the impact of diversity on news coverage. Among the journalists with whom I spoke, there was almost no evidence of blatant racism. Nonetheless, many downplayed the poten-tial impact of race on their news judgment, reporting, and coverage. Several suggested that the media's commitment to fairness and accuracy means that coverage is, in essence, colour-blind. Given that my own analysis of media portrayals found some fairly persuasive patterns of racial differentiation, this lack of self-reflection on the impact of race and diversity was somewhat surprising. It was less so when I looked at guidelines and training for report-ing on diversity. In general, race and diversity are not well covered in the curriculum at Canadian journalism schools, and journalists receive minimal workplace training about reporting on these topics. Guidelines produced by the Canadian Press and at the newsroom level are imprecise and open to interpretation. Interviewees confirmed this, but also noted that exercis-ing judgment is an important part of being a journalist. Journalists are not robots, and the stories they tell have many facets, different layers, and vary-ing interpretations. It is telling, however, that when a story does include a visible minority subject, its form, focus and framing are different – and importantly, more racialized – from a similar story about a white subject.

The media's portrayal of race has negative effects on public discourse, electoral representation, and democracy in Canada. As I detail in Chapter 1, racialized coverage can influence voters' decision making, discourage poten-tial candidates from running for office, hamper the recruitment of a diverse candidate slate, and diminish the achievement of equality in the electoral arena. I return to this point in the book's conclusion, where I argue that politics are not race-neutral. Race influences media coverage, political aspirations and experiences, and the exercise of democracy. Visible minor-ities are portrayed differently from their white counterparts and can expect their news coverage to be framed according to stereotypical assumptions about their socio-demographic backgrounds, viability, and policy expertise.

Nevertheless, our discourse is marked by a profound silence about the effects of race, the persistence of racialization, and the potential for racially based thinking to colour our judgment. Instead of confronting the persistent racial gaps that characterize the practice of politics, we mythologize multiculturalism and resort to tropes about colour-blindness, equality, and inclusion.

I argue that when we see racialized coverage, we should not simply blame the media. Indeed, to understand the relationship between race and politics in Canada, we must cast our gaze much more broadly and consider how political parties, candidates, and the public contribute to the continued salience of race. Each of us plays a role in the patterns identified in this book. In the conclusion, I offer some suggestions to counter racial mediation. This grounding is an important practical contribution of the study, but my prognosis is somewhat grim. While some measures can be taken to produce political news coverage that is less racialized, widespread change really demands a cultural shift. We need to acknowledge racial thinking, problematize race-differentiated coverage, and resist racialized assumptions about diversity, minorities, and politics in Canada. This shift requires an honesty and openness that Canadians have thus far been reluctant to embrace. As a result, visible minorities suffer, as do our democratic institutions, which remain only partially representative and devoid of the full range of diversity that so many of us proudly claim as quintessentially Canadian.

1
Understanding Racial Mediation

"There's something systemically wrong within the media and politics in general. We are just so used to having white, middle-aged men that it's become part of the DNA. You walk through the halls, and the photos of the speakers and the premiers are all of white men. The media are used to that image, and that image just hasn't changed at all."

– Interview with a political staffer and visible minority woman

The media have been referred to as "democracy's oxygen" (Winter 1997), meaning it is through the media that our democratic politics are given life. One of democracy's central tenets is the notion of equality. This notion is borne out in the principle of "one person, one vote," the extension of a universal franchise, and efforts to ensure fairness in the electoral system. When elements of inequality creep in – when there is coercion, gerrymandering, or the perception of vote-rigging, for example – trust, confidence, and legitimacy are undermined. Citizens expect that political actors will be treated equitably, and yet, as this book details, the media's coverage of Canadian politics does not always live up to this standard. Instead, candidates are covered in different ways, according to subjective assessments of what is newsworthy or important, with their race, gender, or other characteristics often influencing these judgments.

In recent years, we have seen media stories about controversies surrounding veiled Muslim voters, the potential for so-called ethnic voting blocks to exploit democratic nomination processes, and politicians' pandering to immigrant and minority voters (Cowan 2004; Gardner 2007; Markusoff 2008; Young 2008). Even if the coverage is not overtly *racist*, race influences the stories' framing, angle, discourse, and effect. As Liberal member of Parliament Mark Holland has observed, when fellow MP Omar Alghabra – a Muslim – spoke out against provisions in the Anti-Terrorism Act, "his motives were questioned. Certain media outlets speculated that Omar's position was driven by a personal and ideological agenda." Similarly, media reports suggested that MP Navdeep Bains's questioning of the act was linked to his Sikhism, a narrative accompanied by the allegation that his father-in-law was on a list of potential interviewees in the Air India case, and Bains was thus seeking to protect him. Holland, who is of Irish and German origin, notes that "when Nav and Omar organize, it's ethnic politics; when I organize, I'm just a good organizer. When Omar or Nav express concerns about anti-terrorism or foreign policy, it's because of their ancestry or religion; when I question it ... I'm debating hard choices" (Holland 2007, A15). What Holland is making clear is that media coverage results only partly from the raw materials that candidates provide: their actions, personalities, and communications. The way that the media use these inputs is not the same for all politicians or public figures. Rather, mediation is occurring. This fact raises questions about whether political news coverage is equitable and fair, or if it is biased against certain participants.

Mediating Politics

The media make a number of choices related to the production of the news. These involve the selection of a particular news item, the resources that will be devoted to its coverage, the sources that will be consulted, the visuals that will be used, the angle that will be taken, and the length, depth, and prominence of the finished product. The selection, construction, production, and consumption of the news is referred to as mediation (Allen 2004). Shannon Sampert and Linda Trimble (2010a, 2) note that news mediation has three core elements: "the selection and framing of stories by the press; the instrumental use of mass media by political actors; and the ways in which the structure and organization of media shape news stories." The chapters in this book deal with all three elements. They focus, in particular, on the impact of race on story framing, candidate self-presentation, and journalistic practice. In this chapter, I provide a framework for understanding these choices, drawing on research about gendered news coverage to generate new theoretical insights about racial mediation.

Theories of gendered mediation are well documented and developed in the literature on women in politics (Gidengil and Everitt 1999, 2000, 2003a,

2003b; Goodyear-Grant 2009, 2013; Sreberny-Mohammadi and Ross 1996; Trimble 2007). According to this body of work, the media "filter and shape our understanding of what is politically relevant" through the use of framing, stereotypes, encoded language, and symbols (Gidengil and Everitt 2003b, 197). Goodyear-Grant (2007) provides an excellent enumeration of the key propositions of gendered mediation theory:

1   Masculine narratives inform political coverage, and stereotypes about appropriate male and female behaviours influence the resulting content.
2   When female politicians exhibit behaviour that is stereotypically unfeminine, it will be exaggerated by the media.
3   The coverage of female politicians will be more filtered and mediated than that of male politicians.
4   Female politicians' coverage will disproportionately emphasize their interest in so-called women's issues, like health care and education.
5   Gendered coverage is not (solely) a product of sexist journalists, but rather a reflection of deeply held cultural values and ingrained news norms.

Historically, women faced "symbolic annihilation" (Tuchman 1978), meaning they were virtually invisible in the political arena and thus absent from political news coverage (Gingras 1995; Kahn 1994; Robinson and Saint-Jean 1991, 1995). This invisibility has diminished as women have secured a foothold in electoral politics and, in some cases, actually receive more news coverage than male politicians (Carroll and Schreiber 1997; Goodyear-Grant 2013; Jalalzai 2006). As a result, most researchers now focus less on coverage *quantity* and more on coverage *quality*. Here, there is ample evidence that women are covered differently from men. For example, the media tend to portray female politicians as women first, often by focusing on their demographic characteristics (Trimble and Treiberg 2008).

Women's news coverage often emphasizes their appearance, wardrobe, femininity, and family life (Gidengil and Everitt 2000, 2003a; Heldman, Oliver, and Conroy 2009; Lalancette and Lemarier-Saulnier 2011; Sampert and Trimble 2003; Trimble 2005, 2007). In some cases, media images are hyper-sexualized, with Hillary Clinton referred to as a "cunt," Sarah Palin as a MILF ("Mom I'd Like to Fuck"), and female voters as "hos" (Anderson 2011). Often this type of coverage is initiated outside the mainstream media, but is then picked up and reported on by these outlets. In a further reinforcement of feminine stereotypes, women are portrayed as having "soft" policy interests, and they are positioned as novelties or political amateurs (Gidengil and Everitt 2000, 2003a; Heldman, Oliver, and Conroy 2009; Lalancette and Lemarier-Saulnier 2011; Sampert and Trimble 2003).

The coverage of women is also more likely to be negative than the coverage of men (Heldman, Oliver, and Conroy 2009; Kahn 1994), and female politicians are more likely than male politicians to be portrayed as passive subjects (Goodyear-Grant 2007; Rakow and Kranich 1991). Women are less frequently quoted and more commonly paraphrased, and stories about them are more likely to use non-neutral verbs and less likely to include evidence to support their claims or positions (Gidengil and Everitt 2000, 2003a, 2003b; Goodyear-Grant 2007). Moreover, when women behave counter-stereotypically, such as raising their voices or pointing their fingers, the media give disproportionate emphasis to this behaviour (Gidengil and Everitt 2003a).

Finally, when male and female politicians are evaluated according to the same criteria, men will generally receive more favourable coverage. For example, while male politicians typically benefit from being portrayed as "family men," women are questioned about their ability to combine political life with the traditional roles of wife and mother (Lalancette and Lemarier-Saulnier 2011). We see differential coverage even when female candidates are electorally competitive; in spite of this, they will still be covered as less qualified (Sampert and Trimble 2003). All of this suggests that stereotypic considerations underpin media coverage of politics.

These patterns are found in Canada (Gidengil and Everitt 1999, 2000, 2003a, 2003b; Goodyear-Grant 2009, 2013; Sampert and Trimble 2003; Trimble 2007), as well as in Australia (Jenkins 2007), Britain (Ross 1995), Germany (van Zoonen 2006), Ireland (Ross 2003), New Zealand (Fountaine and McGregor 2002; Trimble and Treiberg 2008), Sweden (Lundell and Ekström 2008), and the United States (Aday and Devitt 2001; Anderson 2011; Gilmartin 2001; Heldman, Carroll, and Olson 2005; Heldman, Oliver, and Conroy 2009; Kahn 1992, 1994), among others. In other words, gendered media coverage is systemic and reflects deeply rooted ideas about patriarchy and the "natural" correspondence between politics and masculinity; this is why it is not confined to a single country or institutional structure. This gendered framing casts doubt on women's political competence, qualifications, and suitability for office. It also raises questions about the coverage of other marginalized groups, including visible minorities.

Insights from the literature on gendered mediation can and should be applied to the situation of visible minorities in politics, for several reasons. First, as Carole Pateman and Charles Mills (2007) argue compellingly in *Contract and Domination,* race – like sex – is a marker of difference that can both oppress and exclude. Just as patriarchy is infused in our culture, values, and institutions, so too are notions of racial supremacy.[1] These ideas underpin deeply rooted stereotypes about the place of women and visible minorities in public life, their qualifications for leadership positions, and their suitability for politics. Second, just as women once faced "symbolic annihilation" from political life, so too did visible minorities. Although both groups increasingly hold public office, neither does so in numbers that mirror their presence in the general population. Women and minorities thus experience parallel underrepresentation. Third, newsrooms exhibit a relative lack of gender and racial diversity; the absence of women and visible minority reporters and editors may either contribute to a silencing of these voices or create the impression that their perspectives do not matter. Fourth, even if there were more female and minority journalists, news norms would favour a masculine and "mainstream" framing of events and actors because of the prevalence of patriarchy and the normalization of whiteness in institutions and society. As a result, media coverage, in general, tends to be both gendered and racialized.

Given these parallels, it is somewhat surprising that researchers have not put forward a theory of racial mediation. Although a number of scholars – particularly in the United States – have noted the propensity towards racialized or race-differentiated coverage, these analyses have not made explicit a theory of racial mediation, nor have they examined the Canadian case (Caliendo and McIlwain 2006; Jeffries 2002; McIlwain and Caliendo 2011; Reeves 1997; Schaffner and Gadson 2004; Schwartz 2011; Swain 1995; Terkildsen and Damore 1999; Zilber and Niven 2000). This study addresses that gap.

Racial Mediation

Drawing on the research on gendered mediation, this book proposes a new framework for understanding the impact of race on political news coverage. This framework, which I refer to as racial mediation, posits that politics are covered in ways that reflect dominant cultural norms, long-standing organizational practices, and the assumption of whiteness as standard. Racial mediation affects which stories are selected, how they are framed, where they are placed, who reads them, how news consumers react, and how politicians respond to these patterns of coverage. Race does not appear organically in stories, but rather is placed there consciously and provides a cue or framework for understanding the story. Racialized coverage is the product of this racial mediation.

RACIALIZED COVERAGE

In my analysis of racial mediation, particularly in Chapters 2 and 3, I look not so much at *racist* coverage, but instead at *racialized* coverage. This distinction is akin to one I drew earlier when I discussed the difference between acting racistly and thinking racially. It is also similar to the contrast between gendered coverage and sexist coverage that can be found in the literature on women in politics. In identifying racialized patterns of coverage, I am not necessarily attributing motive or blame, but rather examining the ways in which candidate race affects media portrayals. When racialization occurs, "individuals and groups are racially coded, that is, identified, named, and categorized, resulting in the imposition of race-based meanings" (Fleras 2011, 58).

My understanding of racialized coverage does not presuppose that racialized coverage is an indicator of media racism nor that the coverage is itself a misrepresentation of reality. Racialized coverage may be unintentional or even an accurate portrayal of a candidate's own presentation. Moreover, as Fleras (2011, 58) points out, "Race-based ideas and ideals are so deeply ingrained within the institutions' structure, functioning and operation that most institutional actors are unaware of how this racialization confers benefits to some and not others." For this reason, I generally do not point a finger at "racist" reporters or "prejudiced" readers.

Racialized media coverage can be understood in two ways. First, we can think of coverage with explicit racial content. Such coverage includes descriptive racial or socio-demographic content related to a candidate's skin colour, ethnicity, linguistic background, or purported interest in so-called minority issues, such as immigration and multiculturalism. This content may be direct, through mentions of race or heritage, or indirect, through photographic cues or references to the subject's support from particular ethnic communities. Although the coverage may be positive, it does inject race into the narrative, which could detract from the subject's other attributes, qualifications, or policy interests. When stories refer explicitly to candidates' socio-demographic difference, the effects can be delegitimizing and distancing.

The second way to think about racialized coverage is more latent and involves looking at how race affects the coverage of otherwise similar subjects. The criterion here is whether candidate race differentiates the types of policy or viability coverage they receive. Are candidates with similar qualifications presented as equally viable? Or, all else being equal, are visible minority candidates portrayed as less qualified or legitimate contenders? To which policy issues are candidates linked? And are these portrayals influenced by racialized assumptions? If two otherwise similar white and visible minority candidates are covered differently, then this suggests that candidate race influences news judgment, assumptions, and reporting.

One critique that has been directed at studies of media coverage is that analysts find the patterns that they do mostly because they go looking for them (Hier 2009). According to this perspective, "Racism and media studies misrepresent the diversity of coverage in the mainstream media ... underrepresent the diversity of media outlets, and remain silent on important patterns of coverage in mainstream and other media pertaining to equity, social justice, and human rights." This is a form of confirmation bias, a cognitive tendency that leads us to search for information and favour evidence consistent with our existing beliefs. Critics claim that researchers who study the media's coverage of race tend to "have a self-avowed commitment to exposing racism in all its forms and manifestations, so they tend to seek out explicit examples of stereotypical, sensational and spectacular media coverage" (Hier and Lett 2013, 124).

This study addresses these challenges in a few ways. First, it looks at the coverage of white and visible minority candidates so that patterns of coverage can be compared. Second, although the focus is on mainstream news, a wide variety of outlets and two different time frames are included, which broadens the scope and depth of the analysis and helps to reveal the diversity of news coverage. Third, rather than just looking at patterns of coverage, the analysis probes the ways in which political actors and journalists feed into these portrayals. This helps contextualize the findings. Finally, while most of the examples highlighted in the chapters that follow illustrate the presence of racialized coverage rather than its absence, care has been taken to showcase portrayals that diverge from our expectations. One way of doing this is to consider what coverage would look like if it *weren't* racialized. It is unrealistic – and even undesirable – to expect coverage that is devoid of racial references and completely blind to race. Instead, what we should seek is coverage that is racially undifferentiated, racially balanced, or race-neutral. So, how might we recognize such coverage?

First, we could say racially undifferentiated coverage exists when race is deemed to be just as relevant for white candidates as it is for visible minority candidates. All of us have racial and socio-demographic backgrounds, and if reporters and editors deem these backgrounds to be newsworthy for some candidates, then they should merit mention for all or, conversely, for none. Stories with a racial angle should not be confined to politicians with a minority racial background. Second, we can look for coverage in which there is some degree of correspondence between candidate presentation and the resulting media portrayal, regardless of whether the candidate is visible minority or white. This does not mean that journalists should be uncritical and non-evaluative or simply repeat what politicians tell them. Rather, the ideal would be coverage where there is no appreciable gap between the racialized components of a candidate's self-presentation and the resulting media portrayal. Third, racially undifferentiated coverage would present people of all races in stories about all kinds of issues. Visible minority candidates should be seen as credible commentators on "mainstream" issues like the economy, while white candidates should have a voice in stories about "minority" issues.

The final way in which to think about racially undifferentiated coverage is as coverage in which racial considerations are evenly applied to news judgment. News judgment includes story choice, sources, decision making, information shortcuts, and language, and although much more difficult for researchers to measure, these subtle processes arguably drive racial differentiation more than any other factor. What leads a journalist to write a particular story? Why does she interview these sources and not others? Why did he quote this candidate but paraphrase that one? Why did the editor choose this headline or include that photo? Why does one story mention a riding's demographic composition when another story does not? Although racial considerations will sometimes motivate stories – reporting on hate crimes or genocide, for example – these considerations should be evenly applied to all candidates in electoral coverage. In short, racially undifferentiated coverage is coverage in which race is treated analogously for all candidates, regardless of skin colour. In a study of racism in Canadian universities, a visible minority faculty member sums this up quite nicely: "The test I do in

my head is to ask myself: would this be said or be done to a White male?'"
(Henry and Tator 2012, 81).

Racialized coverage is not confined to individuals with minority backgrounds. Indeed, in a well-publicized incident during the 2012 Alberta
provincial election, Ron Leech, a candidate in a diverse Calgary riding,
suggested in an interview with an ethnic radio station that "as a Caucasian
I have an advantage. When different community leaders such as a Sikh
leader or a Muslim leader speaks, they really speak *to their own people* ... As
a Caucasian, I believe that I can speak to all the community." Leech went
on to say, "When a Punjabi leader speaks for the Punjabi, the Punjabi are
listening but when a Caucasian speaks on their behalf, *everybody is listening*" (quoted in Gerein 2012; emphasis added). In stories about this interview, there is racialized coverage, but it is directed towards a white candidate
and, incidentally, is also a product of that candidate's self-presentation.
Nonetheless, racialized coverage is likely to be more prevalent in stories
about visible minority candidates. This is because whiteness is the norm
in politics (and in newsrooms), and it is against this backdrop that political
actors are evaluated and political events are understood. Just as female
candidates diverge from a male-centric understanding of politics and are
covered accordingly, visible minorities stand out in an otherwise white,
mainstream narrative.

Rarely do the media tackle systemic questions related to race, with
racial silence more common than investigations into prejudice. When race
is not whitewashed or made invisible by the media, visible minorities
often appear as problems or threats (e.g., terrorists, drug dealers, gangsters,
illegal immigrants, and welfare abusers) or as stereotyped clichés (e.g., hard-
working immigrants, Bollywood actors, belly dancers, rappers, athletes)
(Fleras 2011). White Canadians are shown in advertisements for a wide
range of products, represented in an idealized nuclear family setting and
enjoying "highbrow" culture (Fleras 2011; Henry and Tator 2002; Pottie-
Sherman and Wilkes 2014). Meanwhile, Asian Canadians are stereotyped
as technocrats and are rarely shown in the outdoors, while black Canadians
are typically shown in blue-collar settings like factories and fast-food res-
taurants (Baumann and Ho 2014). Media images remain predominantly
white, and when minorities do appear, they often seem to be little more
than decorative ornamentation: actors who help broadcasters and newspapers meet diversity targets and avoid accusations of racism. To the extent

that minorities are overrepresented in the media, it is "in areas that don't count or count for less, including tourism, sports, international relief, and entertainment" (Fleras 2011, 66). One study of diversity in the Greater Toronto Area (Cukier et al. 2010) found that visible minorities made up just 16.6 percent of broadcast "experts," even though 40 percent of the region's population identified as a visible minority. The same study found that on the print opinion pages, just 3.4 percent of columnists were visible minorities. Even positive coverage of visible minorities may have negative consequences in that it can lead citizens to assume that because these individuals have found success, no problems remain (Fleras 2011). How the media portray race and visible minorities is a matter of choice, and the existence of racialized coverage is evidence of continued racial mediation.

CANDIDATE SELF-PRESENTATION

When thinking about racial mediation, however, it is important to consider not just the content of the coverage, but also the raw materials that feed into the patterns that have been identified. As Goodyear-Grant (2013, 108) points out, "Media content is always a combination of provision and presentation – of real-world events *provided* for coverage and of how those real-world events are selected, interpreted and *presented* by newsmakers." As has been noted, the media's role as a shaper, connector, and mirror of reality is influenced both by cultural norms and assumptions and by the features of the news business itself. However, the news is not created out of nothing. Rather, the news reflects how political actors conduct themselves: the positions they hold, the words that they use, the images they project, and the extent to which they cultivate a media presence. Just as news coverage itself is not neutral, neither is the image that politicians put forward; politicians' messages and behaviours themselves have a racial content. If we were to look only at news coverage, we would miss the racialized aspects of politicians' self-presentation.

Each of us has a racial background, and this background influences our standpoint, our interactions with other citizens, and the opportunities that we may have. In politics, visible minorities may be pigeonholed or choose to run in certain electoral districts – particularly those with high rates of ethnocultural diversity – because they feel they are most likely to garner support in these arenas. They may make reference to their "immigrant story" or status as outsiders, which can solidify a reputation as a hard worker or someone "out of the ordinary." As relatively new political entrants, visible minorities are less likely to be incumbents, more likely to be defeated, and less likely to occupy prominent political positions; as a result, their coverage may portray them as less politically viable, in part because they are. If elected, visible minority politicians may be asked – or request – to oversee a portfolio related to so-called minority issues, and thus may appear most often in stories about immigration, multiculturalism, or foreign affairs.

As was noted by a number of the candidates and politicians that I interviewed, this presentation of self is carefully constructed to elicit the desired response from voters, the media, and other political observers. Self-presentation includes the choice and content of a candidate's messages, as well as tone of voice, body language, physical appearance, clothing, the presence of symbols like flags or "diverse" voters, and the location from which a message will be delivered. All these choices are an attempt to influence the inferences that audiences will draw, whether these pertain to a candidate's qualifications, personality traits, or issue interests (Goffman 1959).

Although a number of the candidates whom I interviewed discussed attempts to cultivate a particular image, some political operatives deny that this is the case. Commenting on research that examined the "traditionally feminine" wardrobe choices of Wildrose leader Danielle Smith during the 2012 Alberta election, the party's spokesperson, Vitor Marciano, argued,

> The [research] paper seems to assume there are committees and strategists and planning attached to what you wear on a given day ... The paper reinforced one of the views I've always had: It's amazing how few [academics] actually know anything at all about electoral politics or campaigning ... They are operating in this weird world of studying [and] writing something for complete outsiders and complete strangers, and they've never done any real observation (quoted in Gerson 2014, A5).

While Smith's handlers say she did not have a committee working on wardrobe selection, image consultants play an increasing role in electoral politics (Marland, Giasson, and Lees-Marshment 2012). Image management is also taught in a number of well-known campaign schools. For example, the annual Washington-based workshop The Art of Political Campaigning includes a workshop entitled "How to Look and Sound Like a Candidate," which offers advice on wardrobe ("Avoid polka dots, stripes and checks"; "Choose ties that enhance your eye colour"; "Know your measurements"; "Make sure you can fit two fingers into the waistband of your pants"; "Never wear shorts"). In a 33-page handbook produced for prospective female candidates, the words "brand" or "image" appear twenty-two times, and readers are instructed to "carefully manage [their] public persona" if they are thinking about entering the electoral arena (Equal Voice 2015, 19). Another handbook counsels, "Be open to changing your image or 'branding,' especially when engaged in party politics" (Nova Scotia Advisory Council on the Status of Women 2014, 7). The handbook also suggests that women candidates seek media training to learn "hand gesturing and voice projection" techniques. Communications consultants will help candidates tailor messages in response to polling and focus groups, and the Women's Campaign School at Yale University has a workshop called "Your Campaign Image."

A candidate's choices may vary depending on the medium and anticipated audience. For example, Gershon (2009) found that politicians tend to present themselves in ways that are consistent with gender stereotypes when they are communicating with potential supporters on their campaign websites, but adopt a more general and broad-based strategy on their official websites. Similarly, in their examination of parliamentary websites and "householders" (i.e., constituency newsletters), Royce Koop and Alex Marland (2012) found that the self-presentation of members of Parliament is "inconsistent," with most presenting themselves as Ottawa insiders on their websites but then as political outsiders who are closely connected to their local constituents in their newsletters. Melanee Thomas and Lisa Lambert's (2013) study of MPs' communications suggests that the presentation of MPs' parental status is conditioned by both gender and party affiliation. Male politicians were much more likely to mention or include photographs of their children on their websites or in their householders; among female MPs, only Conservatives included photographs of their children in their communications, and in all cases, the children were grown, even though women from all parties had children who were, in some cases, very young. In other words, the image that a candidate conveys is not necessarily a true "likeness of self," but rather a strategic (and fluid) construct.

Among visible minority candidates, image management may include westernizing names, seeking endorsements from prominent community leaders, or promoting themselves as politicians who do not speak for one particular community (Biles and Tolley 2008; Bird 2008a; Lapp 1999). The electoral context may influence candidates' self-presentation. For example, candidates running in ridings with large minority populations may put forward an image that stresses their ability to respond to so-called minority interests, while candidates running in ridings with small minority populations will be more likely to practise the "politics of commonality" and emphasize their ability to respond to broad interests (Canon 1999; Citrin, Green, and Sears 1990; Schaffner and Gadson 2004). Variations in self-presentation may be partly a result of a candidate's style and personal preferences, but also a function of careful political calculations about what it takes to appeal to voters and, ultimately, to win. Kristofer Frederick and Judson Jeffries (2009) argue that public image crafting is particularly crucial for minority candidates who must balance their appeals to specific constituencies with a need to attract broader support. This balance requires a "deracialized campaign strategy" and a moderate and non-threatening public image that de-emphasizes race but does not alienate the minority voters who make up their base of support. Choices about image and branding are thus influenced by an understanding of how candidates will naturally be perceived, and campaign teams work within these bounds.

How candidates present themselves is not just cold calculation, however. It is also a means of fitting in, a consideration that is especially salient for non-prototypical candidates. Research on internalized racial oppression suggests that minorities may alter their behaviour, appearance, and language in an attempt to blend in or "pass" (Pyke 2010). They may comply with generally accepted standards of self-presentation and espouse an ideology of fairness and egalitarianism. This practice is adaptive, and it is not surprising that some candidates may deliberately or subconsciously adhere to dominant cultural norms, particularly when trying to gain acceptance in mainstream political institutions. Internalized oppression may also cause minority group members to shy away from leadership positions because they believe they are not qualified, to confine their relations to those within their "own" group because they feel that this is the environment in which they will be most successful, or to avoid behaving in ways that would confirm perceptions about the minority group (Axner 2012). In light of this, we should actually expect minority politicians to present themselves in ways that mirror the self-presentation of other politicians. They may downplay their racial background, shy away from minority issues, and play up their broad appeal.

Although it is important to think about politicians' own self-presentation and their resulting media portrayal in tandem, the impact of individual candidates' behaviour on their actual coverage should not be overstated. Indeed, the literature on women in politics shows that while female politicians strategically engage in some gendered behaviours, there remains a mismatch between their own actions and the coverage that results. In their analysis of federal leaders' debates, Elisabeth Gidengil and Joanna Everitt (2003a, 2003b) found a disconnect between party leaders' actual behaviour and the media's interpretation. They argue that the media tended to emphasize the two female leaders' demonstrations of aggression, such as finger-pointing or interrupting, and that the portrayal was not an accurate reflection of the leaders' own presentation. Importantly, it is not that the female leaders did not engage in aggressive behaviours, but rather that their portrayal was out of sync with their self-presentation, with the media tending to focus predominantly on the behaviours that were counter to ingrained stereotypes. Similarly, although media coverage tends to link female candidates to "softer" policy areas (Goodyear-Grant 2013; Heldman, Oliver, and Conroy 2009; Lalancette and Lemarier-Saulnier 2011), at least one study of candidate issue priorities found that women's policy interests were quite similar to those of their male colleagues (Dolan 2005). In another study on the portrayal and self-presentation of members of the US Congress, David Niven and Jeremy Zilber (2001) found that while female members place a greater emphasis than their male colleagues on so-called women's issues, media coverage exaggerated this difference. Similarly, in their comparison of African American Congressmen's self-presentation and media portrayal, Zilber and Niven (2000) found that reporters tended to give far more emphasis to race and politicians' purported interest in minority issues than the politicians did themselves.

In Chapter 4, I provide additional evidence on the self-presentation and media portrayal of visible minority candidates, arguing that while visible minority candidates do engage in strategic image management, their media coverage tends to portray them in terms of their ethnocultural background more than their self-presentation might imply. This tendency suggests that racial mediation is occurring and that the framing of electoral candidates is not merely a neutral reflection, but rather a function of choices, choices that are influenced by candidate race.

Framing Candidates in Canadian Politics

The concept of framing is central to this study. As was discussed in the introduction, frames facilitate the packaging and consumption of news stories because they provide an interpretative lens for navigating issues, events, and actors. Framing is useful because it helps put the news into a digestible and understandable format. Nonetheless, framing can also encourage complacency because it allows journalists and news consumers to fall back onto recognizable tropes, to accept things as common sense, and to avoid asking or answering critical questions about root causes, possible solutions, and broader implications. The propensity of journalists to frame politics as a game or battle instead of a debate about ideas is especially problematic because it reduces political discourse to tactics, conflict, and winners and losers. Candidates are players, journalists are referees, and citizens become mere spectators (Jamieson 1992, 166–67, employs a similar metaphor).

The framing literature spans several fields of study, and scholars often disagree about what constitutes a frame, what components must be included in a frame, and how one should properly measure frames (Matthes 2009). The political science literature seems to take a fairly broad approach; in political news coverage, some of the most common frames include a focus on the horse race and strategy, personalities, scandal, and conflict. As I argue, however, the media's framing of stories about politics is also influenced by the race of the candidates on which they are reporting. Below, I introduce three racialized frames that can be found in political news coverage; in Chapter 2, I provide a more detailed description and operationalization of each. These three frames may be applied to candidates with white or visible minority backgrounds, they are not mutually exclusive, and stories may include more than a single frame. However, for conceptual clarity, I refer to them separately as the socio-demographic frame, the political viability frame, and the policy issues frame.[2]

Socio-demographic Frame

As the name implies, the socio-demographic frame highlights candidates' demographic characteristics. This might be an explicit description of a candidate's race, such as black, South Asian, Anglo-Saxon, or visible minority, or it might be more implicit, such as a reference to a politician's country of origin or religious affiliation (McIlwain and Caliendo 2011; Terkildsen and Damore 1999). The coverage may draw attention to candidates' support from particular ethnic communities or describe the racial composition of their constituencies, thereby reinforcing the particular appeal of their candidacy (McIlwain and Caliendo 2011; Terkildsen and Damore 1999; Zilber and Niven 2000). The inclusion of a candidate's photograph may further aid in the transmission of a socio-demographic frame because it provides clues about a candidate's skin colour and, sometimes, his or her religion (Jeffries 2002). Stories about minority candidates more often include photographs than do stories about white candidates, possibly because a picture is a means of communicating demographic information without raising it explicitly (Caliendo and McIlwain 2006). When stories do contain visual elements, they are less likely to depict minority candidates in a positive light (Caliendo and McIlwain 2006; Major and Coleman 2008).

Research suggests the socio-demographic frame is more likely to be applied to visible minority candidates than white candidates, and when a candidate's race is mentioned, it is typically because he or she is a minority (Zilber and Niven 2000). Moreover, the coverage of electoral contests with at least one minority candidate is more likely to draw attention to race than those where the candidates are all white; in these cases, it is the race of the minority candidate that is most often mentioned (Caliendo and McIlwain 2006; Terkildsen and Damore 1999). When political analysis does employ racial explanations, these are typically only applied to minority candidates. White candidates are viewed as succeeding on their own merits (i.e., for non-racial reasons), while minority candidates' outcomes are interpreted as a function of their race. This kind of coverage encourages voters to see visible minority candidates as a product of their race. When visible minority candidates win, it is because (or even in spite) of their race, and not because of their other skills or qualifications (Yuen 2009). Their success may be viewed as a product of the support they have from other minority constituents rather than a result of broad-based public appeal.

POLITICAL VIABILITY FRAME

The second frame I examine when looking at news coverage is a political viability frame. This frame emphasizes candidates' electoral chances and qualifications for office. Candidates may be portrayed as insiders or outsiders, as experienced or amateurs, and as likely to win or face defeat (Zilber and Niven 2000). References to polls and strategy may be less frequent in their coverage and thus leave readers with the impression that these candidates are not political players (Goodyear-Grant 2013). When there is a desire for change, this kind of framing could work to the advantage of visible minority politicians, but they may still have to overcome suspicions about their credentials or motives for entering politics. This is because visible minority candidates are often viewed as intruders with less dedication to their party and politics (Sayers and Jetha 2002). Indeed, the viability frame may highlight visible minority candidates' novelty, trail-blazing, or famous "firsts," which can leave voters with the impression that these candidates are political anomalies who do not necessarily belong in electoral institutions (Braden 1996; Gidengil and Everitt 2003b; Heldman, Oliver, and Conroy 2009; Zilber and Niven 2000). As Yasmin Jiwani (2006, 39) points out, "When racialized individuals attain an extraordinary standard of achievement in an uncommon venue, they are likely to receive extensive media attention. The underlying expectation is that such individuals or groups are generally incapable of rising to such standards, or come from cultural traditions antithetical to the particular avenues in which they excel." That said, a candidate's novelty status could also be an advantage because it provides an angle for a story that would not otherwise exist. However, that story is not about a candidate's policy agenda or qualifications – characteristics that voters weigh when making electoral decisions – but instead about the candidate's difference.

The impact of viability coverage may also be affected by what is referred to as the distribution effect, which suggests that when a profession is associated with particular attributes, these characteristics may subsequently be viewed as necessary for the job. If individuals are believed to not possess these characteristics, then they are less likely to be viewed as qualified or appropriate. As a result, unless other information counters this assessment, the group that typically dominates a profession will be assumed to be more qualified (Eagly and Mladinic 1989; Zilber and Niven 2000). In politics, this works to the advantage of white candidates, who are most numerous and thus less likely to be portrayed as atypical and outside the mould.

POLICY ISSUES FRAME

The third frame is a policy issues frame, which focuses on substantive policy matters, ideological positions, and candidates' issue priorities. Although many visible minority candidates bring a diverse set of policy interests to the table, media coverage may suggest that they in fact concentrate on a narrow set of so-called minority issues, such as immigration, multiculturalism, discrimination, racial profiling, and civil rights (Schaffner and Gadson 2004; Zilber and Niven 2000). Overreporting on crimes committed by minority suspects (often black, with white victims) has contributed to a connection between visible minorities and crime (Entman 1993; Fleras 2011; Henry and Tator 2002), while the media's focus on the "undeserving" black poor in the United States has led citizens to see poverty and associated policy responses as an African American problem (Gilens 1996, 2003). The linking of visible minorities to so-called minority issues is akin to the media's coverage of female politicians, which tends to situate them as most qualified to address such "soft" policy issues as education, health care, abortion, and child care. Brian Schaffner and Mark Gadson connect this tendency to journalistic practice and, in particular, the time constraints that reporters face. They suggest that "reporters who hastily prepare stories for the evening newscast may carelessly stereotype the local delegate. They contact the African-American legislator to record a sound bite for a story on racial profiling while contacting non-black legislators for responses on other issues" (Schaffner and Gadson 2004, 619). In one survey of journalists, Meta Carstarphen (2009, 415) found that "when asked, 'Who makes the best sources for stories about race?' the highest number of responses, thirty-four percent, rated people of colour or minorities."

Framing that disproportionately aligns visible minority candidates with a narrow set of "minority" policy issues suggests that these candidates are not interested in, or are ill-equipped to deal with, broader "mainstream" issues. This alignment is particularly problematic if visible minority candidates are in fact interested in other policy spheres, as researchers have found (Schaffner and Gadson 2004; Zilber and Niven 2000). It also plays into voters' fears of racial threat, including the perception that, once in office, such candidates will enact self-interested policies (Rivlin 1992; Sonnenshein 1994). We must consider the compounding impact of such narrow coverage. For example, Carol Sigelman et al. (1995) found that even when minority politicians are stereotyped in positive ways, such as being more capable of handling social justice issues, the effects of that coverage are usually offset by perceptions of incompetence in other areas. In other words, candidates have difficulty overcoming coverage that suggests they are not able to deal with key policy issues.

The Effects of Racialized Coverage

This book does not offer a direct test of the effects of media coverage on voter behaviour or electoral outcomes. Instead it uses the ample existing evidence to demonstrate the key role that the media play in reflecting cultural norms, connecting us to political events, and shaping our understanding of the world around us. This research allows us to make several assertions about the impact of racialized coverage on candidates, voters, politics, and democracy.

First, racialized coverage puts the focus on race and introduces a new set of criteria for evaluating political candidates. Such coverage may lead voters to see the objects of racialized coverage – most typically visible minorities – as exotic outsiders, novelties, inexperienced amateurs, or parochial interlopers. It sets them apart from other political actors, who are presented according to normalized or so-called whitestream narratives that emphasize politically salient features rather than socio-demographics.

Second, by situating candidates within a racialized frame, media coverage marginalizes them from mainstream politics. This marginalization can occur even when the coverage is positive or ostensibly neutral. Examples include coverage of visible minority candidates as the first Tamil MP, the first Muslim woman in Parliament, or the first Japanese Canadian cabinet minister. These portrayals of unusualness or atypicality signal the candidates as individuals who inherently do not belong (Zilber and Niven 2000). Similarly, the media's propensity to seek out minority politicians for reactions to stories about so-called minority issues, or to portray them (competently) tackling problems related to multiculturalism, immigration, or minority rights may reinforce voters' beliefs that visible minority candidates are most capable of addressing these issues rather than other big-picture policy concerns (Schaffner and Gadson 2004; Zilber and Niven 2000).

Third, voters' stereotypes about candidates' beliefs and competencies influence vote choice (Huddy and Terkildsen 1993; Sanbonmatsu 2002). The literature on heuristics is quite compelling in this regard. It shows that we tend to seek out the most economical means of obtaining, storing, and evaluating information. We do this by extrapolating from what we already know and applying these cues, stereotypes, and schemas to new situations (Fiske and Taylor 1991; Lau and Redlawsk 2001). Heuristic cues are most likely to be employed in low-information settings (e.g., when little else is known about the candidates) and when voters are asked to make complex decisions (e.g., to select between a number of candidates) (Fiske and Taylor 1991; Lau and Redlawsk 2001; McDermott 1997). Among other things, heuristics influence our judgment on the likelihood (availability) and categorization (representativeness) of events.

In the first place, events that conform to images or messages already familiar to individuals – those that are most "cognitively available" – will be perceived as most likely (Shoemaker 1991; Shoemaker and Vos 2009; Tversky and Kahneman 1974). When making election predictions, we tend to consider candidates who have won in the past. As an example, while the face of politics is changing, the prototypical elected official is still a white, middle-aged man. Voters (and journalists!) use what they know about the typical "winning" politician – our available information – to make judgments about who is most likely to succeed in politics. This unconscious cognitive reasoning leads us to believe certain candidates are more likely to succeed than others. Media coverage can influence this process by making available criteria – such as a candidate's race, age, or gender – that are associated with perceptions of electability and political success or failure.

In the second place, heuristics can facilitate the categorization of information. Specifically, voters use probabilistic reasoning to ascertain whether a particular item belongs to a given class; they do this by asking whether the item is similar to other items in that category (Tversky and Kahneman 1974). Items that share characteristics with things that are already in a category will be placed in that same category. In a political context, party affiliation serves as an important cognitive shortcut, with voters often choosing local candidates on the basis of their affinity for the party or its leader, and the assumption that all members of a particular party are analogous and thus belong in the same category. The representativeness heuristic may similarly cause voters and journalists to lump visible minorities into stereotypic categories (e.g., passive Asians, pushy Indians, ethnic brokers) that influence how candidates are perceived even if they display none of these characteristics.

By highlighting and making particular characteristics more salient, media coverage can influence voters' assessments of the likelihood of an event and its categorization. On the basis of these cues, voters infer information about candidates, connect this to their own issue preferences, and render an electoral decision. We know, for example, that voters make political decisions on the basis of their socio-demographic similarity to, or difference from, the candidates, which Cutler (2002, 467) refers to as the "simplest shortcut of all." Socio-demographic distance may be an important factor in voters' political calculus either because they automatically or subconsciously attribute more desirable traits to individuals with demographic features similar to their own, or because they believe that someone from their own socio-demographic group is most likely to promote their interests (Cutler 2002; see also Fiske 1998; Johnston et al. 1992).

Racialized coverage and coverage that draws attention to other demographic markers, such as gender, age, religion, sexual orientation, and occupation, may also cue inferences about candidates' traits and beliefs. For example, female elected officials are seen as more liberal and feminist than their male counterparts (Huddy and Terkildsen 1993; Koch 2000; McDermott 1998), and as more ethical and committed to honest government (Dolan 1998; McDermott 1998). Male candidates are viewed as "tough, aggressive, self-confident and assertive, while their female counterparts are described as warm, compassionate, people-oriented, gentle, passive, caring and sensitive" (Banducci et al. 2008, 904). Women are also viewed as more qualified to deal with "softer" policy issues, like health, poverty, or women's issues, while men are seen as more capable of addressing crime, defence, and foreign policy (Huddy and Terkildsen 1993; Sanbonmatsu 2002).

Meanwhile, candidates who look older are given higher personality evaluations than those who look younger (Banducci et al. 2008). Evangelical Christian candidates are viewed as more conservative, competent, and trustworthy than other candidates (McDermott 2009), while candidates who wear head coverings, such as a turban or veil, are evaluated less positively than candidates who do not (Banducci et al. 2008). In addition, voters may infer information about a candidate's qualifications from their occupation (McDermott 2005) or sexual orientation (Golebiowska 2001), and they are likely to evaluate physically attractive candidates more positively (Sigelman, Sigelman, and Fowler 1987).

Visible minority candidates are seen as more liberal than white candidates and are thought to be most qualified to address so-called minority issues (McDermott 1998). Voters are likely to see visible minority candidates as singularly interested in the concerns of their particular ethnocultural communities (Zilber and Niven 2000), and they may be viewed as politically ineffective, inexperienced outsiders (Haynie 2002; Zilber and Niven 2000). All of this is to say that when the media draw attention to a candidate's demographic characteristics, they provide cues from which voters can – and do – infer information about candidate traits and beliefs. These cues thus affect how and on what basis citizens evaluate candidates and politicians.

A fourth and final reason to consider racialized coverage is that apart from influencing voters, such coverage may affect candidates' decisions to run for office, or party elites' propensity to recruit them. As David Campbell and Christina Wolbrecht (2006) point out, girls see themselves as potential candidates not because of the aggregate number of female politicians, but rather the overall visibility of women in the media's coverage of politics. This finding has implications for visible minorities; it is particularly problematic given that the most marginalized groups are the least likely to be recruited, precisely because elites do not consider them winners. Indeed,

Kira Sanbonmatsu (2006) found that party leaders do not accurately estimate women's electoral chances, while Richard Fox and Jennifer Lawless (2004) suggest that not only are women less likely than men to be recruited into politics or encouraged to run, but they are also less likely to view themselves as qualified candidates even when their credentials and characteristics rival those of their male counterparts. Similarly, visible minorities in Canada do not run in numbers that reflect their presence in the general population, and they tend to be recruited in a limited number of highly diverse ridings, which limits their electoral opportunities (Black and Hicks 2006). Media coverage that reinforces stereotypes about electability, presents visible minorities as atypical, or unnecessarily shines a light on their race and minority status may contribute to electoral underrepresentation either by discouraging candidacies or dampening recruitment.

The effects of racialized coverage are thus potentially far-reaching and have implications for candidates, voters, political attitudes, electoral outcomes, and democracy in general. In Chapters 2 and 3, I provide a detailed assessment of the media's portrayal of candidates in Canadian politics to understand whether and when racialized coverage occurs. This examination suggests that race does matter to media coverage. As I argue in subsequent chapters, racialized coverage is only partly a function of candidate self-presentation, and not exclusively so. The media make choices: some reflect candidates' self-presentations, while others respond to societal values, cultural norms, or readers' perceived interests. Regardless, it is plainly evident that racial mediation is occurring.

2
Racialized Media Coverage in Canadian Politics

"News is the first rough draft of history."
– Philip Graham, newspaper publisher

Does race influence the media's selection, interpretation, and shaping of stories? This chapter answers that question through a systematic comparison of the news coverage of white and visible minority candidates in Canadian politics. It is a comprehensive assessment of the *form* that candidates' coverage takes, including the amount, prominence, tone, visuals, and presence of quotations, as well as its *focus*, including attention to candidates' socio-demographics, perceived viability, and policy interests. I find that visible minority candidates' coverage is more negative, less prominent, more filtered, and more likely to include a photograph (a subtle way of cuing candidate race) than is the case for white candidates. Not only does the form of candidates' coverage vary by race, but so too does its focus, with visible minority candidates' coverage more likely to highlight their socio-demographic characteristics and less likely to portray them as interested in policy issues that "matter." While viability coverage does not, overall, vary by candidate race, visible minority candidates do need to first prove themselves as incumbents or potential electoral winners. These findings underscore not only the ways that race matters, but also the subtle ways in which the coverage of Canadian politics is racially differentiated. Although factors outside the media's purview doubtless influence these patterns, it is not possible to simply write them off as a product of candidate self-presentation, a point taken up in Chapter 4.

My conclusions are drawn from an analysis of 980 stories that appeared in eighteen of the country's largest English-language print dailies during the 2008 federal election.[1] The sample includes the country's largest circulating papers; Canada's "paper of record," the *Globe and Mail*; regional representation through several dailies; and stories written by some of the country's top political reporters. Given the complexities of studying racialization and the potential for implicit meanings to be lost in translation, French- and foreign-language papers have been excluded from this study, a feature that some may find limiting. Sean Hier and Daniel Lett (2013) argue, for example, that by focusing on a narrow swath of media outlets or a single news medium, analysts risk overstating the extent to which news coverage is racially biased. Concerns about sampling and generalizability should not be brushed off, but there is good reason to believe that the racialized patterns that I uncover here would be found in other media. In an analysis of the English- and French-language reporting on Hérouxville's Code of Life – a 2007 document aimed at immigrants that outlined the behaviour expected of citizens and stipulated, for example, that women should not be stoned – similar patterns of coverage emerged irrespective of the language of the news story (Pottie-Sherman and Wilkes 2014). Other analyses suggest that the portrayal of immigrants and minorities may be more hardened, and arguably problematic, in French-language media given anxieties over minority accommodation and the status of francophones in Quebec (Bouchard and Taylor 2008; Potvin 2012; Potvin 2014).

In the ethnic press, while there is a stronger emphasis on political integration and information than is the case in mainstream media, one study of news coverage during the 2008 federal election found that attention to minority issues and Korean Canadian candidates was higher in the Korean-language press than in the mainstream media (Yu and Ahadi 2010; see also Lindgren 2014). In other words, racialization occurs even in the ethnic media. Moreover, examinations of the portrayal of female politicians in social media suggest that if anything this medium lends itself to more sexist and gendered coverage than its mainstream alternatives; this would probably be the case were we to look at racialized coverage (Anderson 2011; Heldman, Oliver, and Conroy 2009). These studies suggest that norms of coverage – particularly as they relate to race and gender – are surprisingly consistent across media.

A study's conclusions are bounded by the confines of its research design, which includes case selection, sampling strategy, and method, and the research presented here is no exception. However, the ubiquity of racialized media coverage, irrespective of outlet, medium, or language, is not simply an artifact of research design, but rather a reflection of the cultural and institutional embeddedness of race. This is why analysts outside Canada also find racialized coverage when they examine the media's coverage of minorities (Bleich, Bloemraad, and de Graauw 2015). While encouraging researchers to look at other forms and types of media, we can nonetheless assume with some certainty that the racialization identified in this analysis of English-language print news coverage is not unique to this context.

The print media were selected for study because newspapers are where local candidates are most likely to receive coverage. Television coverage tends to focus more on the national campaign and the leaders' tours, with much less attention given to local candidates, so a focus on broadcast news would probably result in a media sample without sufficient coverage of the local candidates who are at the centre of this study. Second, the less restrictive space constraints of the print media allow for a more extensive treatment of individual politicians. Print journalists thus have more latitude to frame their subjects, build narratives, and prime citizens with information about their elected representatives. Third, although readership is declining, newspapers remain an important source of information about politics (O'Neill 2009). Many digital platforms have print origins or serve as aggregators of coverage from a broad swath of sources including newspapers. In addition, newspapers continue to play an important investigative function. Print reporters have broken some of the biggest political news stories in recent history, including the misallocation of funds through the federal government's sponsorship program, evidence of drug use by then Toronto mayor Rob Ford, and fraudulent "robocalls" during the 2011 federal elections. In short, the print media remain a relevant and important source for political information. They also offer an efficient way to study news coverage because they provide more of it for any given story, candidate, or event.

To capture candidate-centred election coverage, I chose a sample of thirty-four visible minority and thirty-four white candidates who ran in ridings outside Quebec to become the focus of the media study.[2] Establishing the race of candidates can be somewhat problematic, and there is no registry of visible minority candidates. The collection of race-based data also raises important normative questions, which Robert Entman and Andrew Rojecki note in their study of racialized news coverage. They point out that "since racial distinctions are heavily cultural if not arbitrary, we must acknowledge that even in writing about and especially coding media texts in terms of race and attributes like skin color, we face the danger of perpetuating the very distinctions we want to overcome." They go on to say, however, "We are writing about how people come to classify themselves and others into categories called 'race,' not about what race people 'really' are" (Entman and Rojecki 2000, 242n10). In identifying the processes of racialization and representation, this study follows their lead and understands race as a socially constructed but not reified category.

To establish the racial backgrounds of candidates, I relied on published biographies, media accounts, and photographs. Although there are some ambiguous cases, the results are in line with those obtained by Jerome Black (2008a, 2011) and Karen Bird (2008b) who have also studied the presence of visible minorities in Canadian politics. The candidate sample was stratified so it would include individuals who had won and lost in ridings with varying levels of diversity. Within these categories, the sampling was random, and there is variation with respect to candidate gender, incumbency, and electoral outcome. While there is variation along party lines, the sample includes only those who ran for the Conservative, Liberal, and New Democratic parties and who were thus most likely to receive media coverage. Unlike a simple random sample, which may have resulted in too few visible minority candidates to even permit an analysis, this stratified strategy ensured sufficient variation along the main categories of interest (see also Schwartz 2011). The characteristics of candidates included in the analysis are shown in Table 1.

Using the names of these candidates and the dates of the campaign period (September 7 to October 14, 2008) as the search parameters, full-text articles were retrieved from Canadian Newsstand and Eureka.[3] All news stories were included, with the exception of letters to the editor or simple lists of riding candidates. This search returned a total of 980 stories. The largest number of stories (11.6 percent) appeared in the *Toronto Star,* which in part reflects the fact that many of the candidates included in the sample ran in Toronto ridings; 9.8 percent of the stories came from the *Globe and Mail,* 9.6 percent from the *Vancouver Province,* 8.9 percent from the *Calgary Herald,* 7.8 percent from the *Ottawa Citizen,* 7.3 percent from the *Vancouver Sun,* and 6.8 percent from the *Edmonton Journal.* Coverage patterns did not vary significantly among outlets, suggesting that racial mediation is more than an organizational or ideological phenomenon.

The stories were analyzed by three coders who were trained using a comprehensive coding scheme with forty-seven variables that probed various aspects of candidate coverage, article tone, framing, and candidate

TABLE 1

Candidate characteristics

	Candidates (n)		
	Visible minority	White	All
Number	34	34	68
Province			
Ontario	14	16	30
British Columbia	10	7	17
Alberta	6	3	9
Saskatchewan	1	1	2
Manitoba	1	3	4
Nova Scotia	2	1	3
New Brunswick		1	1
Prince Edward Island		1	1
Newfoundland and Labrador		1	1
Visible minority population in riding			
> 50%	17	16	33
15.1%–49.9%	7	8	15
< 15%	10	10	20
Gender			
Male	22	22	44
Female	12	12	24
Party			
Conservative	17	10	27
Liberal	13	17	30
NDP	4	7	11
Incumbency			
Incumbents	18	20	38
Non-incumbents	16	14	30
Election outcome			
Elected	17	28	45
Defeated	17	6	23

characteristics.[4] Many of the variables asked coders to code for "mentions" of a particular phenomenon. A "mention" was defined as "a direct reference to or evidence of the item in question," and coders were instructed to code only what was contained in the article itself. To improve reliability, coders were asked not to infer from the articles nor to code on the basis of information that they might already possess (i.e., their own personal knowledge of the candidates). Coders received approximately twenty-five hours of training using articles from outside the study sample.[5] During this pilot coding phase, intercoder reliability was checked, and coders worked independently once an acceptable level had been reached.[6] After training was completed, my own involvement in the substantive aspects of the coding was limited, which helps to minimize the influence of researcher bias.

Each coder coded approximately 455 randomly assigned articles. In each coder's set were approximately 260 unique articles, in addition to 195 articles that were the same for all three coders; this set of common articles composed 20 percent of the total article sample and was used to check reliability.[7] Once reliability was checked, the common articles were incorporated into the main data set; if the coders disagreed on these common articles, a majority rule was imposed to determine which code would be included in the main data set. The use of three coders in this fashion is an acceptable means for measuring reliability (Krippendorff 2004; Neuendorf 2002), while ensuring coders have a manageable number of units to code.[8]

On the basis of this analysis, we can draw reliable and valid conclusions about the coverage of white and visible minority candidates during the 2008 Canadian election.[9] Here, the analysis I provide is largely quantitative, although quotations from a number of media stories are used to illustrate candidates' coverage.[10] A more discursive and qualitative approach is taken when examining the coverage of visible minority women in politics (Chapter 3). In the remainder of this chapter, I discuss both the form and focus of coverage with a particular interest in how candidates' socio-demographics, viability and policy interests are reported on. In essence, I am testing whether candidate race has any significant impact on the ways in which those candidates are portrayed in the media. I begin with the quantity of candidate coverage.

Quantity of Candidate Coverage

Although visible minorities were at one time almost completely absent from political news coverage – owing in part to their near invisibility in the political arena itself – that is changing. Indeed, there is only a small difference between the amount of coverage received by the white candidates in the story sample and that received by the visible minority candidates; specifically, white candidates are mentioned in 53.7 percent of stories, while visible minority candidates are mentioned in 46.3 percent. Stories average just over

674 words in length, and candidate race does not correlate in any way with average story length. With respect to the type of news coverage that candidates receive, the bulk of the stories in the sample (83.2 percent) are news articles, while 14.9 percent are columns and just 1.9 percent are editorials. White candidates are mentioned more frequently than visible minority candidates in all three categories, with the largest difference occurring in the editorial category, where 57.9 percent of editorials mention white candidates compared to 42.1 percent for visible minority candidates. Given that editorials are where newspapers typically offer their endorsements of particular candidates, this finding provides some clues about how candidate race may affect the *type* of coverage they receive, a hypothesis that is tested throughout the remainder of this chapter.

Prominence and Placement of Coverage

Even if candidates receive roughly equivalent amounts of coverage irrespective of their race, there may still be differences in the prominence of their coverage because most stories mention more than one candidate. A story could be mostly about a particular candidate with another candidate mentioned fleetingly. For this reason, coders noted whether or not the candidate was the main subject of the article. To qualify as being "mostly" about the candidate, the story had to devote more attention to that candidate than it did to other candidates or subjects; if it did, the coder would code "yes." Examples of articles that led coders to code "no" were riding profiles that devoted relatively equal attention to all the candidates, stories about candidate debates that outlined in roughly equal proportions how each candidate performed, and stories that were largely about a candidate outside of the study sample but that quoted or mentioned one of the sampled candidates. There are no statistically significant differences on this measure.[11] That is, whether the candidate is white or visible minority, upwards of 90 percent of stories do not focus mostly on him or her.

Nonetheless, it is still possible that stories that mention visible minority candidates are less prominently placed in the newspaper than stories that mention white candidates (Chaudhary 1980). To assess this, the placement of coverage was divided into two categories: coverage that appears on the front page of the paper (i.e., A1) versus coverage that appears on all other pages of the paper.[12] The bulk of candidate coverage (90.5 percent) appears in the inside pages of the paper, and just 9.5 percent appears on the front page. However, the vast majority (66.7 percent) of front-page stories are

TABLE 2

Prominence of coverage, by candidate race

	Front-page stories	Inside-page stories
Stories	%	%
White candidate	11.8	88.2
Visible minority candidate	6.8	93.2
All candidate	9.5	90.5

NOTE: chi-square = 6.976; $p < .01$; df = 1; phi = 0.084.

about white candidates, while just 33.3 percent are about visible minority candidates. As shown in Table 2, if you are a visible minority candidate, you can expect about 6.8 percent of your stories to end up on the front page, compared to 11.8 percent if you are a white candidate, a statistically significant difference. This suggests that while candidates receive roughly the same amount of coverage, the placement of white candidates' coverage is more prominent than that of visible minority candidates. Of course, this prominence may not be the result of any "hidden agenda" on the part of the media, but simply a reflection of the fact that many key political players, including cabinet ministers, incumbents, and long-serving MPs, are not visible minorities. As one journalist noted in an interview with me, "We certainly are not equal opportunity coverers, as in we're not paid to change the playing field to a level one, when it isn't."

Does that explanation hold water? Is the more prominent coverage accorded to white candidates a function of them occupying more prominent political positions? While the white candidates in the sample held slightly more high-profile positions at the time of the election, the differences are not dramatic. For example, three of the candidates were cabinet ministers, one of whom was a visible minority. Sixteen other candidates had previously sat in cabinet; half were visible minorities and half were white. Of the thirty-eight incumbents in the sample, twenty were white and eighteen were visible minorities, although before the election, the white incumbents had held office for an average of 10.6 years, compared to 6.8 years for visible minority incumbents. Nonetheless, differences in the prominence of candidates' coverage appear somewhat more marked than differences in their "objective" prominence.

When cabinet ministers are removed from the sample, white candidates' coverage is still more likely to appear on the front page than visible minority candidates' coverage, although the gap narrows slightly. Among non-ministers, 64.4 percent of front-page stories are about white candidates, compared to 35.6 percent for visible minorities. White non-ministers can expect 12.4 percent of their stories to land on the front page, while 6.9 percent of stories about visible minority non-ministers will get top billing. When incumbents are removed from the sample, the gap widens somewhat, with white non-incumbents garnering 76.3 percent of front-page stories, compared to 23.7 percent for visible minority non-incumbents. White non-incumbents will see their stories on page one 13.8 percent of the time, compared to 7.4 percent for visible minority non-incumbents. In other words, while white candidates' more prominent coverage could, to some degree, be attributed to their comparative political prominence, something else is driving the difference.

As a result of this coverage gap, when Canadians skim the newspaper, the front pages are unlikely to show examples of visible minorities in politics. This has the potential to reinforce the notion that visible minorities are political outsiders, less viable, and less central to the political process. Moreover, if the coverage that appears on the front page is positive, white candidates benefit doubly because they not only appear in the most visible section of the paper, but are also shown in a positive light.

Tone of Coverage

Coders determined the tone of each candidate's coverage by assessing whether the portrayal of any sampled candidate in a given story was mostly positive, mostly negative, or neutral. Neutral coverage was assumed to be the default; positive and negative tones were coded only if such coverage was readily apparent. As one might expect, the vast majority of candidate coverage (89.1 percent) is neutral. Nonetheless, as Table 3 shows, when coverage is negative, it is most likely to affect visible minority candidates. Meanwhile, when coverage is positive, it is most likely to be directed at white candidates. White candidates are 1.75 times more likely to be covered positively than are visible minority candidates. This racial differentiation is notable given that the bar for assessing non-neutral coverage was quite high. Consequently there is little nuance; visible minority candidates' negative coverage is unambiguous.

TABLE 3

Tone of coverage, by candidate race

Stories	Mostly negative %	Neutral %	Mostly positive %
White candidate	4.2	89.4	6.5
Visible minority candidate	7.5	88.8	3.7
All candidate	5.7	89.1	5.2

NOTE: chi-square = 8.134; $p < .05$; df = 2; Cramer's V = 0.091.

Often, negative stories report on criticisms candidates have faced. For example, in its report on a Surrey riding, one article notes:

> A campaign to get more ethnic signs has uncovered a surprising trend ... Liberal MP Sukh Dhaliwal and Conservative candidate Sandeep Pandher have been criticized in the Indo-Canadian community for not having bilingual signs featuring Punjabi script ... The only Newton-North Delta candidate of the three big parties to include the script known as Gurmukhi on her signs is the NDP's Teresa Townsley, a non-Punjabi. (*Vancouver Province* 2008, A14)

Another draws attention to accusations that Conservative candidate Alice Wong is a member of the Canadian Alliance for Social Justice and Family Values Association, "an extreme fundamentalist organization," that has opposed legal protections for hate crimes and hate speech directed at gays and lesbians (Mercer 2008, A8). Some negative stories simply offer a prediction of the candidate's defeat, typically via a quotation from an opposing camp (e.g., Bermingham 2008). There are also stories that provide a negative account of several candidates in one fell swoop. For example, when Conservative candidate Lee Richardson made some comments about immigrants and crime that led the Liberals and NDP to call for his resignation, a story notes, "The Conservatives shot back with a statement accusing the Liberals of hypocrisy and questioning whether Liberal candidates Hedy Fry, Garth Turner and Keith Martin would be dropped for quoted statements linking immigrants and crime" (Proudfoot 2008, A5).

In a number of stories in which candidates are reported on negatively, the reporter can deny culpability because the negative remarks come from an outside source. Generally, if asked, most campaigns would foretell the demise of their opponents, and quite a few would happily cast doubt on another party's campaign. That said, it is reporters who decide which leads to pursue, whom to ask, and what quotations to include. That visible minority candidates are more often the subject of negative coverage is telling. Although media reports, by and large, offer a neutral take on political events, when they stray from neutrality and provide a critical perspective, that lens is more often focused on visible minorities than on their white counterparts.

Filtering Candidates through Quotes and Paraphrases

As the preceding discussion makes clear, stories are not told only through the voices of reporters. Quotations and paraphrases allow journalists to inject the voices of others into the account. But to what extent are candidates shown speaking *for themselves* as opposed to being the subject of others' commentary? This question stems from research that suggests lower-status speakers, such as women and visible minorities, are less likely to be quoted; as a result, their coverage tends to be more filtered (Gidengil and Everitt 2000, 2003a, 2003b; Van Dijk 1991). That is, these candidates' stories are told *about* them rather than *by* them. To examine this question, coders looked for instances of quotations from candidates and about candidates, as well as for paraphrased statements about a candidate's position, background, or interests.[13]

With respect to quotations *about* candidates, visible minority candidates are just as likely as white candidates to be "talked about" by others; such quotes can be found in about 9 percent of all stories. An analysis of quotations *from* candidates and paraphrases about their positions, however, suggests that visible minority candidates are less likely to be quoted than white candidates. Specifically, 22.7 percent of all stories include a quote from a white candidate while 14.6 percent of stories include a quote from a visible minority candidate. As is shown in Table 4, 42.2 percent of white candidates' stories include a quotation from them, compared to 31.5 percent of visible minority candidates' stories. White candidates are thus more likely to have their positions and ideas communicated directly using their own words, which leaves less room for journalistic interpretation. As Davis (1985) suggests, the relative absence of filtering also gives the speaker more authority and legitimacy.

Table 4 also shows that white candidates' stories more often paraphrase one or more of their policy positions than is the case for visible minority

TABLE 4

Quotes and paraphrases, by candidate race

Stories	Quote from candidate[a] %	Paraphrase about candidate's policy position[b] %
White candidate	42.2	32.9
Visible minority candidate	31.4	26.4
All candidate	37.2	29.9

a　chi-square = 11.953; $p < .01$; df = 1; phi = −0.110.
b　chi-square = 4.849; $p < .05$; df = 1; phi = −0.070.

candidates. This means that even when white candidates are not being directly quoted, their substantive interests are highlighted in paraphrases more
frequently than is the case for visible minority candidates. Of course, the
difference in policy paraphrases could be driven by the presence of cabinet
ministers in the sample, given that these are the politicians most likely to
speak to policy issues and, perhaps more to the point, two of the three cabinet members in the sample were white. To test this hypothesis, I excluded
the cabinet ministers from the sample and reran the analysis. Although this
narrows the gap somewhat, white non-ministers are still more likely than
visible minority non-ministers to receive policy paraphrases. Specifically,
55.6 percent of non-ministerial policy paraphrases are dedicated to white
candidates, compared to 44.4 percent for visible minorities, a statistically significant difference. In short, white candidates can expect to be quoted more
frequently than their visible minority counterparts and, irrespective of ministerial status, are more likely to have their substantive issues and interests
covered. Why are visible minority candidates less likely to be quoted than
white candidates? In the first place, it may simply be a matter of journalistic
convenience, with reporters tending to go to familiar sources when seeking
quotations (Zilber and Niven 2000). It could also be a result of assumptions
about status (Van Dijk 1991) or, as one journalist suggested to me, perceptions of candidate "quoteability." In this reporter's view, visible minority candidates may not be directly quoted as often because of issues related to their
language proficiency, whether real or perceived. Visible minority candidates
with whom I spoke also suggested that reporters often seem surprised when
a minority turns out to be well-spoken; one staffer mentioned that visible

minorities are sometimes even explicitly described as "articulate" in their coverage, as though this is newsworthy. For example, a profile about Olivia Chow contains no fewer than five references to her communication skills: "she speaks in brief bursts, rather than expansive paragraphs"; "off teleprompter, she is less impressive"; "[Layton] was the orator, she was the organizer"; "struggled to learn English"; and "whether she has the rhetorical passion to cut through the verbal sparring and connect with voters outside her left-of-centre base is another question. If she is to make history as the first Chinese-born mayor of Canada's largest city, being a 'doer' may not be enough" (Martin 2014, M1). These descriptions are indicative of some of the assumptions that underscore journalists' decisions about a story's content and the voice that is given to their subjects.

Communicating Race through Photographs

Content goes beyond words, and visuals are an important aspect of media portrayal. Indeed, 15 percent of candidates' stories include their photograph. Some of these are simply headshots, while others show the candidate on the campaign trail. The presence of photos is important because images allow journalists to communicate information about candidates without saying a word. Rather than stating outright that a candidate is not white and thus opening themselves up to accusations of racism or bias, journalists can convey this information through a simple photograph. Race can thus be conveyed implicitly and under the cover of objectivity. Past research (Caliendo and McIlwain 2006) shows that photographs of visible minority candidates appear more frequently than photographs of white candidates, and my analysis confirms this conclusion: 18.3 percent of stories mentioning visible minorities include a photo of the visible minority candidate, while only 12.2 percent of white candidates' stories similarly depict them photographically, a difference that is statistically significant.

This finding bears reflection for several reasons. First, whether a story includes a photograph is a conscious decision. If such decisions were purely objective, visible minority and white candidates would appear in photographs at exactly the same rate. Instead, the media choose to include photos of visible minority candidates more frequently than photos of white candidates. In my interviews with journalists, I asked why visible minority candidates may appear in photographs more often. One reporter suggested that newspapers are always trying to show diversity on their pages and, because the majority of politicians are white, editors jump at any opportunity to show a visible minority. In this reporter's view, there is not "any kind of nefarious agenda here." This opinion was seconded by another reporter who noted that because most photographs in the newspaper are "headshots of white men," when there is a chance to include photos that are more representative of Canada's diversity, "they're keen" to do so.

This explanation seems plausible, but somewhat surprisingly, I do not also find a gender difference in candidate photographs. Like visible minorities, women are underrepresented in politics, and if there is a diversity and inclusion agenda at work, presumably editors would be equally motivated to include photos of female politicians whenever they could. This is not evident in my sample. Perhaps, however, critiques of gendered media coverage have permeated newsrooms to the extent that when editors select story visuals, they are conscious of not *over*representing female politicians, a consciousness that has not yet manifested itself when thinking about how to cover other marginalized groups. It is also possible that political parties are driving the presence of visible minorities in photographs because, as another journalist noted, at media events involving leaders and "so-called star candidates, ... party spin doctors always make sure that they're surrounded by groups that include visible minorities and women." Again, however, we should then also expect to see gender differences in candidate photographs, which is not the case.

A second reason to consider the use of photographs in candidate stories is that information about candidates' race (in addition to characteristics such as gender, age, and even religion if, for example, the candidate wears a turban or head scarf) is communicated by a photograph implicitly rather than explicitly. In one experimental study (Unkelbach, Forgas, and Denson 2008), research participants played a computer game in which they shot at different people carrying guns, coffee mugs, or pop bottles. Some of the targets were wearing turbans or head scarves, while others were bare-headed. Participants were told to shoot only at those who were armed. To simulate the kind of quick decision making that occurs in the real world, the game was timed and points were awarded. Noting a clear "turban effect," the study's authors found that participants were much more likely to shoot those wearing religious head coverings, regardless of whether the target was armed or male or female, and irrespective of the participant's stated egalitarianism. This tendency is indicative of both our implicit stereotypes and the strong and persuasive power of visual cues. In the electoral arena, such cues are important because while verbal appeals can activate voters' equality norms and thus reduce the effectiveness of racial priming, subtle visual cues can make race salient while simultaneously concealing the racial intent of the appeal (Mendelberg 2001). In other words, *showing* that a candidate is a visible minority may engage voters' racial considerations more effectively than simply *saying* that the candidate is not white. As a result, the inclusion of a candidate's photograph is not a neutral choice nor is it without consequence. The upshot can be effective and insidious.

Reasoning that there are some factors that render candidates more "photoworthy" and that these may be correlated with race, I looked at a few other possible explanations. First, I found that non-incumbents are more likely to be depicted in photographs than incumbents (18.4 percent versus 13.3 percent, a difference that is statistically significant). This may be because journalists assume that a photograph of a (known) incumbent is not needed. A photograph is one means of acquainting voters with challengers whom they might not recognize. Disaggregating these results by candidate race, I found that visible minority non-incumbents' stories are more likely to include a photograph than white non-incumbents' stories (24.8 percent versus 14.8 percent, a difference that is statistically significant). This further suggests that assumptions about a candidate's recognizability may underpin, at least in part, visible minorities' photographic coverage.

I next looked at gender. Given what we know about gendered mediation, I expected to see women depicted more frequently in photos than men. However, as noted above, there is no statistically significant difference. That is, male candidates are just as likely to be shown in photographs as female candidates. There may be a few reasons for this. First, underscoring a point made above, critiques from academics and political observers may have made journalists more conscious of the way in which female politicians are portrayed, and the media have thus sought to avoid the kind of gendered portrayals that we have seen in the past. Second, although I do not find quantitative differences in the photograph coverage of male and female candidates, there may be qualitative differences. The photographs of female candidates may be more sexualized or less flattering. They may be depicted in more passive positions or alone, rather than surrounded by supporters. Although these are important questions, one limitation of this data set is that the databases from which the stories were drawn do not include actual photographs, but rather a photo notation and the caption. As a result, we are not able to judge gendered (or racialized) differences in the depiction of candidates in photographs.

Nonetheless, perhaps the most persuasive explanation for the opposing findings on race and gender differentiation in candidate photos is that while gender can be easily communicated without a photograph – often just through the candidate's name or the use of a pronoun – race is more complicated. Although voters may recognize some names as Chinese, South Asian, or non-European, this is not always the case, nor is there any pronoun to signify "non-white." A photograph, however, offers a way of clearly communicating information about candidate race without drawing explicit attention to it. Photographs may substitute or supplement framing centring on candidates' socio-demographics.

Socio-demographic Framing

A focus on candidates' demographic characteristics is one of the most basic ways in which racialized coverage can manifest itself. Candidates' socio-demographic coverage was examined using seven variables. The first five relate to a candidate's personal characteristics: mentions of a candidate's race (either white or visible minority), birthplace (either Canadian- or foreign-born), religion (either Judeo-Christian or non-Judeo-Christian, such as Sikh, Muslim, or Hindu), language (either English/French or other), and the birthplace of a candidate's parents (either Canadian- or foreign-born). Two additional variables relate to the characteristics of a candidate's riding or supporters: mentions of the demographic composition of a constituency or of a candidate's supporters (either minority or "mainstream").

Mentions of candidate religion, language, and parents' birthplace turned out to be relatively rare (each occurred in twelve articles or fewer). Possibly, attributes such as candidate birthplace or race are taken as "stand-ins" or proxies for characteristics such as religion or language, which therefore need not be discussed. Alternatively, journalists may feel uncomfortable discussing candidates' religion, or it may be more difficult for them to determine a candidate's religion or parents' place of birth. Regardless of the reason, coverage of these attributes is uncommon, and these results are not discussed in detail. Instead, I focus on mentions of candidate race and birthplace, as well as mentions of riding composition and community support.

Some socio-demographic framing is quite explicit. Take, for example, the description of Conservative candidate Tim Uppal as "the bearded, turbaned

Sikh [who] was still in his 20s when he challenged then Liberal cabinet minister David Kilgour" (Henton 2008, A4). A more recent profile of the MP notes, "Mr. Uppal is nothing if not distinctive in the Commons ... In a body full of white, middle-aged males, Mr. Uppal is that young man (he sports a remarkably bushy beard) wearing the vibrant Tory blue turban" (Taber 2011). The same story describes Mr. Uppal as a former DJ for a "multilingual radio station" who spun "mostly hip-hop Punjabi mix music." Note that the article does not describe Mr. Uppal simply as a DJ or a broadcaster, but rather draws marked attention to the "ethnic" nature of his former profession. Another article offsets a Sikh candidate's diversity with a reference to his Canadianness: "Although he wears a turban, 32-year-old Jagmeet Singh, the New Democratic Party candidate, points out he's very much a modern Canadian as he was born and educated here" (Crawford 2011, U8). Meanwhile, a story about Liberal incumbent Omar Alghabra does not explicitly refer to his race, instead saying, "Born in Saudi Arabia to Syrian parents, Alghabra came to Toronto alone as a teenager to find opportunity in Canada" (Wilkes 2008, M8). This story also includes a photo of Alghabra.

References to candidates' support in particular communities are another way of cuing a candidate's background, which is the implied reason for the connection between the candidate and an ethnocultural community. One example of this kind of coverage can be found in an article about Liberal candidate Raymond Simard, who ran in Saint Boniface. The story quotes a commentator who notes that "Mr. Simard is very strong in the francophone community" (Coutts 2008, A6). Alternatively, the journalist may draw attention to the socio-demographic composition of the candidate's riding either as a means of distinguishing the candidate from his or her voters or as a way of highlighting their similarities. Take, for example, an article by Doug Ward on six electoral races in British Columbia. Reporting on the riding of Richmond, Ward (2008, A5) notes, "Conservative leader Harper probably won some support in the riding's huge Chinese Canadian community with his party's apology for the Chinese head tax," while in Burnaby–Douglas, Ward suggests, "Leung's social conservatism could win him votes in the riding's growing Asian community." Other articles mention a riding's "diversity" or "growing immigrant population" as a means of describing the voters who live there.

In short, there are a variety of ways to draw attention to socio-demographics. So how frequent are these mentions? I found that 14.4

Figure 1

Proportion of socio-demographic mentions, by candidate race

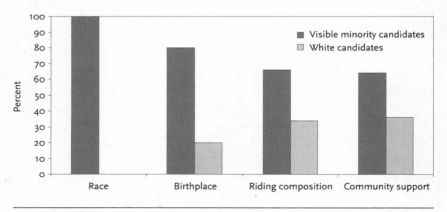

NOTE: Race: chi-square = 37.090; $p < .01$; df = 1; phi = 0.195; birthplace: chi-square = 17.649; $p < .01$; df = 1; phi = 0.134; riding composition: chi-square = 7.242; $p < .05$; df = 2; phi = 0.086; community support: no statistically significant relationship between mentions of community support and candidate race.

percent of all stories include at least one socio-demographic variable. The most common type of socio-demographic mention is a reference to the composition of the candidate's riding, found in 8.1 percent of all stories. References to a candidate's race appear in 3.2 percent of stories, while references to a candidate's place of birth can be found in 2 percent of stories. The least common type of socio-demographic mention (apart from references to religion, language and parents' birthplace) are discussions of a candidate's support for particular communities, which occur in 1.1 percent of candidate stories. As Figure 1 illustrates, however, the distribution of socio-demographic mentions varies greatly by candidate race.

Tellingly, *all* mentions of candidate race are made in relation to visible minority candidates. In terms of magnitude, 6.8 percent of stories about visible minority candidates make some reference to their race, while no stories about white candidates do so. The majority of coverage of candidate birthplace (80 percent) is also in reference to visible minority candidates; these mentions appear in 3.5 percent of stories about visible minority candidates. When visible minority candidates' birthplace is mentioned, it is nearly always foreign; only one article mentions a visible minority candidate's Canadian birthplace. In only four cases is the birthplace of white candidates mentioned (generally to signal whether the candidate was born in the riding).

Similarly, references to the demographic composition of a candidate's riding are firmly targeted at visible minority candidates, with two-thirds of these mentions appearing in articles about visible minority candidates. Taken together, 10.6 percent of articles about visible minority candidates mention the demographic composition of their ridings, compared to only 5.9 percent of articles about white candidates. Among visible minority candidates, nearly all mentions of riding composition (96 percent) emphasize minority socio-demographics, including the proportion of immigrants, ethnocultural minorities, and citizens of non-Judeo-Christian faiths. Meanwhile, 75 percent of mentions of white candidates' riding composition refer to minority socio-demographics; many of these are situated within a context of "ethnic targeting" (e.g., Martin 2008b; Moloney 2008; Ward and Lai 2008). In other words, when riding composition is covered, the focus is almost always the community's non-white/non-mainstream makeup, no matter the race of the candidate. White candidates' socio-demographic backgrounds are apparently not newsworthy, nor are the demographics of ridings with predominantly white voters. This just underscores the extent to which whiteness is viewed as natural and neutral, while minority statuses are deemed different and thus merit coverage. Such an assumption leads to coverage that is racially differentiated.

Another way of cuing race is to refer to the communities from which candidates are drawing most of their support. References to candidates' clout in particular communities are relatively rare (only about 1 percent of any candidate's coverage), and there is no statistically significant correlation with candidate race. However, most mentions of community support (72.7 percent) pertain to support from minority communities and, of these, 87.5 percent are made in reference to visible minority candidates, while the remainder (12.5 percent) refer to white candidates' support from minority communities. This difference is statistically significant, meaning that when there are mentions of community support, these generally refer to minority communities, which tend to be linked to visible minority candidates.

If these socio-demographic variables are combined – that is, all variables related to candidates' socio-demographic characteristics, riding composition, and community support – 3.2 percent of white candidate stories refer to majority or mainstream characteristics. By contrast, 15.6 percent of stories about visible minority candidates mention minority characteristics. This suggests that when socio-demographic framing is employed, it is firmly targeted at visible minority candidates.

It is also significant that discussions of riding composition tend to reinforce visible minority candidates' minority status, while the coverage of white candidates emphasizes their ability to appeal to voters unlike themselves. This tendency echoes the sentiment expressed by Ron Leech, the Alberta Wildrose candidate mentioned in Chapter 1, who asserted that minority candidates represent minorities while white candidates can represent everyone. Coverage characterizing candidates as cultural bridge-builders is almost exclusively confined to white candidates; visible minority candidates are more commonly portrayed as co-ethnic capitalizers who win primarily because of support from their "own" communities. In reference to a particularly heated nomination battle, Scott Young (2008, A13) observes, "Ethnic communities wield significant political power. Residents of Fleetwood–Port Kells will remember the 2004 federal election, when busloads of immigrant South Asian Tory members descended on the party nomination to vote for Nina Grewal." Young goes on to say that nominations are "easily exploited by non-citizens ... Immigrants in that riding made a sham of our electoral system."

This framing is cause for concern not only because it applies a different standard to white and visible minority candidates, but also because the notion that visible minority candidates win primarily on the basis of a co-ethnic voting block is empirically dubious. There is only one riding in Canada where a single visible minority group forms a majority: Richmond, in British Columbia, where voters of Chinese descent make up 50.3 percent of the population. In six other ridings, a single visible minority group makes up one-third of the population. This means that in order to win, visible minority candidates, just like their white counterparts, must bring together diverse coalitions of voters, a shared imperative that is rarely depicted in news coverage.[14] In addition, very little is made of the fact that other, much larger, voting blocks exist. For example, during the 2008 election, Catholic voters formed a majority in 93 (30 percent) of the country's 308 electoral ridings, including 37 where they represented 90 percent or more of the population. Protestant voters, meanwhile, formed a majority in 45 ridings

(14.6 percent). These sizable voting blocks are given far less media attention, and little is made of the fact that white candidates may play on their "natural" constituencies to garner an electoral win.

Instead, white candidates appear as cultural ambassadors, a trope typified by the coverage of Jason Kenney, then the minister of citizenship, immigration and multiculturalism. In one profile of Kenney, the *Toronto Star* notes, "The MP for Calgary Southeast has become a fixture at dragon boat races, Ukrainian folk dances, Macedonian dinners and Diwali celebrations. He pops up everywhere, tweeting as he goes and earning the nickname (courtesy of erstwhile colleague Rahim Jaffer) 'the minister for curry in a hurry' ... It's been a slog, he says, riding by riding, samosa by cheese perogy by pot sticker dumpling" (Diebel 2011a; for a similar profile in the *Globe and Mail*, see Jimenez 2008). References to food and dance ("saris, samosas and steel bands") are the stock in trade of stories on minorities in politics, and the "curry in a hurry" moniker is repeated in a number of stories about Kenney. Of course, reporters are quick to point out that it was not *them*, but one of the minister's colleagues (and a visible minority one at that) who bestowed the nickname; this provides them with a justification for unproblematically using it. My analysis did not uncover the use of equivalent monikers for politicians who focus their attention on business executives, industry professionals, or the corporate elite. Indeed, it is rare to find the courting of "mainstream" voters presented in terms that mirror the "wooing" of minority voters, who are often presented as passive and easily persuaded.

Stories written outside of the 2008 campaign only underscore the pervasiveness of this framing. For example, in an article about a 2011 campaign stop by Stephen Harper in Brampton–Springdale, the reporter notes, "Every time the Conservative leader emphasized a point, bearded men in turbans clapped and *droned in unison*" (Grewal 2011, GT2; emphasis added). This imagery is echoed in a column about "Liberal ethno-politics," which describes one-time leadership candidate Gerard Kennedy as someone who had "been staked out early by ethno-politicians as an empty vessel into which they could pour their parochial agendas" (Kay 2007, A20). The columnist goes on to liken "ethnic" party members to cattle: "The Montreal Liberal convention was a close-fought thing, and the mass migration of hundreds of well-herded delegates along ethnic lines was likely the deciding factor." Reporting on a 2004 Liberal nomination contest in Don Valley East, a riding with a large visible minority population, James Cowan (2004, A10) maintains, "These demographics dictated not only the issues discussed by the candidates, but also the machinations taking place in the backrooms. There were allegations that the South Asian community stacked the membership list with illegitimate forms. There were cheat sheets to help first-generation immigrants understand the complex balloting process." Allegations of illegitimacy and cheating are portrayed as though they are a natural consequence of the involvement of immigrants and minorities in politics.

Reflecting on Harinder Takhar's 2013 Ontario Liberal leadership bid, one columnist writes that the candidate's "almost exclusive reliance on South Asian support makes a mockery of multiculturalism (ghettoizing himself rather than broadening his base with multi-ethnic outreach)" (Cohn 2013, A6). Again, there is the suggestion that an "ethnic" politician is playing the "race card" by encouraging South Asian Canadians to support his campaign. Another columnist notes, however, that Takhar is simply "a savvy guy who has cleverly worked within ... [the] leadership-selection process." Takhar

> does not deny that he has pulled most of his support from a small number of immigrant communities. But that doesn't entirely set him apart from the rest of the leadership field. "Charles Sousa went to his community and got votes," Mr. Takhar said in an interview, referring to the fifth-place candidate's focus on fellow Portuguese-Canadians. "He's not being targeted because he's not the same colour I am."

The column goes on to say that the campaign's two front-runners, Kathleen Wynne and Sandra Pupatello, have also "disproportionately drawn support from relatively narrow demographics" even though they have tried to appear more broad-based in their appeals (Radwanski 2013, A9). They faced little backlash as a result of these tactics.

These portrayals are indicative of a distinction – raised in the literature on social capital – between bridgers and bonders (Putnam 2000). Cultural bridgers are those who build and retain diverse social networks made up of individuals from a range of socioeconomic and ethnocultural backgrounds, while cultural bonders are those who generally have ties only with people from backgrounds similar to their own. In political news coverage of community support, white candidates are framed as cultural bridgers who appeal to a diverse group of voters – often people unlike themselves – while visible minority candidates are framed as cultural bonders who mostly appeal to people like themselves.

While explicit mentions of candidates' support among members of specific ethnocultural groups is relatively rare (occurring in just 1.1 percent of all articles), these references most commonly highlight the connection between a visible minority candidate and a minority ethnocultural community. Mentions of visible minority candidates' support within minority communities occur twice as often as mentions of white candidates' support within majority communities; that is, 1.5 percent of visible minority candidates' stories include a mention of support from minority communities, while 0.6 percent of white candidates' stories include a mention of support from majority communities, a difference that is statistically significant. In other words, visible minority candidates are more likely than white candidates to be positioned as candidates who succeed on the basis of their ties to their "own" communities.

The characterization of visible minority candidates as cultural bonders is illustrated in a story about Newton–North Delta, a riding in British Columbia's lower mainland:

> This is another true three-way race, with incumbent Liberal Sukh Dhaliwal under threat from Conservative candidate Sandeep Pandher and New Democrat Teresa Townsley ... The NDP finished second [in 2006] and has high hopes for Townsley, a nurse who is vice-chairwoman of the Delta board of education. The Tories hope that having a Sikh candidate this time will cut into Dhaliwal's support in the riding's Indo-Canadian community. (Ward 2008, A5)

Here, it is assumed that the "Indo-Canadian community" will naturally support either Dhaliwal or Pandher – both of South Asian descent – although the reporter carefully positions this as the party's opinion, not his own. What is problematic is the fact that discussions of co-ethnic voting allegiances rarely appear in articles about white candidates who receive significant support from white voters (Tolley and Goodyear-Grant 2014). There is thus a disparity in portrayal.

A similar "ethnic" narrative is employed in a story about Conservative candidate Devinder Shory. Shory, of Indian heritage, ran against Roger

Richard, an independent candidate with Anglo-European origins. Richard's campaign manager, Perry Cavanagh, claims that "Shory won his party's nomination with non-citizen teenage voters and through other sketchy techniques," inflammatory language that does not appear in quotation marks, suggesting these are the words of the reporter and not a direct quote. The story goes on to say that "Shory refused to comment on Cavanagh's remark, or on any aspect of the Richard campaign. Flipping back and forth between Punjabi and English in his rally speech, the 50 year old lawyer avoided mention of any of his rivals" (Markusoff 2008, A6). The references to "non-citizen teenage voters," "sketchy techniques," and Shory's use of Punjabi in his rally speech are framing that positions visible minorities as parochial candidates who win unfairly or because of their minority ties.

Among the stories examined for this study, not a single one mentions any visible minority candidate's support from majority (i.e., white) communities.[15] Overall, however, journalists appear more comfortable implying a candidate's support from particular communities by drawing attention to the characteristics of the riding in which the candidate is running, rather than through an explicit mention. Again, white candidates' coverage is more likely than that of visible minority candidates to show them "reaching" into racially different ridings. Among white candidates, 4.6 percent of their articles mention the minority dimensions of their constituencies. A white candidate running in a riding with a large visible minority population is quoted as saying, "It is important to fight for immigrants" (Keung 2008, M7), while a story about Liberal candidate Andrew Kania, who is white, notes, "About one third of the riding's 170,000 residents are South Asian, and many are involved in Mr. Kania's campaign. Mr. Kania, who was chair of John Manley's Liberal leadership bid, has courted Sikh supporters, attending their weddings and birthday parties, and getting to know them through the area's gurdwara, the largest in Canada" (Jimenez 2008, A13). By contrast, an article about Liberal Omar Alghabra says, "Alghabra, born in Saudi Arabia to Syrian parents, has built a solid support base among new Canadians" (Wilkes 2008, U11). Meanwhile, a story about a South Asian candidate points out that she "may not have the political experience of her opponent but she's a household name nonetheless among the riding's large South Asian population. The 32-year-old is former host of Bollywood Boulevard" (Ferenc 2008, M7). In other words, the white candidates may not look like their prospective constituents, but they "fight for them," "court them," and "get to know them," while the visible minority candidates largely represent those like them-selves: in these cases, South Asians and new Canadians.

Although it is relatively common for stories about white candidates to mention the minority demographics of their ridings, just two articles mention the majority dimensions of a visible minority candidate's riding. Meanwhile, 10.6 percent of visible minority candidates' stories mention the minority dimensions of their ridings. This reinforces the notion that, unlike white candidates, visible minorities are not cultural bridgers. Of course, this difference is partly a function of the ridings in which particular candidates run. Visible minority candidates are most likely to run in ridings with sig-nificant visible minority populations. In addition, white candidates are more likely to run in ridings with significant minority populations than visible minorities are to run in ridings with significant white populations. Even so, if journalists really are just pointing out the newsworthiness of a candidate who comes from a different socio-demographic background from that of his or her constituents, we should expect to see a roughly equal number of men-tions in the coverage of visible minority candidates who ran in ridings with large white populations as we do when white candidates run in ridings with large visible minority populations. Is that the case? In the candidate sample, ten visible minorities ran in ridings with large white populations, compared to sixteen white candidates who ran in ridings with significant visible min-ority populations. However, mentions of riding composition are not at all equitable. White candidates receive coverage as cultural bridgers in visible minority ridings, but visible minority candidates receive almost no such coverage in white ridings.

On a number of fronts, it is therefore evident that reporting on candi-date socio-demographics is racially differentiated. Coverage is more likely to mention the race and birthplace of visible minority candidates than those of white candidates. Discussions of riding composition and commun-ity support tend to pigeonhole visible minority candidates as narrow and inward-looking, while white candidates are portrayed as cross-culturally appealing. This kind of coverage may cue voters to see particular candidates as unlike them and thus less capable of representing their interests, which may dampen visible minorities' electoral prospects and political recruit-ment. These effects would only be exacerbated by coverage that positions visible minority candidates as less electorally competitive, the question to which I turn next.

Political Viability Framing

To assess the framing of candidates' political viability, coders looked at reporting on three criteria: a candidate's insider status, quality, and novelty. These three components capture key elements of a candidate's experience, qualifications, and atypicality in the political arena. To assess insider coverage, coders looked for stories that mentioned whether candidates are incumbents, have held previous electoral office, have been involved with their party for some time, have support from party elites, or are superior political strategists. Most insider coverage employed simple descriptors like "the sitting MP" or adjectives like "veteran" and "long-serving," which were relatively straightforward to code. Coding the coverage of candidate quality proved to be more difficult because of its relative subjectivity; as a result, a somewhat narrow definition of "quality" was eventually adopted. Specifically, "quality" was taken to mean a candidate's high profile or prominence, service to the community, being established in the community, or garnering respect.[16] Quality candidates may be described as having long roots in the community, as stars, or as sought-after; they may also be portrayed as having been recruited to run. Coders looked for such words and phrases as "admired," "touted," "esteemed," "a heavyweight," "highly sought," "influential," "outstanding," "popular," "having a strong network," "well-known," "high-status," "renowned," "well-respected," "successful," and "a strong candidate." Finally, novelty coverage included mentions of a candidate being the first to accomplish something or as having a distinctive occupational status or personal accomplishments. In general, if the candidate was portrayed as being the first, top, or one of a few to have done something, the coverage was coded as novel.

The viability frame is often somewhat mundane, providing a "just the facts" account of a candidate's electoral experience. Some stories do, however, offset candidates' viability coverage with mentions of other evaluative criteria, such as this column by the *Globe and Mail*'s Jeffrey Simpson:

> Liberal MP Hedy Fry has never in Ottawa fulfilled the lofty expectations she brought in 1993, her first of five consecutive electoral victories. No matter. In Vancouver Centre, she's been unbeatable. Every election, she is deemed to be in trouble, only to confound the skeptics ... This time, though, she's running in the teeth of ill winds from the national campaign. And she's got two experienced politicians against her ... If things look generally bleak for the

Liberals in BC, luck just might hand [the NDP] a seat they did not expect to win. (Simpson 2008, A21)

Here, the columnist notes that while Fry is a five-time electoral winner, she has her critics and has never really met expectations. Moreover, she is running against tough opponents and for a party whose popularity in British Columbia is waning. Thus, while her electoral history positions her as a viable candidate, it may be diminished by other factors, which the columnist is quick to mention. This is probably an attempt to achieve balance; nonetheless, because the article does mention Fry's long tenure in politics, even if alongside other factors, it would be coded as viability framing.

Another type of viability framing, quite common among visible minority candidates, positions them as "model minorities" or "immigrant success stories." This is typified in a story about Sikh candidates that appeared in the *Globe and Mail:*

More than two dozen Indo-Canadian candidates are running for next month's federal election, contesting ridings from Halifax to Vancouver ... a phenomenal success story for this ethnic community. Most are Sikhs, by far the most savvy campaigners and aggressive political organizers of any visible minority group in Canada ... Many factors account for the electoral success of Sikh Canadians. They are relatively affluent, speak English, and come from the world's most populous democracy, India. (Jimenez 2008, A13)[17]

A *National Post* editorial about Liberal MP Ruby Dhalla, which appeared during the 2004 federal election, further exemplifies this, mixing socio-demographic mentions with coverage of the candidate's viability:

She's a girl from Winnipeg who bears both the brightness and the burden of being one of Prime Minister Paul Martin's star candidates. Ruby Dhalla seems to have all that a prime minister would want in a candidate – she's bright, young, active in Sikh and Liberal circles and brings health care experience as a chiropractor. Oh, and she's also a model and star of Bollywood movies.

Referring to the thirty-something Dhalla as a "girl" juvenilizes her and subtly calls her qualifications into question. Moreover, although the candidate is a

practising chiropractor, the editorial's headline downplays her professional occupation and instead underscores the more titillating aspects of her
résumé, blaring "Sikh Actor Is a Model Liberal Candidate Who Offers
Health Care expertise, too" (*National Post* 2004, A8).

Mentions of a candidate's viability are quite common, with this kind
of coverage appearing in almost two-thirds of all stories in the sample
(64.4 percent of stories include an insider or quality mention or both).
Mentions of candidate quality are much less frequent than mentions of
candidates' insider status, however. There is a reference to candidate quality
in just 6.4 percent of stories, compared to 62.6 percent of stories in which a
candidate's insider status is mentioned.[18] It is possible that journalists are
reluctant to comment on candidates' subjective qualifications for office,
choosing instead to highlight more objective criteria such as their previous
electoral experience and connections to the party. Moreover, the relative
frequency of insider mentions is probably a reflection of which candidates
are most likely to receive media coverage, namely incumbents and those
who are well-known in political circles.

The bigger question, of course, is whether there are racially differentiated patterns in viability framing. When the frequency of insider and quality
coverage is examined by candidate race, there is no statistically significant
difference. Regardless of race, about two-thirds of coverage mentions a
candidate's viability. In the aggregate, then, candidate race does not exert
an influence on the coverage of political viability. This finding diverges
somewhat from my expectation that visible minority candidates would be
portrayed more frequently as politically inexperienced outsiders than their
white counterparts, and runs counter to findings by Jeremy Zilber and David
Niven (2000). Why might that be?

One problem with looking at aggregate patterns of coverage – the
approach taken here – is that it can obscure differences between candidates. We know that the media are more likely to cover those candidates
who are well-known and, because coverage is a necessary prerequisite for
inclusion in this study, the sample is thus biased towards the most politically viable. Because coders only looked for positive viability framing and
did not code for mentions of outsider status or a lack of quality, we will have
missed coverage that positions candidates less favourably. That is, the types
of candidates who are *least* likely to receive positive viability coverage –
the non-incumbents and lesser-known candidates – are also the *least* likely
to receive any coverage at all. In other words, the sampling strategy is, by

Table 5

Viability coverage, by incumbency

	Insider mentions (% of stories)[a]	Quality mentions (% of stories)[b]
White incumbents	82.6	6.6
Visible minority incumbents	86.8	5.7
White challengers	27.1	7.6
Visible minority challengers	5.0	2.5

a   chi-square = 404.1; $p < .001$; df = 1; Cramer's $V = 0.642$.
b   Results do not achieve conventionally accepted levels of statistical significance.

design, picking up those visible minority candidates who have made inroads in the electoral arena and are thus portrayed quite positively. As a result, the results could overstate the similarity between white and visible minority candidates' viability coverage. This explanation is bolstered by the finding that incumbency improves viability coverage, particularly for visible minority candidates, a pattern that is shown in Table 5.

Table 5 clearly shows that white challengers (i.e., non-incumbents) receive significantly more viability coverage than visible minority challengers. The most dramatic difference pertains to candidates' insider coverage, with 27.1 percent of white challengers' coverage mentioning their insider ties, compared with just 5.0 percent for visible minority challengers. White challengers also receive slightly more quality coverage than visible minority incumbents (7.6 percent of all white candidate stories, compared to 2.5 percent of all visible minority candidate stories). In other words, white challengers receive significantly more insider and quality coverage than visible minority challengers, but incumbency closes that gap. Among incumbents, we see little difference in viability framing, regardless of candidate race.

Two important observations can be made. First, incumbent visible minority candidates seem to be accorded more viability coverage than white candidates. Second, visible minority candidates' viability coverage suffers considerably when they are not incumbents, in which case they are much less likely than white candidates to be portrayed as political insiders. This suggests that once visible minorities have, in effect, proven themselves, they are just as likely as white candidates to receive positive viability coverage. When they are not "known commodities," however, visible minority candidates appear not to be given the benefit of the doubt. To put it plainly, if you want to be portrayed as a qualified insider, being an incumbent does matter, but it matters most for visible minority candidates. This point is underscored in Chapter 4, which presents an index that measures candidates' electoral prospects using incumbency, electoral outcome, and party competitiveness as the indicators. On this basis, I assess candidates' actual viability – a measure of self-presentation – against their media portrayals. Again, according to this yardstick, white challengers receive more positive viability coverage than their visible minority counterparts, but incumbency washes away the difference, a finding that confirms the patterns identified in Table 5.

Part of this may have to do with expectations of candidates' political success. Given that visible minorities are less common in Canadian politics, the framing of their viability may reflect the subtle assumption that they are less likely to win than their more typical white counterparts. The findings on novelty coverage are indicative of this assumption, in that all novelty mentions appear in stories about visible minority candidates, although these stories represent less than 1 percent of their total coverage. Nonetheless, because these mentions set visible minority candidates apart as atypical and uncommon, their effects are potentially powerful. This type of coverage is illustrated in a story about Rahim Jaffer: "Jaffer has been [Edmonton–Strathcona's] member of Parliament through four consecutive elections. He has been a star: In 1997, when he was first elected at age 25, his Muslim heritage set him apart from typical Reformers of the day" (Audette 2008, A4). Such coverage, while favourable in that it positions Jaffer as a "star," also characterizes him as a novelty, a Muslim different from "typical" Reform Party members.

Novelty coverage, in a sense, offers a mixed blessing for candidates. In some cases, candidates who would not otherwise attract much notice become the subject of stories – often lengthy features – that provide exposure and potential name recognition. One has to ask whether this is desirable exposure, however. Do candidates benefit when they are framed as atypical? This query is not definitively resolved here, but certainly we should not simply assume that any news is good news, particularly when it sets visible minorities apart from their white counterparts or implies that their minority status is relevant to their political persona. This kind of coverage not only positions visible minority candidates as atypical, but also draws a link – often inappropriately – between their socio-demographics and their political experience or agenda. This point is reinforced when we examine the policy issues to which candidates are most frequently connected.

Policy Issue Framing

To assess policy issue coverage, coders looked for references to the candidate's interest in, support for, or involvement in various aspects of public policy. These included instances of candidates speaking out on issues, mentions of their role as a cabinet minister or party critic for a particular portfolio, or mentions of their membership on a standing committee of the House. In a number of cases, the candidate was quoted in relation to a riding-specific issue or spoke in support of a plank of the party's platform. Coders looked specifically for policy mentions related to crime, social welfare, and immigration and multiculturalism – the so-called minority issues – as well as for mentions of other policy areas, which I reservedly refer to as "mainstream" policy issues. Examples include the economy, natural resources, and health care; a full list can be found in the appendix.

Much has been said about the absence of policy discourse in Canadian elections (Bastedo, Chu, and Hilderman 2012), but policy mentions are in fact fairly common in candidates' coverage, with 39.7 percent of all articles connecting candidates to at least one policy issue. There is no statistically significant pattern in terms of the propensity of coverage to link particular types of candidates to policy issues: 41.4 percent of all stories about white candidates include a policy mention, compared to 37.7 percent for visible minority candidates. As is shown in Table 6, however, there is some racial differentiation in terms of the types of policy issues to which white and visible minority candidates are connected.

For example, visible minority candidates are more likely than white candidates to be connected to crime issues, a finding that is consistent with past research (Entman and Rojecki 2000; Fleras 2011; Henry and Tator 2002). Specifically, 12.3 percent of stories about visible minority candidates link them to crime policy issues, compared to 7.4 percent of stories about white candidates. An example of this linkage can be found in the reporting on a story involving Lee Richardson, a white Conservative candidate who ran in a Calgary riding with a large immigrant population and made comments that drew attention to the portrayal of minorities in crime stories. In an interview with a community newspaper, which was later reported by the national news media, Richardson linked immigration and crime: "Particularly in big cities, we've got people that have grown up in a different culture ... They don't have the same background in terms of the stable communities we had 20, 30 years ago in our cities ... and [they] don't have the same respect

Table 6

Policy mentions in candidate coverage, by story and candidate race

		Candidates				
	White		Visible minority		All	
	n	Stories (%) (n = 526)	n	Stories (%) (n = 454)	n	Stories (%) (n = 980)
Economy	77	14.6***	36	7.9***	113	11.5***
Crime	39	7.4***	56	12.3***	95	9.7***
Environment	45	8.6**	24	5.3**	69	7.0**
Immigration and multiculturalism[1]	31	5.9	35	7.7	66	6.7
Families and seniors	32	6.1	24	5.3	56	5.7
Government	24	4.6	16	3.5	40	4.1
Health	18	3.4	21	4.6	39	4.0
Cities and infrastructure	19	3.6	15	3.3	34	3.5
Transportation	18	3.4	10	2.2	28	2.9
Social welfare	17	3.2	9	2.0	26	2.7
Foreign affairs	11	2.1	14	3.1	25	2.6
Employment and labour	13	2.5	8	1.8	21	2.1
Defence and security	10	1.9	8	1.8	18	1.8
Education	11	2.1	7	1.5	18	1.8
Agriculture, forestry, fishing, mining	8	1.5	9	2.0	17	1.7
Energy, electricity, hydro, gas	11	2.1	6	1.3	17	1.7
Trade and industry	8	1.5	6	1.3	14	1.4
Gay and lesbian rights	2	0.4**	12	2.6**	14	1.4**
Intergovernmental relations	5	1.0	3	0.7	8	0.8
Aboriginal issues	1	0.2*	5	1.1*	6	0.6*
Democratic reform	0	0	2	0.4	2	0.2
Other	12	2.3	6	1.3	18	1.8
Stories with at least one issue mention	218	41.4	171	37.7	389	39.7

notes: Some stories included mentions of more than one policy issue.

Statistically significant at * $p < .10$; ** $p < .05$; *** $p < .01$.

1 These results include stories about Jason Kenney, who is white, and was then the minister of citizenship, immigration, and multiculturalism. When Kenney's stories are removed from the sample, there is a statistically significant relationship between candidate race and stories on immigration and multiculturalism issues.

for authority or people's person or property." He added, "Talk to the police. Look at who's committing these crimes. They're not the kid that grew up next door." Richardson's two main opponents were both immigrants, including one who is a visible minority. They roundly criticized the remarks, and Richardson later apologized. He said that his views are based on what he hears from his constituents and admitted that "what their comments are based on is probably anecdotal – what they read in the newspapers" (quoted in Klaszus 2008). It is notable that Richardson says explicitly that his information comes not from crime statistics or research, but from what he hears, which depends heavily on what his constituents read in the news. News coverage matters.

Diverging from American research (Gilens 1996, 2003), visible minorities are no more likely to appear in stories about social welfare than are their white counterparts, at least not in a political context. On immigration and multiculturalism issues, there is also no statistically significant relationship between these mentions and candidate race, which again was somewhat counter to my expectations. However, this is probably because the sample of white candidates includes Jason Kenney, then the minister of citizenship, immigration, and multiculturalism. Given his portfolio, a large number of his stories connected him to immigration and multiculturalism issues. Indeed, 28 percent of all such mentions were in stories about Kenney. To assess the magnitude of the "Kenney effect," I removed him from the sample. Without Kenney, there was a statistically significant relationship between candidate race and mentions of immigration and multiculturalism issues. Specifically, such mentions appear in 7.7 percent of visible minority candidates' stories, compared to 2.8 percent of white candidates' stories. Given this, the initial finding that visible minorities are no more likely than white candidates to appear in stories about immigration and multiculturalism issues should appear with a caveat that this may be the case only when the minister responsible for these issues is a media-savvy white candidate.

We can draw a few conclusions from these data. First, the link between race and so-called minority issues, which is prevalent in the American research, appears only partially applicable in Canada. On matters of social welfare, the lack of racial variation could be a result of Canadians' comparatively more positive orientation towards social welfare issues, which could depress negative associations between visible minorities and perceptions of dependency. On immigration and multiculturalism issues, there is the "Kenney effect," but also the fact that the sampling strategy targeted white candidates who ran in highly diverse ridings. These are constituencies where immigration and multiculturalism issues are presumably salient, and candidates – regardless of race – may be more likely to discuss them. On crime issues, visible minority candidates are more likely than white candidates to appear in such stories and, in the 2008 election, at least a portion of this discussion revolved around an incident in which a (white) candidate argued that rising crime rates are the result of increased immigration. This suggests that, as in the United States, crime is a racialized policy issue in Canada.

Mainstream policy mentions, meanwhile, appear in 35.7 percent of white candidates' coverage, compared to 28.4 percent of visible minority candidates' coverage, a difference that is statistically significant. Put another way, 59.3 percent of mainstream policy mentions are connected to white candidates, while 40.7 percent are connected to visible minority candidates. Table 6 shows which mainstream issues candidates are most likely to be connected with.

Clearly, when visible minorities do receive policy issue coverage, it is less likely to relate to mainstream issues than is the case for white candidates. Not only that, but visible minorities are much less likely to appear in stories about the economy and the environment, which were among the key issues in the 2008 election campaign (Gidengil et al. 2012). For example, whereas 68.1 percent of economic policy mentions were in reference to white candidates, just 31.9 percent were in reference to visible minority candidates. The relative absence of visible minorities from economic policy discussions is important given how centrally the economy figures in electoral campaigns, and particularly in 2008, which was the height of a global recession and an election in which the Conservatives' Economic Action Plan was a key policy plank (Gidengil et al. 2012; see also Soroka 2002). The findings suggest that visible minority candidates largely do not figure in coverage about an election's "quintessential valence issue" (Gidengil et al. 2012, 13)

The tendency for visible minority candidates to appear less often in stories about the "issues that matter" may leave voters with the impression that these candidates are not tuned into the key policy issues, that they have a narrow focus, or that they will be less able to respond to voter concerns. The problem is compounded if that coverage reinforces voters' stereotypes about candidates' capabilities. For example, Monica Schneider and Angela Bos's (2011) analysis of politician stereotypes in the United States suggests that black politicians are seen as less capable of handling policy related to taxes, the economy, education, and the military.

Of course, we must look at the coverage of candidates' policy interests in tandem with their stated policy priorities; if visible minority candidates are less interested in economic issues, then such coverage is not a function of mediation but merely a reflection of reality. This task is taken up in Chapter 4, where I look at candidate self-presentation. I turn first, however, to other factors that may contribute to differences in candidate coverage, beginning with gender effects.

Gender Effects

Socio-demographic Coverage

Research presented in Chapter 1 shows that female candidates typically receive more socio-demographic coverage than their male counterparts, and the results presented earlier in this chapter suggest that the same may be true of visible minorities. By inference, then, visible minority women might be expected to receive the most socio-demographic coverage. To assess this, I split socio-demographic coverage into two types: personal and political. This split draws on literature about the public-private divide, which situates men in the public realm of politics and decision making, and women in the private domain of home and family (Elshtain 1993; Pateman 1988). Personal socio-demographic coverage includes mentions of a candidate's race, birthplace, religion, language, and birthplace of parents, while political socio-demographic coverage includes mentions of the candidate's riding composition or community support. Arguably, the latter are more politically salient.

Somewhat surprisingly, it is male candidates who receive more personal socio-demographic coverage; specifically, 6.8 percent of stories about male candidates include at least one personal socio-demographic mention, compared to 2.8 percent of stories about female candidates, a statistically significant difference. In contrast to the literature on gendered mediation, we thus find more focus on the personal features of male candidates than female candidates. Moreover, political socio-demographic coverage shows no statistically significant gender differences, suggesting that female candidates are no less likely to receive coverage of these politically salient characteristics. Male candidates are no more likely to be cast as political operatives than their female counterparts, at least not on the dimensions included in this study.

To see if there are any racialized gender differences in socio-demographic coverage, I looked specifically at stories about visible minority candidates. There are no statistically significant gender differences in visible minority candidates' personal or political socio-demographic coverage. That is, visible minority women – possessors of two minority statuses – are not more often the subject of racialized socio-demographic coverage. There is no "multiplier" effect (Fleras 2011). This may be because for women candidates, gender is viewed as the key socio-demographic variable, and thus socio-demographic mentions focus on this factor, rather than on racial characteristics, although that is purely speculative. An alternative explanation is that aggregate statistical analysis does not tell the whole story. Indeed, as is shown in Chapter 3, a more qualitative and discursive reading of visible minority women's media coverage provides a compelling account of the intersecting roles played by race and gender.

POLITICAL VIABILITY COVERAGE

Do these racialized and gendered intersections play out in the coverage of candidates' viability? Based on existing research, we might expect female candidates to receive less viability coverage than male candidates, and visible minority women to receive the least. Looking first at gender, male candidates indeed come out on top: 68.5 percent of male candidates' stories include at least one viability mention, compared to 57.2 percent of stories about female candidates, a difference that is statistically significant. Men are more likely to be portrayed as political insiders than are women (67.3 percent of male candidates' stories, compared to 54.4 percent for female candidates), while women are more likely to be portrayed as novelties (1.1 percent of female candidates' stories, compared to none for male candidates). That said, there is no statisticially significant gender difference in quality mentions. This could be because the media are hesitant to impose specific evaluations of candidate quality, as noted above, given the subjective nature of such assessments; by contrast, mentions of a candidate's insider status or novelty can be justified as ostensibly factual given a candidate's limited electoral experience or recruitment from outside politics. Bolstering this conjecture are the data on policy mentions, where we see that male candidates receive the most policy issue coverage, a finding that I discuss in greater detail below. Again, however, unlike subjective assessments of quality, linking a candidate to a particular policy issue appears neutral, which makes the narrative safer and thus potentially more appealing to journalists.

When race is added to the equation, the relationship changes somewhat, with visible minority women getting a boost in viability coverage. As we might expect, white men still receive the most viability coverage (73.7 percent of their stories include at least one such mention), but they are followed closely by visible minority women (71.0 percent). Visible minority men are next, with 63.5 percent of their stories including at least one viability mention, while white women receive the least viability coverage (just 48.6 percent of their stories include a viability mention). To the extent that there is a race-gender multiplier effect, then, it appears to advantage visible minority women. In light of Black's (2008b) observation that "double minority" candidates have to be more qualified than other candidates in order to succeed politically, the viability coverage that visible minority women receive may in fact be a reflection of reality. This possibility is explored more fully in Chapter 4, where I compare candidates' "objective" viability to their resulting viability coverage. I find that while aggregate coverage of visible minority women's viability roughly approximates their actual viability, the least viable visible minority women can expect to receive much less positive viability coverage than similarly situated visible minority men or any white candidate. This suggests not only that mediation is occurring but, moreover, that race matters to candidate coverage.

Such a conclusion is also apparent when we look at racialized and gendered differences in the coverage of candidates' novelty. Indeed, visible minority women are the only candidates to receive novelty coverage. Although such mentions occur in just a small proportion (2.9 percent) of all stories about visible minority women, the relationship is statistically significant. Moreover, as is discussed further in Chapter 3, visible minority women's atypicality is presented in distinctly racialized and gendered ways, highlighting their exoticism, appearance in Bollywood films, or standing on *Maxim*'s list of the "world's hottest politicians" (e.g., Martin 2008b).

POLICY ISSUE COVERAGE

A final way in which racialized and gendered differences may manifest themselves is through candidates' policy issue coverage. On the one hand, gendered mediation theory suggests that female candidates' coverage will emphasize their interest in so-called women's issues, while my theorization of racial mediation suggests that visible minority candidates will be more closely connected to so-called minority issues, such as immigration, crime, and social welfare. As was noted earlier in this chapter, this latter hypothesis was not fully supported, although I did find that visible minority candidates' coverage was less likely to discuss the most electorally salient policy issues such as the economy or the environment. Overall, male candidates receive the most policy issue coverage: 43.3 percent of their stories contain such mentions, compared to 33.6 percent for female candidates, a difference that is statistically significant. This suggests that male candidates figure more prominently in policy discussions.

With respect to the mainstream policy areas to which male and female candidates are most often connected, statistically significant differences exist only on issues related to natural resources (e.g., agriculture, forestry, fishing and mining) as well as the economy. Natural resource policy issues appear in only a small number of stories (2.3 percent of male candidate stories and 0.8 percent of female candidate stories), but when they do appear, 82.4 percent of mentions are connected to male candidates compared to 17.6 percent for female candidates. Economic issues appear in a much larger proportion of stories (13.9 percent of male candidate stories and 7.5 percent of female candidate stories) but, again, a large majority of these mentions (76.4 percent) are in stories about male candidates.[19] This finding is in line with past research, which suggests that "harder" policy areas are stereotyped as "masculine" (Dolan 2005; Huddy and Terkildsen 1993; Schneider 2009). This stereotyping provides a partial explanation for why more men hold portfolios in these policy areas, although certainly men may also simply be more interested in or qualified to speak to these issues. Stereotyping may also lead the media to contact male candidates to comment on stories about "masculine" policy issues, a situation that is augmented by the tendency of media sources in general to be male, even in stories about so-called women's issues (Farhi 2012). For all these reasons, we might have expected to find a connection between male candidates and more "masculine" policy coverage.

What is perhaps more surprising is that no statistically significant gender differences exist in the coverage of such so-called women's issues as health, education, and families. The literature on gendered mediation leads us to believe that these are the issues in which female candidates should figure the most prominently, but this appears not to be the case. On each of these three issues – health, education, and families – there are a few reasons that we may not find significant gender differentiation. First, because I was not explicitly interested in gendered coverage, coders did not look specifically for mentions of "women's" issues. Rather, they looked for mentions of broad policy areas, and I am using health, education, and families and seniors as a proxy for women's issues. Although the "families and seniors" category did include mentions of child care, abortion, and other women-centric policy areas, the fact that women's issues were not a separate and distinct category might conceal some of the mentions of gendered policy areas.[20]

Second, within the specific areas I looked at, some issues were connected to one or two prominent candidate spokespeople, and their sociodemographic characteristics could affect the extent to which issues appear to be gendered. For example, nearly one-third of the coverage on health issues was connected to Ujjal Dosanjh. Although Dosanjh was not at the time the Liberal Party health critic, he had been the minister of health when the Liberals lost power in 2006 and had served as the premier of British Columbia before entering federal politics. Given his knowledge of the policy file and the fact that health care falls under provincial jurisdiction, he may have a special interest in health care or be viewed by reporters as a natural spokesperson on such issues. Physicians Keith Martin and Benson Lau – both male – also received some coverage on health policy, although interestingly neither Hedy Fry, a physician, nor Ruby Dhalla, a chiropractor, had coverage that connected them to these issues. That said, if I remove all the medical doctors from the sample, 60.9 percent of health policy mentions are connected to women, compared to the 39.1 percent that are connected to men, and the difference is statistically significant. This suggests that when occupational credentials are removed from the equation, health remains a gendered policy issue.

In contrast to health, my candidate sample contained no "natural" spokespeople for either education or families and seniors issues. No candidates had been minister for these portfolios, nor are there parliamentary committees that directly touch on these issues. Thus, there was no clear affinity between any of the candidates and these two policy areas, nor was either a clear campaign priority. Coverage of both areas is rather generic, with male and female candidates speaking about each in roughly equal proportions. When candidates do make reference to these policy areas, it is often simply to signal their importance, perhaps because the federal government does not have explicit jurisdiction over either. In the sample, thirteen candidates (seven men and six women) refer to education policy; coverage is evenly split among these candidates, with none really standing out as the dominant contributor. Coverage on issues related to families and seniors is also fairly broad, with 32 candidates referring to these policy areas. The largest contributors to the discussion were Jason Kenney and Olivia Chow, who respectively garnered 10.7 percent and 7.1 percent of coverage in this area. This coverage is largely a result of debate around changes to the Immigration and Refugee Protection Act that would limit the ability of Canadians to sponsor parents and grandparents through family reunification provisions. This issue was coded as related both to immigration and multiculturalism, as well as to families and seniors. Other candidates mention families and seniors issues much more generically, with coverage spread evenly among them.

When the coverage of so-called minority policy issues is considered in the aggregate, there are similarly no statistically significant gender differences. Overall, male and female candidates are about as likely to be connected to these issues. Nonetheless, some gendered differences exist in the coverage of crime and social welfare issues. Specifically, male candidates are more likely than female candidates to appear in coverage related to crime issues, with 12.3 percent of their coverage focusing on this area, compared to 5.3 percent for female candidates. Put another way, 80 percent of all crime mentions are linked to male candidates. Partly, this might reflect the fact that fully 70 percent of the Conservative candidates in the sample are male. This is important because male candidates are stereotyped as most capable of dealing with crime policy (Schneider 2009), and the Conservatives also ran on a "tough on crime" platform. Thus the high proportion of male Conservatives may be driving the association between crime policy mentions and male candidates.

In contrast, female candidates are significantly more likely than male candidates to appear in stories about social welfare, which includes issues related to social assistance, social housing, homelessness, poverty, and pensions, with 4.2 percent of their coverage focusing on this area, compared to 1.8 percent for male candidates. When issues related to social welfare are raised, 57.7 percent of the time, they are linked to a female candidate. The characteristics of the sampled candidates do not offer any clear explanations for this association. For example, given that the NDP is more likely to stress issues related to welfare, poverty, and homelessness, a large number of female NDP candidates in the sample could have driven the results. However, only one-quarter of the NDP candidates in the sample are women, so there is no notable overrepresentation. In addition, at the time of the election, the minister of human resources and skills development – the government portfolio most closely related to social welfare issues – was a man and not included in my sample, so this is not the driver either. I conclude, then, that some policy issues remain gendered. Although there are no significant gender differences on traditional women's issues like health, education, and families and seniors, women are still more associated with social welfare than are men, and this arguably falls under the "caring" rubric. In contrast, men are more likely to be associated with the rough and tumble world of crime policy.

There are thus gendered and racialized differences in policy issue coverage, which raises a second question about intersectionality. Looking only at visible minority candidates, there are no statistically significant gender differences in the overall amount of policy mentions (38 percent of male visible minority candidate stories include as least one policy mention, compared to 37 percent for female visible minority candidates). Among white candidates, however, statistically significant differences exist with respect to the frequency of policy issue coverage; specifically, 28.1 percent of white male candidates' stories include a policy mention compared to 13.3 percent of white female candidates' stories. This finding suggests that where there is gender differentiation in overall policy mentions, it is being driven by white candidates, with white male candidates more likely to be covered talking about policy issues than their female counterparts. Policy, in other words, may be a man's game, but only among white candidates. Does this hold when we drill down and look not just at the amount of policy coverage that candidates receive, but more specifically at its type? Here, much starker gender differences emerge among visible minority candidates.

In particular, visible minority men are more likely than visible minority women to be connected to crime policy, while visible minority women figure more prominently than their male counterparts in the coverage of social welfare and immigration and multiculturalism policy issues. Specifically, 14.6 percent of visible minority men's coverage touches on crime policy issues, compared to 7.2 percent of visible minority women's coverage. With respect to social welfare issues, visible minority women receive two-thirds of this coverage, with 4.3 percent of their stories touching on this policy area, compared to 0.9 percent for male visible minority candidates. Immigration and multiculturalism issues feature in 10.9 percent of visible minority women's coverage, compared to 6.3 percent for visible minority male candidates. Visible minority men are also more likely to be connected to natural resource policy issues (2.8 percent of their coverage) than their female counterparts (no coverage). Finally, male visible minority candidates are more likely than their female counterparts to be connected to health policy issues, with 4.0 percent of the former's coverage highlighting this area, compared to 0.7 percent of the latter's, although this difference was largely driven by the prominence of Ujjal Dosanjh – a visible minority man – in the coverage of health policy issues. There are no statistically significant gender differences among visible minority candidates in any of the other mainstream policy issues. Thus, to the extent that there are gender differences in policy issue coverage among visible minority candidates, it is in a few policy areas – namely crime, natural resources, social welfare, and health – and in only the last are the differences somewhat inconsistent with what the literature on gendered mediation would have us believe.

In sum, the coverage of policy issues is gendered, and the intersection of gender and race augments the effects in some cases. Overall, male candidates are more likely to be associated with "masculine" policy issues like the economy, natural resources, and crime. While there are no statistically significant gender differences in the coverage of issues related to health, education, and families, women candidates are more likely to be connected to social welfare issues, which arguably fall within the "caring" domain. As the earlier discussion on policy issues suggests, race does influence the extent to which candidates are connected to policy in general, and to particular issues specifically. Gender appears to multiply these effects in a few cases, including in the coverage of crime, social welfare, natural resources, and health.

Constituency Effects

Apart from candidates' personal characteristics, the diversity of the constituencies in which they run may also affect coverage. One compelling suggestion is that to the extent that racialized coverage exists, it is a function of a riding's diversity and not the result of a focus on the candidate's race or difference. For example, greater discussion of minority policy issues might be expected among candidates – both white and visible minority – who run in ethnoculturally diverse ridings, given that these issues are presumably of some interest to those constituents. Meanwhile, socio-demographic coverage may vary with riding diversity, although it is difficult to predict in which direction. On the one hand, newspapers in a less diverse riding might find a visible minority candidate's socio-demographic background different and newsworthy, while on the other hand, to avoid charges of racism, they may avoid such discussion altogether. Conversely, the media in highly diverse ridings may draw attention to candidates' racial backgrounds because race is probably quite salient to voters who are themselves visible minorities. That said, because many of the candidates in highly diverse ridings are from minority backgrounds, drawing attention to socio-demographics is perhaps not newsworthy.

To test these propositions, I examined candidates' coverage by riding diversity. As was shown in Table 1, there are thirty-four visible minority candidates in the candidate sample. Of these, seventeen ran in constituencies with visible minority populations that exceeded 50 percent (highly diverse ridings), seven ran in constituencies with visible minority populations between 15.1 percent and 49.9 percent (moderately diverse ridings), and ten ran in constituencies with visible minority populations of 15 percent or lower (homogeneous ridings). The distribution of the thirty-four white candidates is roughly the same, with sixteen having run in highly diverse ridings, eight in moderately diverse ridings, and ten in homogeneous ridings.

For both white and visible minority candidates, there is a statistically significant relationship between mentions of their riding's demographic composition and the diversity of the riding. In particular, candidates who run in highly diverse ridings are most likely to receive coverage that mentions the demographic composition of their constituency; this seems intuitive. Among white candidates, 64.5 percent of all mentions of riding composition are directed towards candidates who ran in highly diverse ridings. By comparison, 79.2 percent of mentions of riding composition are directed at visible minorities who ran in highly diverse ridings. This tells us that in the highly diverse ridings that are most likely to pique the media's interest in riding composition, news coverage will focus more on visible minority candidates than on their white counterparts – even though many white candidates run in these highly diverse ridings. In other words, coverage is racially differentiated, and the driver is the candidate's race.

The pattern holds when we look at socio-demographic coverage by candidate race and riding diversity. Visible minority candidates – especially those who run in highly diverse ridings – are much more likely to receive coverage of their race, religion, language, and birthplace than other candidates. Visible minorities who run in highly diverse ridings receive about twice as much coverage of their socio-demographic backgrounds (13.8 percent of all their coverage) as do visible minorities who run in moderately diverse and homogeneous ridings, where such mentions make up 7.0 percent and 7.6 percent of those candidates' coverage, respectively. I do not find this pattern in the coverage of white candidates who run in highly diverse ridings. That is, the media do not disproportionately discuss the socio-demographic backgrounds of white candidates who run in diverse ridings, even though these candidates are racially distinct from their voters, a feature that might merit coverage. This silence suggests that whiteness is viewed as neutral or non-newsworthy. Again, the driver behind visible minority candidates' socio-demographic coverage is their race, not the diversity of their ridings.

Moreover, among white candidates, there is no statistically significant relationship between riding diversity and mentions of community support. White candidates' coverage is about as likely (or, really, unlikely) to mention community support, regardless of the diversity of the riding. Among visible minority candidates, however, there is a statistically significant relationship: the coverage of visible minorities running in highly diverse ridings is much more likely to mention support from particular communities – minority communities, specifically – than if the candidate runs in a less diverse riding. That is, 85.7 percent of mentions of visible minority candidates' support from particular communities occur in ridings with visible minority populations that exceed 50 percent. Much of this coverage implies that visible minority candidates running in such ridings will benefit from the support of their "co-ethnics." In other words, while the discussion of objective facts like riding composition is evenly spread among white and visible minority candidates, it is the latter – and particularly those visible minorities who run in highly diverse ridings – who receive coverage about their propensity to garner the support of (minority) communities.

While, on the surface, this coverage may be viewed as positive in that it conveys the impression that the candidate has support among voters, it is also problematic because it reinforces the impression that visible minority candidates run to represent those like them and win because of support from "their own." This is the kind of parochial portrayal that Jeremy Zilber and David Niven (2000) found in their examination of media coverage of black members of Congress. Such coverage leaves voters with the impression that visible minority candidates are inward-looking and cannot play the cultural bridging role that white candidates do. Moreover, it suggests that racial explanations, not objective qualifications, can account for visible minorities' success. Visible minorities are portrayed as winning because of what they are and who they know, not the skills and qualifications they bring to the table. This narrative is echoed in the coverage of party efforts to appeal to minority voters, to which I turn next.

Party Effects

During the 2008 election, increased attention was paid to so-called ethnic targeting strategies, which observers suggested the Conservative Party, in particular, was employing (Flanagan 2011).[21] Ethnic targeting involves the identification of residentially concentrated pockets of voters who are perceived to be like-minded – often from the same ethnic group – and who can be mobilized through messaging that appeals to their priorities and values; such messages often include policy announcements related to immigration or multiculturalism. Sometimes, but not always, a candidate from the same ethnic group will be selected to run in the riding. The strategy can be successful because it matches candidates and their messaging to the perceived preferences of voters.

Given what has been said about the Conservatives' use of ethnic targeting, we might expect party affiliation to affect socio-demographic coverage, but, surprisingly, with the exception of mentions of riding composition, partisanship and coverage appear to be unrelated. Among Liberal candidates, 10.4 percent of stories include a mention of the riding's demographic composition, compared to 7.3 percent for Conservative candidates and 4.1 percent for NDP candidates, a difference that is statistically significant. Of those stories mentioning a riding's demographic composition, the vast majority (87.8 percent) pertain to minority demographic mentions. That is, the article suggests that the riding has high proportions of visible minorities, immigrants, or other minority groups. Of these minority demographic mentions, 52.8 percent pertain to Liberal candidates, while 38.9 percent are in relation to Conservative candidates and 8.3 percent are directed at NDP candidates. In other words, Liberal candidates' coverage is somewhat more likely to mention that the riding has a significant minority population, in spite of the attention given to the Conservatives' ethnic targeting strategy.

This finding probably relates to the types of candidates who were fielded by each party. Although the Conservatives are increasingly running high-profile candidates in the so-called ethnic battlegrounds – the ridings in which the media would be most likely to make mention of minority demographics – this phenomenon is relatively recent. In 2008, even though the party had begun to implement a more concerted ethnic targeting strategy, the Conservative candidates in diverse ridings were still lower-profile than the Liberal candidates, who were often long-time incumbents and thus more likely to secure media coverage. The bulk of these high-profile Liberal candidates are also white, a finding that is bolstered when I look at mentions of candidate race, birthplace, and community support by political party. Here, I find no statistically significant differences, suggesting that the media are commenting on the riding's makeup, which is diverse and therefore newsworthy, while the backgrounds of the relevant candidates – mostly white – are thought not to be. That said, because the 2011 election saw increased use of ethnic targeting strategies with more high-profile Conservative candidates running in ridings with large minority populations, we may expect to find a stronger relationship between political party and socio-demographic coverage in that context.

Because ethnic targeting strategies typically include a policy component, we might also expect to see a relationship between political party and policy issue coverage. Given the Liberal Party's historical reputation as the "party of immigrants," I wondered if Liberal candidates would be more strongly connected to immigration and multiculturalism policy issues than candidates from the other two parties, or if the Conservative Party had succeeded in carving out a portion of this policy space. In fact, there are no statistically significant differences, meaning that all candidates, regardless of party, are about as likely to receive coverage on immigration and multiculturalism policy issues (see also Black and Hicks 2008). Although this contradicts conventional wisdom about the Liberal Party's stranglehold on immigrant and ethnic voters, it is consistent with the narrative of the 2008 election, which increasingly positioned the Conservatives as the new party of immigrants and minorities (Marwah, Triadafilopoulos, and White 2013; Tolley 2013).

It also bears repeating that the candidate sample included the minister of citizenship, immigration and multiculturalism – a white Conservative candidate – and a large proportion of the Conservatives' immigration and multiculturalism issue mentions were directly connected to Jason Kenney. Research on additional elections could be instructive, especially since it really seems to matter which candidates occupy key positions in their parties. For example, were the minister of citizenship, immigration and multiculturalism a visible minority, the results presented here might be quite different. For the time being, however, we can conclude that the traditional narrative of Liberals as the protector and promoter of immigrants and minorities may no longer hold.

Canadian Politics in Black and White

What should be made of the broad swath of data presented in this chapter? The results show that while the media provide balanced or race-neutral reporting in the majority of stories, the coverage of candidates in Canadian politics is race-differentiated in a number of ways. First, the coverage of visible minority candidates is more racialized than the coverage of white candidates. The socio-demographic characteristics of visible minority candidates are mentioned more frequently than those of their white counterparts, and visible minority candidates are more likely to appear in accompanying photographs, a pattern that provides readers with additional clues about their racial backgrounds. This focus on candidates' ethnocultural characteristics may cue negative associations for voters or induce them to think of visible minorities simply in terms of their demography rather than their skills and qualifications for office.

Second, there are very few aggregate differences in the coverage of white and visible minority candidates' political viability. Contrary to some of the previous research in the field, this study does not find that visible minorities are less likely than their white counterparts to be portrayed as insiders or candidates of high quality. However, a deeper look reveals that positive viability coverage generally accrues to visible minority candidates only when they are known commodities with at least one electoral win under their belts. This finding suggests that visible minority candidates need to prove themselves before receiving positive viability coverage, a point that I take up further in Chapter 4.

Third, visible minority candidates are more likely to be portrayed as novelties, a tendency noted in Chapter 1 and one that contributes to narratives about visible minorities being atypical, unusual, or unexpected in the political arena. As a consequence, voters may be left with the impression that visible minority candidates do not really belong in politics.

Fourth, visible minority candidates are less frequently positioned in stories about the most electorally salient issues. Although visible minorities do not necessarily appear more frequently in stories about so-called minority issues, they are less likely to appear in stories about high-valence policy issues. During the 2008 electoral campaign, these were the economy and the environment, a function of the impending global recession as well as the Liberal Party's focus on the "Green Shift." Removing visible minority candidates from discussions about the most salient policy issues further distances them from the political arena.

Fifth, not only is the focus of visible minority candidates' coverage different from that of their white counterparts, so too is its form. Although there are no real racial differences in the amount of coverage that candidates receive, when visible minorities do appear in the media, they can expect their coverage to be less prominent and more negative than that of their white counterparts. They are also less likely to be quoted directly, meaning that they have fewer opportunities than white candidates to appeal to voters through their own words; this may be a result of judgments about visible minority candidates' quoteability and communication skills, a point to which I return in Chapter 4.

Finally, it appears that candidate race – not the characteristics of the ridings in which candidates run – is driving the racialized coverage to which this chapter points. Yes, racialized coverage is higher, in general, in ridings with large visible minority populations, but it is highest when a visible minority candidate is running in such a riding. In other words, the media's focus on race is not just due to incidental geographic characteristics, but rather is influenced by assumptions about the candidates running in those ridings. Even in highly diverse ridings, coverage of white candidates is not nearly as racialized as that of visible minority candidates. This suggests news judgment is based not only on the objective characteristics of the riding but also on subjective assumptions about the relevance of candidate race.

Of course, one reaction to these findings is that even if racialized coverage does exist, it represents only a portion of all candidates' coverage. Skeptics will point out, for example, that socio-demographic coverage occurs in "just 14.4%" of all candidate stories so, to the extent that the media focus on racial aspects of a candidate's background, it is in less than one-fifth of stories. The bulk of reporting is on other, non-racial characteristics. Be that as it may, this critique ignores that the amount of space devoted to *any* one subject is very limited. This point comes out plainly when we examine the coverage devoted to individual policy issues, shown in Table 6. Even the most prominent electoral issue – the economy – appeared in just 11.1 percent of candidates' stories, meaning that the most significant policy area is discussed in fewer stories than candidates' ethnocultural backgrounds. In this context, the amount of attention devoted to candidates' socio-demographic characteristics is actually quite significant.

Moreover, frames do not need to be ubiquitous in order to have an impact. As Karrin Anderson (2011) points out in her study of the "pornification" of women's political news coverage, part of the resonance of such framing is, first, that it is present and, second, that it is palatable. In other words, a frame is not important because of its prominence or frequency, but rather because of the extent to which it fits with conventional understandings of politics and social relationships. This is the case with racialized framing in that it is neither the most common frame nor even that remarkable. But the coverage of visible minority candidates picks up on themes and narratives that fit with our understandings of race, multiculturalism, diversity, and politics. These include the assumption of whiteness as standard, tropes about "deserving immigrants" and "benevolent Canadians," and judgments about what it takes to succeed in Canadian politics. Racialized framing is likely to have an impact precisely because it is so ordinary, so everyday.

Consider, as well, that the standards adopted for the identification of racialized coverage were rather high in that they required *explicit* mentions; coders were not to read into the data.[22] This requirement may mean that the resulting estimates of racialized coverage are in fact conservative. Critics may further suggest that if racialized coverage is so subtle even trained coders do not uniformly detect it then it is likely to also be missed by members of the public. Such a critique positions "conscious recognition" as the appropriate test of impact, which ignores existing research showing that implicit appeals are in fact more influential than explicit appeals because they do not activate egalitarian impulses that might counter the racial message (Mendelberg 2001). Moreover, psychologists have found that citizens are more sensitive to implicit negative stimuli than implicit positive stimuli, again suggesting that messages may affect us in ways that we do not realize, particularly when the appeal is negative (Nasrallah, Carmel, and Lavie 2009). As a result, the fact that racialization may be hidden or even go unnoticed is not a sufficient test of impact.

We need to ask questions about the fairness of coverage, its consistency, and the ways in which media portrayals are differentiated by candidate race. That socio-demographics are mentioned in much smaller proportion of white candidates' stories is significant because it suggests that a different standard of newsworthiness is being applied when a candidate is a visible minority. Moreover, that visible minority candidates' stories are routinely more negative, less prominent, more filtered, and less likely to cover the most salient electoral issues suggests that candidates are covered differently depending on the colour of their skin. In a competitive electoral environment, even small differences can matter, and we should not turn a blind eye to these.

That these differences may systematically disadvantage visible minority candidates is a cause for concern. Indeed, racialized coverage is not evenly distributed nor in any way random. Mentions of candidate race appear only in stories about visible minority candidates, 80 percent of references to candidate birthplace appear in stories about visible minority candidates, and, while rare, all novelty coverage is confined to visible minority women. In other words, racialized coverage disproportionately affects visible minority candidates more than white candidates.

Beyond arguments of fairness and electoral consequences, racialized coverage has an impact on the lives of real people. As is discussed in Chapter 4, a number of visible minority candidates believe they are held to a higher standard and are treated differently in the electoral arena because of their race. In a democracy, that alone is cause for concern. Yes, we should applaud the print media for reporting that is fair and even – a finding that is relatively unsurprising in a country with a highly trained and professional news corps – but we cannot be complacent about the presence of racialized coverage. Although racial framing can be subtle, this chapter and those that follow provide persuasive and consistent evidence that racial imbalance exists in news coverage and disproportionately affects visible minority candidates.

3
Portrayals of Visible Minority Women in Political News Coverage

"To be Black and female in a society which is both racist and sexist is to be in the unique position of having nowhere to go but up."

– Rosemary Brown, former member of the
Legislative Assembly of British Columbia

In 2013, when Canada's provincial and territorial leaders met in Niagara-on-the-Lake, Ontario, for their annual summer meeting, the group photograph included a record number of six women. Never before had so many provinces and territories been governed by female leaders, a fact that was highly touted by the media (Benzie 2013). The presence of women in these positions of power was viewed as evidence of the shattering of the proverbial glass ceiling, but within a year of that photo being taken, only two of those female premiers – Christy Clark and Kathleen Wynne – remained in office. This turn of events illustrates two things. First, representational gains are often fragile, and we should not expect a slow and steady progression towards political equality. Second, although women have made a number of important electoral gains, those who have succeeded have almost always been white. Among the female leaders who posed for that 2013 photo op, only one – Eva Aariak, who is Inuit – could be described as having non-European origins. This latter observation raises important questions about what could be called the "stained glass ceiling." This term has been used to describe the limited opportunities available to clergywomen, but I appropriate it to refer to the obstacles confronted by visible minority women who break the political mould in two ways: first, on account of their gender and, second, on account of their race.

The intersection of these two identities provides an opportunity for the media to introduce narratives about femininity, exoticism, foreignness, sexuality, suitability, and loyalty. This is plainly evident in the coverage of Rathika Sitsabaiesan, a New Democratic MP who was elected in 2011. At a 2012 press conference, Sitsabaiesan offhandedly (and erroneously) said that Canada's population was nine million people. One columnist used the incident to simultaneously draw attention to the politician's age, ethnicity and novelty: "Rathika Sitsabaiesan, at 31 the youngest MP in the Toronto area and the first MP of Tamil heritage, was elected last year to represent Scarborough–Rouge River." The story observes that while Sitsabaiesan was "born in Sri Lanka, she grew up in Canada, attended U of T, graduated from Ottawa's Carleton University, and has a master's from Queen's. So she's no dummy." This juxtaposition of Sitsabaiesan's foreign birthplace and her intelligence suggests that these two traits in tandem are somewhat surprising, a point that is reinforced when the columnist goes on to chastise Sitsabaiesan for not knowing "basic facts" about "the country she has been elected to serve."[1] Finally, by quoting a Korean War veteran who "is aghast at what he sees as political ignorance," the story not only further undercuts Sitsabaiesan's intelligence but also her Canadianness (Worthington 2012).

This story is a provocative example of the insidiousness of gendered and racialized portrayals, here cloaked under the guise of "competence" and "dedication." By imbuing the discussion of Sitsabaiesan's suitability for office with references to her age, immigration status, and heritage, the story cues readers to connect these identifiers to the evaluation of the MP as unsuitable. Comments on the online version of the story suggest that readers picked up on this. For example, a number question Sitsabaiesan's loyalty to Canada, invoking language about "duty" and "service." One commentator observed, "I bet if she were tested, this woman knows far more about Sri Lanka than Canada. It may have been to serve Canada that voters elected her, but serving Sri Lanka was her probable motive for running." Several readers suggested that candidates who are not born in Canada should not be allowed to vote or run for office, a nod to their perceived unsuitability for political life in this country. Finally, a number of commentators drew attention to Sitsabaiesan's racialized and gendered identity, with one writing, "Yep. Play the 'I'm just a girl' card, followed with 'I'm the traumatized victim of a violent impoverished childhood,' blend in 'woman just struggling to get by in a man's world' with some 'poor misunderstood victim of systemic Anglo-Saxon racism' and you got bullet-proof 101." Readers thus tapped into issues that the columnist raised and echoed the narrative to which the story gave rise. That narrative suggests that just as politics is not gender-blind, neither is it race-blind. Indeed, the intersection of Sitsabaiesan's racialized and gendered identities appears to amplify rather than mute experiences of marginalization. In spite of this, very little research has been devoted to the experiences of visible minority women in politics, nor to the ways in which their double differentiation affects their media coverage.

Given this gap, this chapter looks specifically at the media's coverage of visible minority women in Canada. It builds on the findings presented in Chapter 2, which suggested that race does matter in candidate coverage. However, the approach adopted in this chapter differs in two important ways. First, it focuses only on visible minority women, providing a case study of the coverage of politicians who are often identified as different on account of both their gender and their race. Second, the analysis is much more qualitative. Instead of relying on statistics and tables as in Chapter 2, this chapter provides quotations and passages to illustrate the findings. In so doing, the findings support the broad conclusions reached in Chapter 2, while also providing rich contextual detail about the language, imagery, and rhetorical strategies that distinguish the coverage of visible minority women in politics. I point to several racialized and gendered frames. These include references to "exotic" appearances and other markers of feminine difference, a reliance on mythologies about "good" and "bad" minorities and an "us" versus "them" discourse, as well as an attendant inclination to focus on mistakes while minimizing successes. Although some of these frames can be found in stories about candidates who are not visible minority women – indeed, the media's focus on mistakes is arguably universal – the effects of this coverage may have a deeper impact on visible minority women because it exists in combination with, and may even confirm, stereotypes about both their race and their gender.

Visible Minority Women in Canadian Politics

Visible minority women broke an important electoral barrier in 1993 when Jean Augustine and Hedy Fry were elected to Canada's Parliament. Since then, twenty-one women have followed in their footsteps. Following the 2011 federal election, visible minority women made up 4.9 percent of Parliament. This proportion dropped to 4.5 percent several months later when Bev Oda resigned her seat, leaving just one visible minority woman in cabinet. When Olivia Chow left federal politics in 2014 to run in the Toronto municipal election, the remaining visible minority women – thirteen in all – made up 4.2 percent of the House of Commons, an improvement from just two decades earlier when visible minority women made up less than 1 percent of MPs, but still far from proportionate.

Visible minority women MPs have had diverse origins: Chinese, South Asian, Black, West Asian, Arab, Southeast Asian, Latin American, and Japanese. They are no doubt trail-blazers – counting among them the country's first black and first Japanese cabinet ministers as well as the first Sikh, first Muslim, first Chinese, and first Vietnamese women elected to Parliament – but like their white female counterparts, visible minority women's presence in Parliament is roughly half their share of the Canadian population.[2] Visible minority women have to confront both racialized and gendered stereotypes (Smooth 2006a). As a result, selection into the political pool may require these women to express higher levels of political ambition and motivation (Frederick 2013), and they are typically more qualified in terms of their experience, education, and occupational backgrounds than their white counterparts (Andrew et al. 2008; Black and Erickson 2006).

Understanding the electoral experiences and prospects of visible minority women is a pressing matter given the rate at which this population is growing. Between 2001 and 2006, when these statistics were last compiled, visible minority women recorded a growth rate of 28 percent, which is thirteen times faster than the 2.1 percent increase recorded by white women in Canada. Projections suggest that by 2031, there will be 6.6 million visible minority women in Canada, and they will account for about 15.7 percent of the country's total population (Malenfant, Lebel, and Martel 2010). If these projections are accurate, visible minorities will make up as much as 31 percent of the total female population by 2031 (Chui and Maheux 2011).

Differences between visible minority and white women are not limited to demographic weight; there are also differences with respect to opportunity and outcome. For example, while visible minority women in Canada are better educated than their white counterparts (26 percent of visible minority women hold a university degree, compared to 16.6 percent of white women), they have higher rates of unemployment and are more likely to work part-time, head single-parent families, and live in poverty (Chui and Maheux 2011). Moreover, gender gaps in employment are larger in the visible minority population than among white Canadians (Chui and Maheux 2011). Given that economic background, education, and occupation are key predictors of electoral involvement (Andrew et al. 2008), these differences between visible minority and white women have potentially important political consequences. So too do women's experiences and perceptions of discrimination.

For example, in the 2009 General Social Survey, visible minorities, regardless of gender, were more likely than other respondents to say they had been discriminated against in the previous five years (25 percent of visible minority respondents versus 13 percent of white respondents). Visible minority women are as likely as white women to report that they were discriminated against because of their sex, but visible minority women are much more likely than white women to say they were discriminated against because of their race, ethnicity, language, and physical appearance (Chui and Maheux 2011). The racial gap in perceptions of discrimination is arguably larger than the gender gap and, at the very least, illustrates the ways that race and gender, in combination, can influence visible minority women's economic, social, and political experiences.

Nonetheless, most accounts of women in Canadian politics do little to reveal the differences between women and, in particular, those that result from experiences of racialized and gendered differentiation and discrimination. Curiously, while feminists critique the male-centric biases of mainstream political science, we have overlooked our own tendency towards deracialized and monochromatic interpretations of the impact of gender on political opportunities and outcomes. In an effort to overcome the weaknesses of universal approaches to political science, many researchers have begun to engage in intersectional analysis, turning their attention to the ways in which our diverse identities influence our political behaviour, electoral experiences, and democratic outcomes. This work reminds us, however, that we cannot simply "add colour and stir." More qualitative and discursive approaches are important to understanding women's experiences in politics. This is particularly true when the focus is on media coverage, where racialized and gendered narratives are often subtle and implicit. A purely quantitative approach could conceal some of the more pernicious ways in which assumptions about visible minority women's backgrounds, political viability, and issue interests are communicated (see Hicks 2009, who provides a discussion of the shortcomings of large-N media analyses). This chapter thus seeks to address not only the methodological limitations of existing research on visible minority women's media coverage, but also shed light on the racialized and gendered silences implicit in the existing research and scholarship on women in politics.

Racialized and Gendered Silences in the Study of Politics

In recent years, scholars have tried to address the complexity of diversity by looking at the dual or multiplicative effects of race and gender on political experiences. These include an interrogation of the "gendered vertical mosaic" (Abu-Laban 2001), efforts to document the presence of minority women in Parliament (Black 2000a, 2001, 2003, 2008a, 2011; Black and Hicks 2006; Black and Lakhani 1997), the charting of the electoral representation of immigrants, minorities, and women in Canada's major urban centres (Andrew et al. 2008), and studies of the impact of candidate race and gender on vote choice (Bird 2011; Tolley and Goodyear-Grant 2014). Intersectional analysis is also evident in the policy sphere. The Government of Canada's guidelines for gender-based analysis counsel policy analysts to consider assumptions related to race, age, sexual orientation, and ability (Status of Women Canada 2013), while the federally funded Metropolis Project oversaw an examination of intersectionality in several policy fields, including political processes (Tolley 2003). Outside Canada, scholars have also engaged in intersectional analysis to shed light on the impact of race and gender on political engagement (Bejarano 2013; Crenshaw 1989; Gay and Tate 1998; Gershon 2012; Major and Coleman 2008; Philpot and Walton 2007; Sanbonmatsu 2015; Simien and Clawson 2004; Smooth 2006b). However, as one observer notes, "Despite the tremendous growth in research on gender and politics that has emerged over the past two decades, we still know relatively little about the experiences of women of color in political life" (Frederick 2013, 116).

The same is true in Canada, where, for the most part, studies of race and gender in politics are a lot like oil and water: they just don't mix. Typically, researchers look mostly at gender or mostly at race, resulting in a siloed and incomplete understanding of both. This extends back into history; for example, the research studies on the Royal Commission on Electoral Reform and Party Financing dealt with women and minorities in two separate volumes (Megyery 1991a, 1991b). A more recent examination of the barriers facing women in politics touches briefly on the descriptive benefits that could accrue from greater ethnocultural diversity, but among the more than two dozen Canadian women politicians listed in the book's index, there is just one visible minority, Rosemary Brown, who was a member of British Columbia's provincial legislature and (unsuccessfully) contested the leadership of the federal New Democratic Party in 1975. All the other women that the book mentions by name are white (Bashevkin 2009). Edited volumes on women in Canadian politics typically include at least a chapter on visible minorities, but again, race is often hived off rather than extending through all analyses. The organization of the Canadian Political Science Association is emblematic of this siloing, with separate sections for the study of Women, Gender and Politics, on the one hand, and Race, Ethnicity and Indigenous Peoples and Power, on the other. Equal Voice, the advocacy group dedicated to increasing women's participation in elected institutions, largely sets aside the question of race, although its Deep Roots, Strong Wings campaign works to engage Aboriginal women in the political process. It is relatively commonplace for studies to chronicle the impact of gender on various political outcomes, but to give nary a mention to the differences *between* women.

Partly, these silences are a matter of practicality and pragmatism. Indeed, empirical examinations of intersectionality are often hampered by the problem of complexity, because each new variable introduces additional analytic categories. In a conventional study of gender, a researcher has to deal with only two categories: male and female. When race is added to the mix, the categories double: white males, white females, non-white males, non-white females. If a more nuanced understanding of race is employed, the categories multiply once again, and even more if additional identity markers are included. Ange-Marie Hancock (2007, 66) argues that this "has led to a rejection of intersectionality by a number of variable-oriented researchers who envision a paralysis emerging from the inclusion of increasing numbers of variables." Although intersectional analysis is more complicated than looking at either race or gender in isolation, it is in fact a more authentic account of how these identities operate. As is discussed in Chapter 4, the visible minority women candidates with whom I spoke had difficulty even separating their race from their gender; these identities (and others) are interlocking and overlapping, which makes it difficult to isolate their independent effects. Instead of struggling futilely to do so, this chapter looks at race and gender in tandem. In doing so, I adopt Smooth's (2006b) perspective that intersectional analysis is "a mess worth making."

Data and Approach

In this chapter, I examine print media coverage of the twenty-three visible minority women who have held seats in the House of Commons since 1993. In contrast to the study presented in Chapter 2, here I look specifically at three of Canada's print dailies: the *Globe and Mail, National Post,* and *Toronto Star.* I chose these outlets because they offer the most complete full-text archival record, but also because they include the country's two "national" newspapers (the *Globe* and the *Post*) and the outlet with the highest circulation (the *Star*). As a result, they arguably have the greatest reaches of any print news source in the country.

Although a focus on large dailies is likely to underestimate the total amount of coverage that visible minority women MPs receive, since these papers will report on the most high-profile politicians, the sample is unlikely to systematically misrepresent the themes or narratives that characterize that content. If anything, a focus on these three papers offers a conservative account of the impact of race and gender on media coverage, given that all three have high standards of professionalism and arguably employ some of the best journalists and editors in the country. By focusing on these three papers, I am in effect offering a "least likely" case study and, as a result, the patterns I uncover here are not only likely to be found in other outlets but may even be amplified. Finally, although each newspaper adopts its own editorial stance and direction, pack journalism and media convergence have resulted in some narrowing. Indeed, PostMedia owns the *National Post* in addition to nine other print dailies, including the *Ottawa Citizen*, *Vancouver Sun*, and *Calgary Herald*. These papers often run similar, if not identical, stories and columns. Thus, while I focus on just three papers, I am in effect harvesting a large swath of the print media landscape.

To construct the story sample, all news articles, columns, and editorials that were six hundred words or longer were retrieved from Newsstand using each visible minority woman MP's name as a search term. I chose to focus on longer stories because these are the articles most likely to include discussion of the MPs' backgrounds, qualifications, interests, and other factors relevant to the discursive focus of this chapter. For each MP, the time frame for analysis was the date of her first election until her departure from federal politics.[3] This resulted in a total of 2,039 stories, including 1,397 news articles (68.5 percent), 590 columns or opinion pieces (28.9 percent), and 52 editorials (2.6 percent).[4]

Table 7 provides a brief overview of the MPs and the population of stories on which this analysis is based. Obviously, visible minority women receive different kinds of coverage, with some achieving much higher levels of media visibility than others. When the number of stories is examined as a proportion of the MP's tenure in office, it becomes clear that it is not simply political longevity that drives media attention. The MPs with the most coverage in relation to their length of time in office are Olivia Chow and Bev Oda. Chow's extensive coverage can be partly explained by her position as wife to the late Jack Layton, who was leader of the NDP and passed away while still in office. Oda, meanwhile, illustrates the potentially negative consequences of extensive media coverage in that a large proportion of her stories focus on the scandals and criticism that dogged her for much of her tenure. This only underscores why the content of coverage is as important as its amount and perhaps even more so.

For this reason, I turn my attention away from measures of quantity, placement, and prominence and instead use discourse analysis to understand the qualitative messages communicated in the media's coverage of visible minority women.[5] Discourse analysis can take a number of different forms, but at its core involves examining how language is used to represent some aspect of social reality (Fairclough 2003). To do this, the analyst identifies the themes, rhetorical devices, grammatical and linguistic structures, or normative claims that are used in the presentation of an issue, event, or actor (Sampert and Trimble 2010b). My analysis focuses on the ways in which visible minority women are represented in popular media, the language that is used to describe them, and the themes on which their coverage focuses. I tie this analysis to broader institutional structures and social relationships. It is important to note that the aim of discourse analysis is not to arrive at *the* meaning of a set of texts, but rather to show how the texts were constructed, what choices were made in that construction, and how those choices reflect and relate to the social context in which the coverage is situated (Cheek 2004). Given the detailed nature of the analysis, I drew a random sample of 408 stories, which represents 20 percent of the original data set. The findings reported in this chapter are based on this sample.

Some observers remain skeptical of discourse analysis, arguing that such an approach is merely one observer's interpretation, and the findings are thus not generalizable. Partly this critique emanates from studies that regrettably provide insufficient information to support the researcher's selection of texts, his or her methods for analysis, and the basis on which the inferences are drawn. In this chapter, I used an open coding approach (Van Gorp 2010), grouping passages by theme and focusing on the language and information contained (and not contained) in the stories. I provide what Cheek (2004, 1147) refers to as a "decision trail," which includes a description of the texts that were analyzed, a justification of how and why they were chosen, and a number of illustrative passages to support the claims I am making. As with any method, while discourse analysis cannot provide definitive closure on all questions related to the print media's coverage of visible minority women, it does shed light on the ways in which media

TABLE 7

Visible minority women MPs, by tenure and media coverage

| | | | | Media coverage (n = 2,039) | | | | | |
| | | | | Amount | | | Types | | |
Name	Party	Year first elected	Tenure (days)	Stories (n)	All stories (%)	Stories as proportion of tenure	News (%)	Column (%)	Editorial (%)
Augustine, Jean	Lib	1993	4,473	190	9.3	0.04	76.8	19.5	3.7
Fry, Hedy	Lib	1993	7,023*	451	22.1	0.06	64.1	32.8	3.1
Jennings, Marlene	Lib	1997	5,082	162	7.9	0.03	71.6	26.5	1.9
Leung, Sophia	Lib	1997	2,583	17	0.8	0.007	64.7	29.4	5.9
Dhalla, Ruby	Lib	2004	2,499	203	10.0	0.08	70.9	26.6	2.5
Faille, Meili	BQ	2004	2,499	20	1.0	0.008	85.0	15.0	–
Grewal, Nina	Con	2004	3,124*	58	2.8	0.02	82.8	13.8	3.4
Oda, Bev	Con	2004	2,956	446	21.9	0.15	61.0	36.1	2.9
Ratansi, Yasmin	Lib	2004	2,499	24	1.2	0.01	79.2	20.8	–
Barbot, Vivian	BQ	2006	995	21	1.0	0.02	81.0	19.0	–
Chow, Olivia	NDP	2006	2,550*	371	18.2	0.15	70.9	27.8	1.3
Mourani, Maria	BQ	2006	2,550*	26	1.3	0.01	76.9	23.1	–
Thi Lac, Ève-Mary Thaï	BQ	2007	1,323	7	0.3	0.005	85.7	14.3	–
Wong, Alice	Con	2008	1,555*	17	0.8	0.01	76.5	23.5	–
Ayala, Paulina	NDP	2011	626*	0	–	–	–	–	–

Name	Party								
Groguhé, Sadia	NDP	2011	626*	0	–	–	–	–	–
Hassainia, Sana	NDP	2011	626*	5	0.2	0.007	80.0	20.0	–
Liu, Laurin	NDP	2011	626*	7	0.3	0.01	57.1	42.9	–
Quach, Anne Minh-Thu	NDP	2011	626*	0	–	–	–	–	–
Sellah, Djaouida	NDP	2011	626*	0	–	–	–	–	–
Sims, Jinny	NDP	2011	626*	2	0.1	0.003	–	50.0	–
Sitsabaiesan, Rathika	NDP	2011	626*	11	0.5	0.02	72.7	18.2	50.0
Young, Wai	Con	2011	626*	1	0.1	0.001	–	100.0	9.1
								100.0	–

(*) denotes sitting MP at the time of analysis. Tenure was calculated up to January 15, 2013.

representations reflect, reinforce, and reconstruct our assumptions about race and gender in the political arena.

Visible Minority Women MPs in Canada's News Media

I have grouped the narratives that characterize the coverage of visible minority women in Canadian politics around eight themes that loosely relate to Chapter 2's focus on socio-demographics, viability, and policy issues. The first three themes ("Exotic breasts and Bollywood princesses," "The 'wife of the party,'" and "Just one of the girls") fall under the rubric of socio-demographic coverage and highlight visible minority women's racialized and gendered features. The next four themes ("Novelty and famous firsts," "Multicultural myth making and the 'good immigrant,'" "Mistakes," and "Minimization") address issues related to viability, broadly conceived. This discussion focuses in particular on the framing of visible minority women's loyalty to their party and to Canada, as well as their deservingness of political office. Considerable attention is given to the media's propensity to highlight mistakes while minimizing the credentials of visible minority women MPs. The final theme ("Serving their own") provides insight into the framing of visible minority women's policy issue interests. Taken together, the analysis of these themes provides powerful evidence of the media's role in constructing racialized and gendered narratives about politics. The findings suggest that this coverage is characterized by racial and gendered mediation.

SOCIO-DEMOGRAPHIC FRAMING

Exotic Breasts and Bollywood Princesses
Consistent with the literature on gendered mediation, the coverage of visible minority women mentions their appearance, clothing, and personal lives. However, visible minority women seem to be framed with an added layer of exoticism. For example, a profile of Rathika Sitsabaiesan ran under the headline "'Why don't you wear a sari?'" (Bardeesy 2011, F3). This sartorial focus parallels the coverage that white women receive, but whereas mentions of blouses or pantsuits draw attention only to the candidate's gender, a reference to a sari presents the candidate as both racialized and gendered – an irresistible and exotic combination. Other references are less overtly racialized, such as an article about Ruby Dhalla that suggests her outfit is indicative of her "spiky indignation." The columnist writes, "There was a

coldness in her attitude. Even what she wore – white and pink – signalled something cold ... She's all ego and entitlement" (Doyle 2009, R3). Whether wearing pink or a pantsuit, a sari or a skirt, visible minority women, like their white counterparts, do not seem able to win.

Journalists may also comment on the physicality of a female MP. For example, Vivian Barbot is described as having a "captivating smoky voice" (Chung 2008, A22), while Bev Oda is a "weak communicator" (Clark 2007, A1). Ruby Dhalla is referred to as "pretty but vain," "beauteous," "a diva," "a young drop-dead gorgeous, Indo-Canadian woman," and "like something out of a Bollywood movie" (Blatchford 2009, A3; Gunter 2009, A18; Taber 2009, F3; Timson 2009, L1). A profile of Hedy Fry reports that at a campaign event, she sang along to the music and "wiggled her hips" (Hutchinson 2006, A1). She is described as "flamboyant" (Travers 2002, A21), and one reporter notes that she "literally sashays up to the microphone" to speak with reporters (Winsor 1999, A11). Sometimes the references are less flattering. For example, reporters drew attention to a blog post authored by a Liberal Party official, entitled "Separated at Birth," that included a photograph of Olivia Chow alongside a picture of a Chinese Chow Chow dog (Vallis 2006).

Meanwhile, one-quarter of stories about Sitsabaiesan mention the airbrushing of her official parliamentary photograph, sometimes with links to her ethnic heritage. As one journalist reports,

> The first Tamil Canadian MP and one of the young stars of the New Democrats' Orange Crush appears on the House of Commons website wearing a sleeveless white top that, in reality, shows the shadow of a modest cleavage. But in the picture that now appears online, her chest has been digitally painted over into a featureless terrain by a House of Commons photographer. (Brean 2011, A8)

Accompanying the story are before and after photographs of the MP's cleavage. A few days later, a wrap-up of subscriber comments on the paper's top stories included an excerpt from a letter to the editor that noted, "Personally, I think Ms. Sitsabaiesan has a nice rack – nothing to be ashamed of but certainly no need to over-expose" (Russell 2011, A21). Underpinning this focus on appearance seems to be the notion that visible minority women do not just have breasts, they have *exotic* breasts.[6]

Even stories that come to the defence of visible minority women in politics nonetheless draw fuel from a sort of "Bollywoodification." Take, for example, a column by Don Martin (2009, A16) that refers to Ruby Dhalla's "undeniable Bollywood-actress good looks" and suggests that she is "precisely the demographic Canada's Parliament needs ... young, female, visible minority." While the column offers support to Dhalla, it is problematic in that the reasons given largely centre on her appearance and demographic background. It is not because of her qualifications or experience that she should be kept in Parliament, but rather because of her looks. A story written before Dhalla was even elected refers to her as "a former model and Bollywood actress" and a "young and successful Sikh" (Harding 2004, A6). Even if the coverage is, on the surface, flattering, it nonetheless frames the MP as a product of her appearance, a shiny object in the rough and tumble world of politics. For example, a headline about Hedy Fry's leadership campaign suggests that the long-time MP is running on her "larger-than-life ebullience" (Mickleburgh 2006, A7). This characterization downplays the candidate's qualifications and, by all accounts, detailed platform, situating her simply as an "enthusiastic" participant. This type of framing delegitimizes their subjects' place in the political arena in a way that is consistent with the findings in Chapter 2.

The "Wife of the Party"

Visible minority women, like their white counterparts, are also subject to coverage that situates them as wives. This is particularly true when they have a political spouse, as in the case of MPs Olivia Chow and Nina Grewal: Chow was married to NDP leader Jack Layton, while Grewal's husband, Gurmant Grewal, was the MP for Newton–North Delta when she was first elected. A number of stories about both Chow and Grewal simply mention their marital partners, while others carry a more evaluative tone, often at the female MP's expense. This type of framing positions the wives as subservient or accessories, which diminishes their role and independence. Although this kind of framing is not explicitly racialized, it does align with coverage that positions immigrants and minorities as passive or easily manipulated. For example, one article says that while Chow has "earned her political cred" in municipal politics and through her grassroots work, "as an NDP stalwart and *leader Jack Layton's wife*, [she] is biased" in her political views (Diebel 2008, A1; emphasis added). This framing suggests that Chow's status as a wife somehow disqualifies her from impartial or independent thought.

Some reporters appear to perceive Chow as simply an accessory to Layton. One article reports that at Layton's 2011 funeral, a family friend was asked by a reporter "whether Chow was a lightweight" (Diebel 2011b, A1). The premise of the question communicates quite clearly exactly what this reporter thought of Chow's abilities. Grewal seems to recognize the potential for conflation with her husband; one story refers to her website, which reads, "Gurmant (Grewal) and I are two separate MPs representing different ridings" (quoted in Chung 2006, A7). Stories about the Grewals, however, typically position Gurmant at the forefront and Nina as the dutiful spouse. For example, a profile of the couple notes that "when they first settled in Canada, Nina was tempted to enter politics but stayed home to raise the children while Gurmant became an MP in 1997" (Hutchinson 2004, A1).

Other articles portray the wives in terms that are more equal with their husbands. For example, a 2011 profile notes, "Ms. Chow was unlike any political wife this country has ever seen. First, she wasn't a wife, she was a partner. That was the way Mr. Layton always referred to her, and it was true on several levels" (Martin 2011, A8). Nonetheless, a number of articles mention Chow's status as Layton's wife even when it is not clear how this fact is relevant to the actual story. Although this type of coverage is more gendered than it is racialized, the portrayal of visible minority women as subservient could reinforce stereotypes of submissive immigrants. This treatment belies the tremendous political acumen that Chow has in her own right. Indeed, while much has been written about Layton's farewell letter, the one in which he reminds Canadians that "hope is better than fear," Chow may have inspired these words; in a victory speech following her 2006 election to the House of Commons, she thanked her constituents for "voting for hope instead of fear" (Lu 2006, B1).

Just One of the Girls

Although much of the socio-demographic coverage of visible minority women includes both racialized and gendered references, some articles actually downplay racial identity and portray visible minority women as women alone. This is the case in a column contrasting the success of Canadian women on the podium at the 2010 Olympics with their relative absence from the political arena. The article employs a sports narrative identified in the gendered mediation literature as characteristic of the masculine assumptions underpinning political news coverage. It quotes Hedy Fry as saying, "Women can be as tough and can be as strong [as men]" (Taber 2010, A8). Fry is the only MP mentioned in the story, and there is no reference to her race even though racialized assumptions similarly underpin the political and athletic arenas. Fry is presented as "just one of the girls."

Meanwhile, Jean Augustine and Olivia Chow are both mentioned in an article entitled "No Breakthrough for Women" describing the outcome of the 2004 election. This story focuses on the electoral barriers faced by female candidates such as difficulty securing the party's nomination, clustering in unwinnable ridings, and discrimination (Black and Monsebraaten 2004). Although these barriers also are relevant to visible minority candidates – who are similarly underrepresented in Canadian politics – the article looks only at gender representation with no mention of the systemic obstacles that may be faced by other traditionally marginalized candidates. Even in a story where race is politically relevant, it is excluded. This absence is suggestive of the discomfort with race that was expressed by candidates and journalists with whom I spoke (as detailed in Chapters 4 and 5).

Many of us seem to struggle between recognizing the impact of race and simultaneously avoiding accusations of racism. As a result, some simply avoid discussions of race altogether, claiming, as some of my interviewees did, that they quite simply do not "see" race. While this may be true, avoiding race altogether denies the significant impact that race can have on social, economic, and political outcomes, particularly for those marked by a min-ority racial status. Toronto writer Desmond Cole criticizes so-called colour-blindness, arguing "white people often go out of their way to say they don't see colour when they look at me – in those moments, I'm tempted to recommend an optometrist. I know they're just expressing a desire for equality, but I don't want to be erased in the process" (Cole 2015). It is notable that the discom-fort I observed in the coverage and conversation about racial issues was not as apparent when dealing with gender and sexism, something I discuss more fully in the chapters that follow.

POLITICAL VIABILITY FRAMING

Novelty and Famous Firsts

As is discussed in Chapter 5, the news business is precisely that: a business. To attract consumers, media outlets need interesting and readable con-tent, and the apparent novelty of a visible minority women's presence in politics appears to provide journalists with just the narrative hook to draw readers in. Many stories present visible minority women as trail-blazers and "famous firsts." For example, an article notes, "Nina Grewal's election as

Conservative MP for Fleetwood–Port Kells, BC, was a bit of a first. She – along with her husband, Gurmant – will become the first concurrently sitting husband and wife team in the House of Commons. She also becomes the first female Indo-Canadian to sit in the House" (Hutchinson 2004, A1). Another story refers to Jean Augustine as "the first black woman in the federal Parliament." In the article, Augustine is quoted as saying, "There is something to being the first of this or the first of [that] elected, it's something of note and provides a good role model. *But I don't think your ethnic origin should be the first thing talked about*" (Thompson 1993, A7; emphasis added). In spite of this remark, it was precisely her race that was mentioned first. Even in articles written on the occasion of Augustine's retirement after more than twelve years in office, reporters refer to her as "one of the few black women to win a seat" (Dawson 2005, A1).

Some may view this kind of framing as relatively benign. After all, Augustine *is* a black woman and she *was* the first to be named to cabinet. This is an accomplishment and so merits mention. The problem, however, is twofold. First, this framing presents subjects through a racialized and gendered lens that would rarely (if ever) be applied to white male politicians. Different news judgment is thus being applied to candidates on the basis of their race and gender. Second, by explicitly mentioning the subject's race and gender, the stories are cuing attributes that may be used by voters to make inferences about the politicians' qualifications, interests, and motivations (Huddy and Terkildsen 1993; McDermott 1998). What is made salient is not the candidate's qualifications but her race and gender. The mention of these attributes not only draws readers' attention to them but may also colour the ways in which other aspects of their political lives are viewed.

This is the case in a story about a rumoured cabinet shuffle. To address the dearth of BC ministers around the executive table, the article comments, "Mr. Chrétien can choose among MPs Hedy Fry and Harbance Dhaliwal and junior minister Raymond Chan, all of whom have the added bonus of being from visible minority communities" (Greenspon 1995, A1). A profile of potential cabinet ministers taps Rahim Jaffer and Bev Oda, because "both visible minority MPs are also proving to be liked by the leader, and could flesh out the diversity of a Harper cabinet" (MacCharles 2005, A8). A story about Ruby Dhalla similarly links her background to her cabinet prospects: "Generally seen as a probable cabinet pick should Ignatieff ever assume power, Dhalla may be coming to be seen as too controversial, despite her photogenic and multicultural appeal. She's the first Sikh woman ever to be elected as an MP" (Delacourt and Brazao 2009, A1). No reference is made to Dhalla's qualifications for cabinet aside from her appearance and background. This sort of framing situates visible minority MPs as tokens and not as individuals who are competent and qualified for reasons that have nothing to do with their race, gender, or atypicality.

Multicultural Myth Making and the "Good Immigrant"

As is suggested by racial mediation theory, visible minority politicians' coverage often draws on an immigrant narrative. When visible minority women are framed in news stories, this narrative often coalesces around a portrayal of some as "good immigrants" and others as somehow falling short of this ideal. These judgments mimic, in some ways, gendered narratives about "good girls" and "bad girls." We see these distinctions being made in the coverage of Jean Augustine, who emerges as a dutiful foot soldier. Nowhere was this more evident than when she agreed to step down from her post as MP so that Michael Ignatieff could run in her riding. One editorial notes, "The first black woman elected to Parliament informed the [Liberal] party [of her retirement] and threw her support behind Michael Ignatieff" (*Globe and Mail* 2005). A second article refers to Augustine as "another black Liberal politician" and states that she "resigned to make way for star candidate Michael Ignatieff" (Gorrie 2006, A1). Because Augustine's race is explicitly mentioned, the framing directly links it to her sacrifice. Articles about Sophia Leung also refer to her "stepping aside" to allow David Emerson to run in her riding; one notes that "her reward will come after the election" (Winsor 2004, A4). However, in contrast to the coverage of Augustine, very little of Leung's coverage makes explicit reference to her race, perhaps because her prototypically Chinese surname makes this unnecessary.

In addition to drawing attention to her race, Augustine's coverage repeatedly refers to her immigration history, which included employment as a "domestic worker, cleaning toilets and working as a maid" (Thompson 1993, A7). One article downplays criticisms of Canada's live-in caregiver program and instead emphasizes its benevolent aspects: "Although the 'domestic scheme' was criticized in some quarters as indentured labour and blamed for causing a brain drain in the Caribbean, it gave Augustine the opportunity to become a leader in her adopted country" (Murray 1999, 1). This phrasing is important not just because it sets aside structural and institutional inequalities but also because it presents Augustine's success as a product of what Canada *gave* her, not what she brought with her to this country. Augustine emerges as the "model immigrant," one who put her head down, worked hard, did not complain, and was subsequently rewarded (Jones 2002, A23).

Hedy Fry, Augustine's predecessor in the multiculturalism portfolio, is framed somewhat differently, with articles describing her as "angry" and "pissed off" after she was excluded from meetings with the heads of Commonwealth governments, although it is Fry herself who notes that she "kicked up a 'stink'" (Taber 2007, A10). A profile suggests Fry has a "reputation as a bit of a loose cannon"; it notes her "vitality and progressive views" but goes on to say, "She is prone to intemperate remarks, has a solid opinion of herself and rarely sees a microphone she doesn't like" (Mickleburgh 2006, A7). In two other stories, Fry is described as "complaining" (*National Post* 2007, A20) and "protesting" (Smyth 2006a, A8). Following a speech launching her bid for the leadership of the Liberal Party, "A reporter asked Dr. Fry to state her age. It is, apparently, a matter of some confusion, although her official Government of Canada biography notes she was born in 1941, in Trinidad. 'You never ask a lady that,' she *snapped*" (Hutchinson 2006, A1; emphasis added). Marlene Jennings, Fry's caucus colleague, who is also black, is said to have "fumed" (Ibbitson 2010, A10) when questioning the speaker of the House about the lack of air conditioning in MPs' offices. She also "reacted with impatience" when asked about a proposed coalition government (Cosh 2009, A10). The choice of non-neutral verbs paints an unflattering portrait of these MPs, even if couched within more complimentary references to their political resilience or skills, as is sometimes the case. Such framing also aligns squarely with stereotypes of the "angry black woman" and thus may subtly confirm biases about visible minority women. The Bollywood princess stereotype is reinforced in a story about Ruby Dhalla that alleges "she was not known as an easy boss" (Delacourt 2009a, A1).

The good/bad juxtaposition is further illustrated in a column that compares Augustine to Fry. A piece entitled "Nice Pictures, Message Needs Work" begins, "Pierre Trudeau's bold plan to make Canada a global village has metamorphosed into a succession of patronizing photo opportunities ... Well-meaning citizens wonder why Canada still needs a ministry of multiculturalism when there is no sign of racism." After critiquing institutional responses to racial discrimination (and grants to support that work), the columnist continues, "Unlike her predecessor Hedy Fry, who saw bigotry even where it didn't exist (she falsely accused residents of Prince George, BC, of racist cross-burnings), Augustine does not think overt discrimination is common. She hasn't encountered much of it" (Goar 2002, A22). This assessment is in contrast to a statement Augustine made shortly after she was elected: "We live in a society where race is not discounted" (quoted in Makin 1993, A17).

The downplaying of racism is evident in a second column entitled "It's Been the Week of the Liar," which describes Fry's inaccurate statement that in the city of Prince George "crosses are being burned on lawns as we speak." The columnist notes, "I don't doubt that Fry believes Canada is pitted with racism," as though discrimination is simply a figment of the MP's imagination (Mallick 2001, F8). Fry later admitted that she had confused the name of the city where she thought crosses were burning with that of another in the BC interior whose mayor had written to her with concerns about Ku Klux Klan activity (Mickleburgh 2006, A7). At the time, few outlets reported this explanation, with the coverage instead criticizing Fry for suggesting that racism might exist in Canada. Fry is painted as an overreactive zealot who "makes up facts" about racism when very little exists (*National Post* 2001, A19). Another article notes, "Dr. Fry has a long record of making unsubstantiated claims about racism in Canada. During her five years as Multiculturalism Minister, she has described Canada's history as one of 'colonial racism and intolerance'" ... [and] she has spoken of a 'very well organized strategic plan' by racist organizations to move into Canada" (Foot, Alberts, and Bell 2001, A4). The story presents these statements as nonsense, even though an article in the same newspaper just one day earlier included commentary from an expert on hate activity stating that "the Klan and other racist organizations such as the Aryan Nations are still trying to recruit members" in this country, an assertion that is overlooked in much of Fry's coverage (Hunter 2001, A6).

Coverage criticizes Fry for presenting a "negative" view of race relations in Canada, with the authors wryly noting that "the city of Vancouver gets more complaints about barking dogs than Canada's combined human rights commissions receive concerning racism in any given year." This article not only uses language that minimizes reports of discrimination, noting that their number is "relatively small," "three provinces had fewer than 100 racism complaints," and "in Ontario there were fewer than 1,000," but also conflates the reporting of racial discrimination with its very existence (Foot, Alberts, and Bell 2001, A4). In doing so, the reporters do precisely what they critique Fry for: namely, they present a distorted view of racism in Canada.

The focus on the specific cross-burning allegation (and its inaccuracy) rather than on broader themes of inequality or prejudice is consistent with Shanto Iyengar's (1991, 1996) distinction between episodic and thematic news frames. Episodic news frames present issues acutely as instances or illustrations, while thematic news frames place them in a historical, social, or political context, drawing out underlying patterns and broad connections. Episodic framing is more common than thematic framing and shapes the way that citizens understand problems. As Iyengar (1996, 70) explains, "By reducing complex issues to the level of anecdotal cases, episodic framing leads viewers to attributions that shield society and government from responsibility ... Viewers come to focus on the particular individuals or groups depicted in the news rather than historical, social, political, or other such structural factors." Racial cues only augment the tendency towards individual attribution, with citizens less likely to recognize systemic or institutional barriers when the subject of a story is a minority (Iyengar 1996). Stories that frame visible minority MPs alternatively as "good" or "bad" immigrants may prime citizens not only to evaluate them this way but also to ignore our own social responsibilities.

Mistakes

The good/bad discourse carries through to the media's reporting of MPs' mistakes, where guilt is typically presumed, and the effects of a gaffe or allegation can linger long after the misstep. This presumption of guilt was apparent when Ruby Dhalla was accused of mistreating caregivers in her family's employ. While journalists admitted that the story was complicated and had many sides, one columnist nonetheless opines, "*Obviously* there's something at the heart of the allegations" (Doyle 2009, R3; emphasis added). A column by Christie Blatchford portrays Dhalla as a tyrant and compares the family's treatment of the caregivers to Blatchford's own treatment of her dog. Throughout the column, Blatchford refers to Dhalla as "I Ruby," censuring the way in which the MP referred to herself in her statement to the committee. The rhetorical device not only mocks the MP but also reinforces Blatchford's argument that Dhalla is self-centred and self-absorbed (Blatchford 2009, A3). The caregivers later settled out of court; Dhalla lost her seat in the next election. Of course the media have a responsibility to report on malfeasance and alleged wrongdoing, but there is a cost to public officials, particularly if the allegations turn out to have been overblown.

Our cognitive biases are such that we are more likely to believe information that confirms our preconceptions and to interpret it in a way that is consistent with these beliefs (Gilovich, Griffin, and Kahneman 2002). A columnist provides an applied understanding of this when she writes, "Communications professionals say that for any story to stick, whether it's a good story or a bad story, it has to be part of a pattern, or 'narrative.'" She goes on to list a series of Dhalla's missteps and then concludes, "The controversies, taken together, paint an unflattering picture of haughtiness, even arrogance. Even if it's a wildly false picture – her friends and supporters say it's totally off the mark – a narrative, once established is hard to shake" (Delacourt 2009b, A19).

The "stickiness" of the narrative seems to affect Hedy Fry's coverage, as well. A profile of the MP on her sixty-fifth birthday says that she "barely noticed" the anniversary because "she was too busy doing what she does best: Causing a stir." This is a nod at Fry's purported troublemaking past, a history that the story digs up when the reporter notes that "the stigma of [Fry's] cross-burning error persists." The reporter even concedes that more than five years after the incident, "Why the media continues to make such a deal of it mystifies many" (Mickleburgh 2006, A7). As Fry observes, "Look at all the politicians who have made the most extraordinary statements. Does anyone repeat their comments over and over again? ... I made one statement and it has continued to dog me, in spite of what my whole life has been about" (quoted in Mickleburgh 2006, A7). A column describes Fry as "spewing her idiocies" (Wells 2001, B1), and in various stories, she is referred to alternately as "stupid," "hapless," a "dunce," and a "prank" that BC Liberals play on the rest of the country.

In my interviews with candidates, which are discussed in Chapter 4, some suggested that long-held stereotypes about minorities fuel these narratives and help make them "stick." Indeed, for all her shortcomings, Bev Oda is described in a number of articles as a solid, competent, and effective minister, but this is not how she will be remembered in the public record. Instead, she has been memorialized as the minister who expensed limousine rides, a $16 glass of orange juice, and the $250 cleaning bill for allegedly smoking in a non-smoking hotel room. In the words of John Ivison (2012, A1), "The country's first Japanese-Canadian MP has done some good things at CIDA [the Canadian International Development Agency, of which she was minister]. Unfortunately, her legacy for most Canadians will be a photograph of her in sunglasses, cigarette dangling from her lips, that makes her look like the driver of the getaway car." Not only does the columnist highlight Oda's negative qualities, but he also inserts her ethnic heritage alongside a description of the wrongdoing and thus places race at the forefront. The story is not just about a minister making mistakes, but a *visible minority* minister doing so. This foregrounding of race is also apparent in a column about Ruby Dhalla: "She's a magnet for partisan cheap shots, personal inquisitions, nasty rumours and apparent anti-immigrant hysteria ... There's definitely something about Ruby Dhalla that attracts controversy like no other ... Problems exploded anew this week [for] Canada's first female Sikh Member of Parliament" (Martin 2009, A16). Again, the framing is such that Dhalla's political problems are not simply those of an elected official, but a female and Sikh politician at that.

While the media's focus on mistakes is not confined to visible minority women and often not even specifically racialized or gendered, the effects can be. This is particularly so when viewed in conjunction with the media's tendency to minimize visible minority women's credentials and qualifications. Indeed, the implicitness of the racialized and gendered assumptions underpinning this kind of coverage is what makes it so effective. That the framing of visible minority women's mistakes is consistent with stereotypical beliefs about "incompetent women," "entitled immigrants," or "shady minorities" increases not only the plausibility that citizens accord to the stories, but the potential that they will make political judgments on the basis of these attributes.

Minimization

The potential damage of this focus on mistakes is compounded if the subject's other coverage does not draw attention to her skills and qualifications. I found several instances where the media downplayed or minimized the credentials of the MPs in my sample. Minimization is particularly apparent in Jean Augustine's coverage, where her cabinet positions are either excluded or accompanied by a "junior minister" label. The double standard is starkly evident when Augustine is presented alongside other cabinet ministers. One article lists several members of cabinet as follows: "Gerry Byrne, Atlantic Development; Ethel Blondin-Andrew, Secretary of State for Children and Youth; Paul DeVillers, Amateur Sport; and Jean Augustine, junior minister for multiculturalism and the status of women" (Clark and Lunman 2003, A1). At the time, Blondin-Andrew, DeVillers, and Augustine were all secretaries of state (that is, junior ministers) and yet this detail is excluded in the labelling of DeVillers, their white male colleague. Another article describes Augustine as a secretary of state and DeVillers as a minister (Curry 2002), again misrepresenting the two MPs' equivalent positions. One story refers to Augustine as a "cabinet underling" who was chastised by David Collenette, a more senior member of the executive, for failing to stand and vote in favour of a government bill (Taber 2003, A4). Several other stories leave out Augustine's ministerial title altogether, presenting her simply as an MP (Dawson 2003; Leong 2002). An article written shortly after her election describes her as a "community activist" instead of as a school principal (Delacourt and Greenspon 1993). Others note that Augustine ascended to office as an "appointed" candidate rather than through a more typical nomination process (Contenta 1993; Speirs 2000).

The medical credentials of another Liberal appointee, Ruby Dhalla, are also disparaged, with Margaret Wente (2009, A17) writing, "Ruby Dhalla (or 'Dr. Ruby Dhalla' as she styles herself)," and later calling her simply "Ruby." Another columnist refers to "Ms. Dhalla" while calling the MP's brother (also a chiropractor) "Dr. Dhalla" (Timson 2009, L1), and a third writes, "Ms. Dhalla (or Dr. Dhalla, as the chiropractor prefers to be called)" (Taber 2009, F3). Even within the same newspaper, Hedy Fry, a physician, is referred to in some articles as "Dr." but in others as "Ms." (Alphonso 2012; Picard 2012).

Fry's coverage includes a number of examples of this minimization. Fry entered politics after defeating sitting prime minister Kim Campbell in the 1993 federal election. Referring to Fry's political acumen, even Svend Robinson, a long-time MP who contested Fry's riding in an attempt to re-enter politics, comments, "You underestimate Hedy Fry at your peril" (quoted in Mickleburgh 2006, A7). Nonetheless, electoral coverage consistently portrays her as electorally vulnerable, with persistent references to the cross-burning incident. One columnist refers to "low-watt Hedy Fry, Secretary of State for Imaginary Cross Burnings" (Martin 2001, A1). Another story, mentioned in Chapter 2, minimizes Fry's decade-plus political tenure, noting she "has never in Ottawa fulfilled the lofty expectations she brought in 1993" (Simpson 2008, A21). Consistent with Zilber and Niven's (2000) observation that African American members of Congress are typically portrayed as Washington outsiders, Fry is framed as a representative who is popular in her BC riding but has had little national impact. In much of the coverage of her bid to succeed Paul Martin as leader of the Liberal party, Fry is portrayed as a long shot with little caucus support and barely passable

French; in the end, she withdrew from the race. Some of this framing is a reflection of self-presentation, but some is a result of mediation.

POLICY ISSUE FRAMING: SERVING THEIR OWN

Stories about visible minority women often portray them as inward looking and parochial, positioning their issue interests as "minority" rather than "mainstream" and framing their successes as accomplishments within their "own" communities rather than achievements with broader societal implications. For example, a story about Jean Augustine's appointment to cabinet looks exclusively at the black community's reaction, with quotations from black community members, as well as other black politicians. Augustine's own statement in the article appears to be an effort to reframe this focus by drawing attention to the wider implications of her appointment: "Being the first black feels good, yes, but more than that, *it says to others* and to ourselves that blacks can be in every place in society ... It's important that no one be able to say that blacks can't perform in every segment of Canadian society because we can" (quoted in Jones 2002, A23; emphasis added). Meanwhile, a story about proposed human smuggling legislation notes, "In Ottawa, NDP MP Olivia Chow accused the government of targeting migrant 'victims' ahead of criminal smugglers. She called the proposed measures 'draconian.' Ms. Chow won't find much traction with that; the proposed act, at least as it was presented yesterday, should find support in *mainstream Canada*" (Hutchinson 2010, A1; emphasis added). No evidence for this perceived "support" is given, but in distinguishing between Chow's views and those of the so-called mainstream, the article situates her on the periphery. Another suggests that the "Asian vote" may help Chow's electoral chances (Vallis 2006, A4).

As is noted in Chapter 5, journalists often refer to a politician's background when they deem it relevant to a story. An article about the flow of illegal migrants from China to Canada refers to Sophia Leung as "the first woman of Chinese-Canadian descent elected to Parliament," and notes that she "made an impassioned plea in Mandarin for officials in Changle to stanch the flow of illegals" because the "fallout from negative coverage of the boat people saga has hurt the interests of her fellow Chinese-Canadians" (Cohn 2000, A1). The problem with this type of coverage is that it is only when politicians have traditionally marginalized identities – as women or minorities, for example – that their socio-demographic backgrounds are deemed to be relevant. When white males discuss economic or military issues – stereotypically "masculine" policy areas – their backgrounds are not mentioned, thus leaving readers with the impression that only minority politicians are influenced by self-interest or their own life experiences. Sometimes, references are oblique and, while not overtly racialized, may prime this type of association (Zilber and Niven 2000). These include descriptions of Jean Augustine as a "social progressive" or a reference to her "large working class riding," or descriptions of Marlene Jennings as an "anti-apartheid activist." These code words cue associations with minority issues.

Of course, the media's framing of politicians is partly a reflection of how individuals present themselves, an issue that is more fully discussed in Chapter 4. In some cases, visible minority women reference their own racialized and gendered characteristics, and it is therefore not surprising that the media report on this. For example, a story about same-sex marriage refers to "Liberal MP Marlene Jennings, who is black, and a strong supporter of same-sex marriage." Jennings is quoted as saying, "I stand before you as a minority to say that once this government even contemplates such an action, where does it stop?" (MacCharles 2003, A8). In other cases, parties may slot MPs into particular roles. This was the case with Nina Grewal who, along with two other Conservative MPs of South Asian origin, accompanied Stephen Harper on a trip to India. A reporter notes that journalists were invited to join the prime minister, his wife and the MPs for a treat of "spicy samosas" (Campion-Smith 2012, A4). Similarly, an article quotes a blog posting from Conservative MP Peter Van Loan discussing the criteria that prime ministers consider when appointing their cabinets: "While merit is an important factor, the nature of our country means that geography, sex and ethnic diversity also play a primary role ... Diane Finley and Bev Oda helped fill the gender balance need, and Bev [Oda], along with Michael Chong would be the two visible minorities in Cabinet" (in Smyth 2006b, A4).

It doesn't help that two of the most recognized visible minority women in Canadian politics – Jean Augustine and Hedy Fry – held the stereotypical multiculturalism portfolio and thus were often closely associated with these issues, while Bev Oda was appointed minister of Canadian heritage, which at the time included responsibility for multiculturalism. In her capacity as NDP critic for immigration, Olivia Chow received significant coverage on issues related to immigration and human rights. When these and other visible minority women MPs held other portfolios, they tended to appear in stories about a broader range of issues. For example, while Fry was in opposition, she held the critic's role for health, and much of her coverage focused on these issues rather than anything related to multiculturalism. Meanwhile, when Marlene Jennings was Liberal justice critic, she appeared in several stories about crime; as deputy house leader, she appeared in stories about a much broader range of issues. This underscores the fact that media coverage is partly mediated – based on choices that journalists and editors make – but also partly a reflection of reality, a distinction to which I return in the next chapter.

Media, Politics, and the Stained Glass Ceiling

The analysis of visible minority women's news coverage presented in this chapter broadly reinforces findings from the larger media study presented in Chapter 2. In particular, this chapter has shown how socio-demographic markers – in this case race and gender – can influence the media's framing of political actors. While this study has not tested the exact effects of such coverage, the existing literature suggests that such framing is likely to cue or prime voters' consideration of these factors when evaluating their political choices. That visible minority women are often presented as racialized and gendered subjects first and political actors second provides voters with a sense of what the media deem matters in the assessment of these MPs.

Second, this analysis draws many parallels to research on gendered mediation, which provides insights into the masculine and sexist narratives that underpin the coverage of women politicians. However, it has also shed light on how the intersection of race and gender can introduce subtle differences into the coverage of women who also happen to be visible minorities. Appeals to notions of exoticism, entitlement, loyalty, and fitness produce patterns of coverage distinct from those identified in the broader literature on women in politics. The "good girl" narrative is interwoven with assumptions about "model minorities" and "hard-working immigrants" and further complicates the delicate terrain that visible minority women must navigate when competing on the political stage. These politicians are judged not only against normative standards about femininity but against assumptions about what it means to be a Canadian and who is qualified and "deserves" to represent us. Visible minority women confront the same gendered barriers as white women, but added to these are a series of contentious and often pernicious racial barriers.

In this way, visible minority women need to crack not merely the glass ceiling, but also the stained glass ceiling. In our efforts to understand the experiences of visible minority women, we cannot simply take existing research on women in politics and "add colour and stir." We must work towards frameworks that take into account the full range of political experiences. This means looking at white and visible minority women, and also examining differences within and between these categories, a task not adequately undertaken here but which should feature in future work.

Third, when set alongside Chapter 2, this chapter underscores the importance of examining media coverage through both qualitative and quantitative lenses. A purely numerical approach could lead observers to argue that racialized and gendered framing makes up only a small portion of the coverage of visible minority women; indeed, there are a number of stories in which neither the politician's race nor her gender is mentioned. The more discursive approach taken in this chapter, however, illustrates that the potential impact of a racialized or gendered frame may not simply be a function of its frequency, but also of its salience. The words used to describe visible minority women are powerful and persuasive. Rather than simply tallying racialized references, research needs to account for the symbolic weight and poignancy of the media's framing. Although the literature on media effects is complex, we know at the very least that news coverage plays a role in shaping our understanding of the world around us (Clark 2002; Toulin 1999). The racialized and gendered media discourses highlighted in this chapter help to establish and maintain existing power dynamics, institutional structures, and inequities. The media are reflecting social norms and relationships, but also helping to reproduce them.

Finally, while it is true that blatant racism and sexism have become much less commonplace, we should not be seduced into thinking that race and gender no longer matter. Carol Aylward, a law professor of mixed West Indian and Mi'kmaq descent, writes that the presence of white women in various institutions has transformed the traditional "old boys club" into the "old boys and new girls club." However, she points out, "We've opened a crack, but that door is still controlled by a white hand ... We are still only the tolerated guests in these institutions" (quoted in Winsor 1999, A11). Visible minority women should no longer be covered in the media as "tolerated guests" but instead as the full-fledged and qualified political actors that they are.

4
Candidate Self-Presentation and Media Portrayal

> "Too often, we talk of hyphenated Canadians and view them primarily through the lens of their ethnicity. In doing so, we fail to see the other qualities they bring. As a result, we deny them the opportunities that exist for the rest of us. No doubt, this is done with the best of intentions; the irony is that visible minorities want to be approached on common ground. They want to be accepted as the rest of us are: simply as Canadian."
>
> – Michael Chong, member of Parliament

The above quotation is taken from an opinion piece written by Michael Chong (2004), a Canadian member of Parliament. Chong's op-ed was a reaction to an article written by *Globe and Mail* reporter John Barber suggesting there should be more Chinese Canadian members of Parliament representing the ridings where large numbers of Chinese Canadian voters live. Chong criticized this perspective, noting that the kind of Canada he wants is one in which identities are not hyphenated, and Canadians with ethnic and visible minority backgrounds are seen as much more than the product of their socio-demographic characteristics. News framing distinguishes visible minority politicians from their white counterparts and provides voters with a racially situated framework from which to evaluate the alternatives before them. The question remains, however, whether these portrayals are an accurate reflection of reality.

Skeptics will assert that visible minority candidates might simply be less interested in economic policy issues than their white counterparts. Maybe they promote themselves as minority representatives or run exclusively in ridings with high visible minority populations and are thus portrayed accordingly. Or perhaps visible minority candidates are less qualified, less articulate, and less prominent than their competitors. Although it is true that the media make choices about how to frame and portray electoral candidates, typically coverage does not emerge out of nothing. Rather, it is based – at least in part – on the raw ingredients that candidates provide. We thus cannot look at media portrayals in a vacuum but must assess them alongside candidates' own self-presentation. That is the objective of this chapter.

Measuring Candidate Self-Presentation

The conclusions reached in this chapter are drawn from two distinct data sources. The first is a series of thirty-three semistructured interviews that were conducted with former candidates, sitting members of Parliament, campaign staffers, and party officials. Many of those interviewed were part of the candidate sample on which the media study was based, but the sample was expanded to include other participants. In addition to my own communications with interviewees, acquaintances in media and political circles introduced me to potential subjects, while press officers in the Liberal and New Democratic parties and a former senior official and a cabinet minister in the Conservative Party all sent information on my behalf to the targeted candidates. As well, I asked all interviewees if they could recommend other subjects; some pulled out their phones and facilitated introductions on the spot. When I did encounter refusals or non-responses, interview fatigue, competing demands, and gatekeeping by staff were among the principal reasons.[1] In addition, the topic of my research – the media – may have led to some reticence on the part of potential respondents given that a number were involved in politics during the long period of minority government in which media communications and interviews in general were discouraged (Campion-Smith 2008).[2] Although my sampling strategy could be categorized primarily as "snowball" or convenience, I made efforts to ensure the interview sample varied on a number of dimensions, including race, gender, party affiliation, electoral record, and region, so as to enrich the data and provide analytic leverage.

The diversity among interview participants allows me to draw conclusions about the factors that affect political experiences, media interactions, and communication strategies, and because I interviewed both white and visible minority candidates, I am able to compare inputs and outcomes on the basis of candidate race. Interviewees had been involved in politics in a number of capacities: twenty-three were former or sitting parliamentarians or provincial legislators (including one senator), six had run as candidates but had never been elected (of these, three had also managed campaigns or worked as political aides), and four had served mainly as political advisors or staffers. Eighteen respondents were visible minorities and fifteen were white, although some of the white staffers had managed campaigns for visible minority candidates and vice versa.[3] Fourteen were women and nineteen were men. Seven of the women were visible minorities. Sixteen participants were from the Liberal Party, nine were from the Conservative Party, and eight were from the New Democratic Party.[4] Most had been actively involved in politics for at least a decade, although some of the candidates – particularly those who had been defeated – had less electoral experience. A few have had political careers that spanned nearly three decades. Candidates and staffers were drawn from a range of electoral districts, including some with large visible minority populations (upwards of 75 percent of the population) and some with much smaller visible minority populations; participants resided in six of the country's ten provinces.

These interviews were conducted between March 2011 and November 2012, with most occurring in the spring, summer, and fall of 2012.[5] Interviews ranged in length from twenty minutes to more than one hour, with one interview occurring in two parts of forty minutes and seventy-five minutes. About half of the interviews were conducted in person, either in the subject's office or in a restaurant or coffee shop of their choosing. The other half were conducted by telephone. Subjects all had some previous experience conducting interviews – typically with journalists – and were quite familiar with the process; differences in interview content, conduct, or comfort did not seem to be related to interview mode. Interviews were conducted in confidence, and participants were assured that their names and identifying details would not be used. Many dismissed the offer of confidentiality, saying they did not mind being identified; as one respondent put it, "If I don't want to be associated with it, I won't say it!" Nonetheless, I have not included any names because the pool of potential interview subjects is quite small – particularly with respect to visible minority candidates – and the inclusion of some names could allow readers to identify even those respondents who wished to remain anonymous.[6] All but one respondent allowed me to audio-record our conversation, and in all but one case respondents gave me permission to quote.

When I initially began contacting potential interviewees, I did not specify my focus on race because I was concerned about priming effects.[7]

Instead, I told interviewees that my research was about the media and politics, and that I was interested in learning about their communications strategies and their experiences in politics. However, after a number of contacts and limited uptake, it was clear that I would need to provide more explicit reasons for wishing to interview each respondent.[8] Respondents were advised that I was interested in how candidates' socio-demographic backgrounds affected their media coverage; where applicable, I also told them that I was interested in speaking to candidates who ran in ethnoculturally diverse ridings. This strategy seemed to increase respondents' interest in the project without specifying my precise interest in race.[9]

Prior to the interview, I sent participants a topic guide, and each interview began with general questions about the respondent's political life, media coverage, and communication strategies. To probe various facets of candidates' self-presentation, I asked a number of different interview questions. They included general queries about candidate branding, the messages that they communicated, the policy issues they emphasized, the methods they used to connect with constituents, and the media strategies they adopted. To elicit more forthright responses, I generally did not ask candidates directly about their self-presentation, but instead asked questions that would provide indications of how they presented themselves, which I later compared to the ways in which the media portrayed them. In the course of the interviews, if subjects did not raise issues related to race on their own, I probed them, often by asking about the effect of constituent diversity on their electoral strategies, about the segments of the population that typically lent them their support, or about the extent to which they felt their personal backgrounds had influenced their coverage. If my review of the candidate's media coverage had revealed some instances of racialization, I would raise these with the respondent and ask him or her to reflect on them.

Recorded interviews were transcribed, and my analysis is consistent with Kvale and Brinkman's (2009) notion of meaning extraction and condensation. Using a memoing technique, I identified points of convergence and divergence in the interviews and connected these to variations in the respondents' demographic and electoral backgrounds. For example, if respondents noted that their coverage had been unfair or inaccurate, I recorded this and also noted relevant demographic or electoral characteristics (e.g., visible minority candidate, woman, defeated, incumbent, etc.). This approach allowed me to assess the extent to which experiences are isolated or correlated in some way with respondent race or other features. Of course, despite my efforts to systematize the analysis of the interviews, the process is at its heart qualitative; the sample is not statistically representative, and the nature and content of the interviews varied across subjects. For this reason, findings from the interviews are also reported qualitatively; I resist the temptation to attach numbers to the results, and instead focus on extracting trends (e.g., "most respondents," "very few participants," etc.), identifying common factors, and using quotations to exemplify or illustrate the major findings.

The presentation of the interview material in this and the following chapter is arguably somewhat unorthodox. Typically, empirical studies that rely on qualitative interviews provide a paraphrased account of interviewees' experiences with selectively chosen quotations spliced in to illustrate the author's principal arguments, but for both methodological and normative reasons, I have opted not to employ such a heavy interpretive hand, choosing instead to provide detailed quotations with much less reliance on my own summation. In doing so, this book highlights the voices and experiences of real people: the politicians, staffers, and journalists who spend their days navigating the political arena. I have several reasons for this choice.

First, this book includes perspectives from individuals who generously recounted their experiences to me. Notable among these are a number of visible minorities as well as journalists who are the focus of the next chapter; these are two groups whose voices have not always been at the forefront of research on the media and politics. In electoral studies, visible minority candidates can be overshadowed or outnumbered by their white peers, while communications researchers often critique the media's end product without discussing its genesis with the journalists who created it. This book provides a space for these voices to be heard. Second, one current that runs throughout this study is a discomfort with the media's propensity to select and make more salient particular aspects of the experiences, expertise, and backgrounds of visible minority candidates. While framing is a necessary part of storytelling, this book provides a number of illustrations of the problematic ways in which visible minorities in politics are portrayed by the media. Among these is a propensity to paraphrase visible minority candidates rather than quoting them directly. This tendency diminishes the status of these candidates and presents their insights through the journalist's interpretative lens. If I were to also paraphrase the interventions of the visible minority candidates whom I interviewed, I would be engaging, somewhat perversely, in the exact kind of framing and interpretation that I criticize the media of performing. A third reason for relying on the first-person accounts of the individuals I interviewed is because these provide a number of stark examples of the racialized treatment to which visible minorities are subjected. Many Canadians wish to deny that prejudice still exists or to assert that it is rare and isolated. The words of those who have experienced prejudice are a powerful statement of its manifestation and magnitude. We need to hear these stories – sometimes multiple times – in order to understand how endemic and cross-cutting racialization really is.

This chapter and the next thus include a number of quotations. These provide a basis for my claims, give voice to respondents who are often silenced in electoral and media studies, and illustrate the propositions emerging from my theorization of racial mediation. To be sure, we should be cognizant of the fact that interviewees are providing a subjective perspective on themselves and their own behaviour, but that is the case with any qualitative interview study. Indeed, the very reason for using an interview methodology is to extract respondents' own perceptions, experiences, and opinions – of which this study offers many. Moreover, while their memories may have faded or they may have withheld information, respondents were provided assurances of confidentiality, and a number provided frank and detailed descriptions of their own performance and strategies. These are set against the ways in which they were portrayed in the media to understand the relationship between candidate self-presentation and media coverage.

In addition to these qualitative interviews, the chapter uses a second data set to assess this relationship. Specifically, it constructs an index that includes measures of candidates' electoral experience, outcomes, and riding competitiveness. These can be thought of as objective indicators of candidate viability. Candidates' actual viability can then be measured against their media coverage to ascertain the extent to which presentation and portrayal converge. The specifics of this index are discussed more fully later on in the chapter.

Based on these two data sources, the chapter argues that all candidates, regardless of race, inject parts of themselves into their messaging and policy issue interests. This is because candidates are storytellers and salespeople, and the personal cannot be separated from the political. Electoral and communication strategies vary depending on a number of candidate-specific and contextual factors, including gender, electoral experience, media market, and riding diversity, but these factors alone do not explain candidates' coverage. Consistent with existing literature, I find that the media tend to overemphasize the socio-demographic backgrounds and stereotypic policy interests of visible minority candidates relative to their self-presentation. My analysis also finds a wide divergence in the viability coverage of white and visible minority non-incumbents. The fact that an electoral win washes away these differences suggests that unless presented with evidence to the contrary, the media views visible minority candidates as unlikely contenders. The racial divergence suggests that journalists are not simply reporting on candidates' objective qualifications, a conclusion that was also drawn in Chapter 2.

The final analysis is clear: media are not passive reflectors. They do not just take candidates' raw ingredients and serve them to voters. Rather, they choose how much of each ingredient will be included, which flavours will be brought forward, and what the final product will ultimately look and taste like. Candidate race appears to be one of the factors influencing these decisions. Exacerbating this is journalists' propensity to draw on simple narratives, which makes it difficult for them to present candidates' multi-dimensionality; this comes out plainly in my interviews with journalists, which are discussed in Chapter 5. Yes, visible minority candidates bring elements of their socio-demographic background and personal narratives to their political lives, but there is not a perfect 1:1 mapping of self-presentation onto media portrayal.

Overall Impressions of Media Coverage

It is important to note that while this chapter raises some concerns about the extent to which race influences a candidate's portrayal in the media, when asked to evaluate their news coverage, most respondents stated – often after some contemplation – that their coverage was satisfactory or neither unfair nor inaccurate, although few provided overwhelmingly positive assessments. Moreover, among those interviewees who said that they thought their coverage was largely fair and accurate, a number asserted that this situation was atypical and that they were somehow exceptional. In other words, while there was no groundswell of negativity towards the media, there was a sense of skepticism and even wariness.

Even those who said their coverage was generally fair argued it was nonetheless often on inconsequential matters. A white candidate who was first elected more than three decades ago said, "The mainstream media will not report on you unless you kill somebody, or they see you going down the street naked. No good news is news." A female one-time candidate and long-time party organizer said, "I don't mean to sound patronizing to the media, but they do lap up stuff that's kind of dumb. You know, if it's a picture of you going to vote with your husband, how stupid is that? But they'll do it. They'll actually [cover] it." Others said that the media provide little space for coverage of substantive policy issues and "reduce the debate to monosyllables instead of intellectual analytical work." In one MP's view, "No media article actually discusses the merits of public policy or a particular bill. It's all about what somebody said that was titillating." Respondents' dismay about the lack of policy coverage is borne out in the findings presented in Chapter 2, which confirmed that very little media attention is devoted to policy issues. This is perhaps because policy discussion is regarded as boring and not in line with news values that privilege sexy, shocking, and dramatic storylines.

Respondents confirmed this tendency, noting that the media place an undue focus on mistakes or gaffes. One visible minority candidate said, "The only way a candidate is going to come to be known during a campaign is for them to say something egregious." A white member of Parliament echoed this view: "My experience is that often [the media] are not really there to help. They would love to get a sound bite or a clip of me screwing up." Interviewees referred to "gotcha moments," the media "frenzy," and "pack journalism." The media's propensity to report on errors, missteps, and conflict affects how candidates campaign; one long-time staffer suggested electoral strategy is largely about damage control. He said, "You're just trying to keep the candidate alert, aware, somewhat rested and not making mistakes or gaffes, not having a temper tantrum caught on tape. You're just trying to hang on a little." In large part, interviewees did not suggest that the media invent stories, but rather that they choose particular aspects to "highlight," which has the effect of "amplifying differences," "facilitating bad blood," and "reinforcing racism."

Some candidates suggested that the tendency to highlight difference is particularly acute once a spotlight has been cast on a mistake or conflict. This is a form of confirmation bias in which more weight is given to information that fits with our existing beliefs than to that which dispels them. For example, one candidate mentioned that his campaign drew the media's attention to his opponent's spotty election debate attendance: "Once it happened once, the media were really looking for it." Another first-time candidate recounted how he was accused of having links to Islamic fundamentalists and, because of his heritage and the fact he was somewhat of an unknown, this allegation perhaps seemed plausible enough for the media to report on it. In our interview, he said, "It was a juicy story. It's an interesting story, and I'm not saying this type of story is not worth covering, but you first do your homework and then if there's absolutely no truth to it, then why would you run it?" He suggested that because of journalists' "prejudicial stereotypes," he was "guilty until proven innocent." Another interviewee suggested that the media are more likely to report on minorities who make a "misstep" because such a story is in line with existing stereotypes. He noted, "The media make it a story because the person is a minority. Chinese or Japanese or Filipino or African, it's a huge story: 'Look at these people acting up again. They've made another mistake. They put their foot in it.'"

Interviewees did not just point to the media's confirmation bias; some suggested that other biases were at play. Some asserted that the media are not seeking the truth but instead hoping that an interview will provide evidence for a predetermined conclusion. For example, a visible minority candidate told me that he was once approached by a reporter from the *Toronto Star* who was curious about the candidate's choice to run for the Conservative Party because of its Reform Party roots and historical perception as an anti-immigrant party. After the interview, the reporter informed the candidate that he would not be proceeding with the story because he had been instructed to write a negative article, and apparently the candidate had not provided quotes to support this angle. The candidate told me, "The media would like to say they give an unbiased view. They would like to say they are unbiased, but we know from experience that is totally nonsense. All media have already made up their mind how the story is going to go." A white candidate from another party echoed this sentiment almost exactly, saying that "the media have their own biases ... I think it's often reflected in the tone of the article. Sometimes they actually make up their mind before they've even had a chance to meet you." A visible minority candidate revealed that she issued news releases to "counter lies, but they were never published. The media were not interested in telling both sides of the story or even seeking out the truth."

Some candidates suggested that the media treated them differently because of ideological or personal biases; these critiques were largely raised by Conservative candidates and staffers. For example, one MP described his first election campaign:

> It was tough because [my opponent] had the media in his back pocket. I would have ministers come to visit my riding, and I'd get almost no publicity at all. He would have backbench colleagues, opposition even, come to visit, and they'd get headlines, they'd get the front page ... So the media in my riding are definitely not Conservative. They claim to be neutral, but they're not. There's no question. They will print anything negative about me or the leader of my party and very seldom will print anything positive.

Another Conservative shared this view: the "media that are more liberal will not like me. Political affiliation also plays a very strong role in the reaction to you." A Liberal candidate, however, also commented that "some journalists have a personal agenda that they're pushing ... A lot of the media personalities, folks who are veterans, who have been around a long time, have a personal agenda, and they paint a certain colour around your comments." Thus, while Conservatives were more likely to mention the media's perceived ideological bias, this perception was not confined to them. On the whole, however, there was not an overwhelming sentiment of ideological bias, particularly not with respect to the print media.

In addition, only a few candidates explicitly recounted especially negative experiences or inaccurate portrayals. However, visible minority candidates, and particularly visible minority women, were most likely to assess their coverage in this way. One visible minority woman said the media unfairly covered a controversy related to her nomination contest and said their "criticism was very biased, unfair and sensationalized." Another said she was "unfairly dismissed" by the media, while a third said she had some fairly negative experiences with the media, including an instance in which reporters "staked out [her] home." Only one white male said he thought his coverage was inaccurate, and he thought it was for ideological reasons, namely a "Liberal bias" in the media. Women and visible minority candidates tended to suggest that unfair or inaccurate coverage was a function of their personal characteristics. A number of candidates – white and visible minority – recognized that even if coverage is generally fair and accurate, it "is not the same across the board. Candidates get attention if there is something peculiar about them, if there is something unique about them as an individual." Interviewees noted that gender, race, or age may be among the things that make a candidate stand out. This assertion is consistent with theories of gendered and racial mediation. While almost no respondents claimed the media were overtly sexist or racist, many drew attention to the subtle ways in which gendered or racialized assumptions influence how the media shape stories about political events and actors.

The Impact of Political Context on Candidate Coverage

Socio-demographic background is not the only thing that can affect news coverage. Interviewees also talked about the impact of political context. For example, several mentioned that being a new candidate can make it more difficult to get coverage or to be covered positively, with a number pointing out that the incumbent has a distinct media advantage. Interviewees suggested that new candidates often do not have strong relationships with journalists, they are less known and therefore not sought out for comment, and they may not be viewed as front-runners, a perception that affects their coverage. One candidate claimed that the media try to "break" new candidates, whom they view as easy targets. In her case, she surmised that once the media "realized they weren't getting anywhere with it, and it wasn't affecting me ... they decided to stop." Some candidates also pointed out that in their first election, they were less media-savvy and not as skilled at communicating messages or providing sound bites. When they developed these skills and forged relationships with journalists, their coverage improved.

Interviewees also recognized that local candidates, in general, do not get a great deal of coverage. Several said that the media's attention is centred on national party leaders. One former MP decried this development, saying:

> Campaigns have shifted to become much more leader-centric, and there is an increasing disinterest in what candidates want to do for their constituents and their country ... The ability of candidates to be agents of change and innovation has been in constant decline to the extent that they are ignored even locally. The content of what a candidate has to offer in a campaign has largely become not of interest and not relevant, while what the leaders are doing has become the issue at the local level as well as at the national level.

Interviewees did not suggest that this development is the fault of the media, but rather a function of structural changes that have centralized power in the leaders' offices. Leader-centric media coverage is in part a reaction to these changes. Local candidates have to compete for media attention not only with leaders, but also with their colleagues who hold cabinet portfolios and critics' roles. One former MP said that in her community newspaper, "Often the critic would get the coverage on an issue rather than the local member ... If the [community newspaper] wants a comment on some federal issue – infrastructure, immigration, environment – why are they going to the critic? Why don't they ask one of the local members?"

The propensity of the media to focus attention on party leaders and those holding prominent political roles decreases the amount of coverage given to local candidates, but also has implications for visible minorities, who are less likely to hold positions of importance in the government (Tolley 2013).[10] A journalist confirmed this: "I'm not running a rainbow newsroom. If parties have immigration critics, they are the people I will talk to [regardless of race] because they are the ones who are versed on the file ... And if I'm covering EI [employment insurance], I'm going to go see the EI critic of a party and, obviously, the human resources minister." In this self-perpetuating cycle, the absence of visible minorities from some of the key cabinet positions reinforces their lack of prominence in news coverage, which I discussed in Chapter 2. It also directs our attention towards those within political parties who select the occupants of cabinet, critic, and committee posts, a point to which I return in the book's concluding chapter.

The Role of Journalists

Most interviewees spoke frankly about the important role that journalists play in their coverage, and many suggested that candidates who have built positive relationships with reporters will receive better media coverage. For example, a white interviewee who had worked as a columnist prior to being elected told me, "I had an advantage because ... I actually knew a lot of the reporters." A visible minority candidate said, "Over time, I was able to build relationships, one-on-one relationships, with lots of reporters. They started taking an interest in the kinds of things I stand for, the issues that I chose to champion." Another visible minority candidate said, "I was very fortunate to have good relations with [the local newspaper] so, generally speaking, I feel they have always given me positive coverage because I have earned that." A white former MP confirmed this sentiment, noting, "The more open and transparent you were, in terms of media calls and media relations, the more likely you were to get coverage." Others suggested that once journalists know candidates, they think twice about covering them negatively; in one visible minority candidate's words, personal relationships with the media "make it more difficult for them to dehumanize you."

In her examination of gendered media coverage, Goodyear-Grant (2007) found that male MPs were much more likely than female MPs to discuss the importance of building relationships with reporters. Among my interviewees, I did not observe a sharp gender divide. Indeed, it was a female staffer to a female candidate who provided the most explicit example of relationship-building: "The minute [the candidate] got elected, we outreached to all of the local media, set up coffees, found out what the local issues were from their eyes and how to work with the media in the community to make sure those issues get raised." That said, although female respondents were about as likely as male respondents to mention the importance of media relationships, the women I interviewed did seem to have a more guarded view. Their references to relationships tended to be couched in protectionist language, which was less common among the men with whom I spoke. The sense among female candidates seemed to be that you must build these relationships *or else* the media will not cover you favourably, while male candidates' references were somewhat less defensive. Similarly, although visible minority candidates were about as likely as white candidates to mention the importance of relationships with journalists, the former were much more likely to note that such relationships had to be *cultivated*. White candidates tended to say that they had connections to journalists and these were useful, while visible minority candidates suggested that *once* they built these relationships, their coverage improved. But those relationships were not pre-existing; they had to be carefully cultivated. This conclusion is in line with the idea that visible minority candidates have a different starting point from white candidates.

It is also noteworthy that some of the respondents who were most critical of the media drew explicit attention to their policy of *not* forging relationships with journalists. As one visible minority candidate put it, "The one good thing about the media was because I didn't want to be a media darling they never covered me, which was fine by me ... I didn't make friends with the media because the media are not your friend. They're there to extract information out of you. So I was very disciplined. I always kept the media at bay." Another visible minority candidate whose coverage suggested she generally did not engage with the mainstream media told me that because they had not covered her fairly, she generally turns down media requests. She said that requests for interviews have decreased as a result, and her decision to not engage with reporters has not necessarily softened the relationship: "I'm very selective in who I talk to with the media, and that is what their problem is. Their problem is that they're really upset because I won't talk to them, because they blew it, okay?"

Nevertheless, a number of interviewees were sympathetic towards journalists. As one staffer put it, "Reporters aren't out to screw you." Many noted the time constraints that journalists face, budget cuts that have reduced the number of reporters available to do in-depth investigative work, the pressure to produce stories that sell, and incentives towards tabloidization and infotainment. Others noted that there are competing stories. As one staffer said, "There were times when we had an issue, we had a press conference or something, and it just didn't get covered because, you know what, the reporter was at a bigger event, or they had something else that they had to put in that day." A staffer and former journalist maintained that journalism is a "manufacturing profession," and a set number of stories is the product: "It's important to understand the constraints on journalists [and] it's especially important to understand what their productivity metrics are. It's as if they are churning out widgets." In his book *Flat Earth News*, reporter Nick Davies (2009) uses the term "churnalism" to refer to the mass production of news content, often with only minimal fact checking. A number of interviewees noted that the twenty-four-hour news cycle and the rise of social media have only exacerbated these challenges and resulted in more simplistic stories.

Portraying the Personal

Interviewees talked about the media's propensity to focus on what one staffer called "biographical trivia." When asked why the media reported on his background, a turbaned Sikh candidate said, "It's just because I stand out, I guess. And when you stand out, if you're from a visible minority, I think that's one of the reasons." Some did not take offence to socio-demographic coverage, saying that it is "factual." When asked about references to her family life, one white legislator said bluntly, "Well, I am a mom. I am a grandma. I am a woman." A visible minority party official noted, "You can't change who you are. You don't develop amnesia at the border when you arrive here. You don't transform through some kind of renovation. You can't change colour. You are who you are."

The focus on socio-demographics was not regarded as wholly neutral, however. Some respondents expressed concern that their race, religion, or gender was sometimes used to approximate or make assumptions about their policy beliefs. As one visible minority legislator said, "If you share [socio-demographic information] as a fact, I have no problem. But if you use that information to colour my statements or views, I will have a problem with that." Similarly, a female candidate said, "What I do find offensive is if [coverage] is superficial about how I look or making an inference that because I'm a woman I don't have the same knowledge of, say, financial issues." A visible minority candidate echoed this concern, noting that as soon as he says his name, people assume his priorities are "Middle East or Muslim stuff." This candidate said references to his immigrant background typically did not bother him, but references to his race or religion were more problematic.

Other candidates said that socio-demographic coverage could actually be quite positive. For example, "If someone wants to report on the fact that I came here at a young age, and I was born in India, that's fine. We had this opportunity, and we made the most of it. It wasn't easy ... but we worked hard. I want Canadians to know that you can do anything." Another visible minority candidate suggested this narrative is attractive to the media because it confirms our own positive perception of ourselves: "We are a country of immigrants ... and maybe it's a point of pride to look at the person who so recently came to Canada or whose parents came to Canada and is now so actively engaged."

There are limits to the kind of coverage the candidates will accept, however. A staffer who had worked for a number of white candidates said that "at a high level," coverage that mentions that a candidate "is a dad or has a dog humanizes him," but most interviewees agreed certain things are out of bounds, including coverage of family feuds or an extensive focus on candidates' children. Most candidates felt the media do respect these limits, although there were references to incidents that suggest there is a grey area. It does seem the media will largely keep a candidate's family out of coverage unless there is a situation that might imperil a candidate's ability to serve or cast doubt on his or her integrity. For example, the media have sometimes chosen to report on a legal matter or family illness, often with reference to the political implications of the situation. White and visible minority candidates were equally likely to raise concerns about the times that the media had "crossed a line" between the political and the personal.

On other fronts, there was less convergence. For example, while white candidates rarely raised concerns about racialized media coverage, both male and female interviewees drew attention to the persistence of gendered coverage. For example, a female candidate who has served in various political capacities over the past three decades told me, "There is definitely a gender bias [in media coverage], but more so in the early years. I think it's covered up a bit better now, but I think it's still there." Another female candidate who has run for multiple levels of government said, "There was, and still is, a double standard in terms of media coverage for women as opposed to men." Like others, this respondent mentioned attention to women's appearance, hair, clothes, marital status, and juggling of family and political responsibilities as indicative of this double standard. She said, "I was described in a way that [the media] would never describe a male even though we were doing exactly the same thing or speaking exactly the same way ... I'd be described as emotional or excited, talking too fast or waving my arms too much."

These sentiments align with the literature on gendered mediation; the interviewees in my study confirmed the already ample evidence that candidate gender affects media coverage. One of the journalists with whom I spoke seconded this, noting while the situation has improved somewhat, the media's coverage is still not "gender-blind." Several interviewees also talked about the effect of candidate age on coverage, with a number suggesting their youthful appearance was used as a heuristic for inexperience. Generally, however, white candidates were silent on the impact of race, and largely rejected any suggestion that their own skin colour might privilege them in the electoral arena. Meanwhile, visible minority candidates talked about the impact of a wide range of characteristics on media coverage, and acknowledged that discrimination can occur on a number of non-racial grounds.

Often references to gender and age were made in tandem with references to race, a point raised in Chapter 3. Consistent with the literature on intersectionality (Collins 1998; Crenshaw 1989, 1991; Lorde 1984), interviewees were unable to separate the independent effects of their identities. This is unsurprising given that our race, gender, age, and other markers of difference do not exist in airtight compartments; they interact, they overlap, and they often change depending on the subject and the context. Said one candidate, "[The media] are attacking me because I'm a woman. Attacking me because I'm a young woman. Attacking me because I'm a racialized young woman." Another visible minority woman asserted that "men can have all kinds of allegations or pasts or histories, and it never gets reported in the media, but you bring in somebody new, somebody young, somebody who is diverse, and somebody who is a woman, and all of a sudden it becomes newsworthy." A third visible minority candidate said that visible minority women are covered differently than white women, but even among visible minority candidates, being male is a "trump card." Each of these quotations illustrates just how interwoven candidates' identities are.

The interviews suggested that references to candidates' backgrounds are fraught, but a number of candidates said that they do draw attention to their family histories and heritage, often using their background as a springboard to talk about their political motivations or policy interests. One of the visible minority candidates with whom I spoke told me that his daughter encouraged him to tell his story:

> She said it's important to give an example of what I went through as an inspiration for other South Asians and other immigrants who come into this country. Because they face discrimination. They lose hope. The struggle becomes very heavy for them. They look around. They look at someone like me who came here and first drove a taxi ... But I found my way out. And I tell them, yes, there is hope.

A strategist who had advised several high-profile parliamentarians pointed out that "politicians seek to connect with people. They seek to touch them ... One form of connecting is the immigrant story because we're a nation of immigrants ... That is one of the key pegs on which we build our story." A visible minority candidate said, "When I'm talking to the media, I'm not talking in a vacuum. It's a way to speak to real people. Connectivity is everything. And people need to relate to you ... Your personal story is always a persuasive point because we love other peoples' stories."

This need to connect is apparent among visible minority candidates who seem to recognize that their backgrounds could be off-putting to some voters, and they therefore confront the issue head-on. For example, during the Calgary mayoral election in 2010, the campaign of Naheed Nenshi, a second-generation Canadian and Ismaili Muslim, created a YouTube video entitled "How Do You Say Naheed?" The video description said, "We get a lot of questions from citizens and the media about Naheed and his Better Ideas for a Better Calgary. This video was created to answer the number one question that we receive from all sources." The video showed Calgarians attempting to pronounce Nenshi's name while cleverly inserting information about the candidate (e.g., "There was a radio program on the CBC a few years ago about urban issues in Canada and for the Calgary person's opinion, they would always call this person and that was, uh, Na-HEED?")

Taking a page out of Nenshi's book, Liberal candidate Omar Alghabra employed a similar tactic in the 2011 federal election, producing a video called "How Do You Pronounce Omar Alghabra (oh-mar al-GAH-bruh)." Children from Alghabra's Mississauga riding tried their hand at it, often with amusing results, including several versions of "Algebra?" and one pint-sized tyke who whispers, "I can't say that." These humorous strategies are an attempt to attract interest to a campaign, but they also serve to defuse suspicions about a candidate's history or motivations, something that is particular to visible minority candidates. Indeed, it is doubtful that you would ever find a "How Do You Say John Smith?" video.

A number of interviewees asserted that references to candidates' socio-demographic backgrounds are "loaded" or skewed towards female and visible minority candidates. One staffer and former candidate, a visible minority woman, pointed to me and said, "So, for example, if you ran as a candidate, even though you're white you have a background – German, Italian, French, whatever – but [journalists] never write that." Another said, "When a Canadian does something, do the media say she's white, she's Jewish, she's born in Israel or whatever? No. Nobody ever says those things." This perspective was reinforced by a visible minority staffer who noted, "The coverage will say 'Muslim, Nigerian-born,' but it never says 'Irish Flaherty' does it? No."[11]

To illustrate this point, one visible minority candidate with whom I spoke contrasted how the media have portrayed various members of Parliament. First, she brought up Rahim Jaffer, a former MP who was found in 2010 to have breached the Lobbyists' Code of Conduct. In this interviewee's opinion, the media made Jaffer "out to be evil" because he "was brown." She observed that Jaffer's "only mistake was that he had not registered as a lobbyist." She contrasted this with the media's treatment of Tony Clement, a Conservative MP and cabinet minister whose riding benefited from a number of capital projects that were financed through the G8 Legacy Infrastructure Fund in a process that the Office of the Auditor General determined lacked transparency and accountability (Fekete 2011). This interviewee said that Clement "created a boondoggle of millions of dollars, but [Jaffer] was ethnic," and that while Clement "has a Greek background, he is white enough." She believed, as well, that ethnicity in part fuelled the coverage of former cabinet minister Bev Oda: "Sixteen-dollar orange juice and she's a moocher of the worst sort?! I mean, give me a break. Why are the media so biased?"

Racialized coverage is not distributed equitably, nor are its effects neutral. For example, one visible minority candidate said that the media's focus on her cultural background made her feel like a "victim": "I was born and raised in Canada and consider myself to be Canadian first." She believed that by focusing on her ethnic heritage, the media painted her as somehow less Canadian than other candidates. Other interviewees said that by focusing on the backgrounds of visible minority candidates more than the backgrounds of candidates with British or European origins, the media exacerbate differences and "perpetuate the notion that there are tiers of Canadians." These reflections are in line with my theorization of racial mediation in that they demonstrate the one-sidedness of racialized coverage. Racialized coverage disproportionately affects visible minorities because race is deemed to be newsworthy largely when the subject is marked by a *minority* race.

Portraying the Political

While most candidates agreed that socio-demographic mentions were common in news reporting, there was a sense that policy issues are not really a focus. As a result, news coverage tends towards the personal rather than the political. There are a few explanations for this. In the first place, some candidates said that they themselves do not talk policy because during elections, voters are not really interested in such discussions. When I asked a long-time MP what policy issues he is most passionate about, he replied, "Doesn't matter. I never talk issues at the door. I have a passion for a couple of things, sure. But at the door, never, never, never do I talk policy." A visible minority candidate said that while she has a personal interest in a number of policy issues, "I think those are not things that are on the minds of everyday, average Canadians." Most interviewees mentioned that a candidate's reputation and credibility are more important than policy interests. For example, one staffer said that "the key thing was to keep the candidate's name in front of people ... Get him quoted ... When we went to frame the pamphlets, it was just name, name, name. We tried to make them more deep policy-wise, but we ended up scrapping that and just going for his picture and information about him."[12]

Those candidates to whom policy was important said that they focus only on the issues that matter to voters. When they talk to seniors, they emphasize seniors' issues; when they talk to immigrants, they emphasize minority issues. At the same time, most interviewees said candidates must understand communities in order to appropriately target their policy messages. A staffer who has worked with a visible minority candidate noted, for example, that Portuguese seniors in the riding are not really interested in seniors' issues, but instead in "their kids' kids' education." A visible minority candidate and a former MP both said that when they communicated with the media and potential supporters, they would ask, "Okay, what kind of messages, what kind of language, what choice of words do we think we need to use to hammer home our messages? What kind of issues are they dealing with here? Maybe the environment isn't as important here, but immigration is, or health care if we are dealing with seniors." There were also interviewees who maintained that policy messages are not really driven by local candidates, but instead by the national campaign. One strategist who had worked on a number of national campaigns noted that local candidates' "job is to be at the doors. You don't need to have their energy worrying about the campaign, or putting together policy briefs." A number of candidates and staffers emphasized that the aspirations of minority Canadians are really just the same as other Canadians.

Several visible minority candidates did mention that they were drawn towards political engagement because of concerns over discrimination, human rights, Islamophobia, or social justice. One said that her political interest was initially piqued when, as a young girl, she became frustrated about having to travel across town to attend her Saturday-morning heritage language classes; this got her thinking about the impact of policy decisions related to public transit and education. Later in her interview she said that, in her childhood, her "house was basically an immigration office ... It [seemed like] it was a required stopover in Canada because my parents were there to help with the integration process, help with the settlement process." Given these motivations, it is perhaps not surprising that the media might focus visible minority candidates' coverage on such issues. However, as one visible minority interviewee pointed out, the media help to entrench perceptions about minority candidates' policy interests by calling on them to comment on such issues "because they felt that's where you're probably most competent to speak, to provide a point of view." This sheds some light on the patterns of policy issue coverage documented in Chapter 2.

While some white candidates also drew a connection between their motivations for entering politics and their own personal experiences – highlighting, for example, their professional expertise or a family history of political engagement – visible minority candidates were more likely to make this link. Nonetheless, I was not left with the impression that visible minority candidates are any less multi-dimensional than other candidates. While their politics are informed by their personal narratives, few seemed singularly focused on minority policy issues. A number either mentioned no explicit policy interests or drew attention to other areas, including the economy, employment, and health care. One visible minority parliamentarian noted that he had done important committee work on issues related to agriculture, banking, and finance, but had never contributed to any formal study related to diversity; nonetheless, when he is mentioned in the media, it is his anti-racism advocacy that is typically highlighted, not his work on these other issues. Moreover, white candidates who ran in ridings with concentrated immigrant or visible minority communities were just as likely as visible minority candidates – and sometimes more likely – to raise immigration and settlement issues as an explicit priority, if they raised any policy issues at all.

The more common reaction when asked about policy interests was for candidates – both white and visible minority – to respond that policy is the stuff of national campaigns, that local contests are not decided on this basis, and that door-knocking and communications must be the local candidate's focus. Rather than candidates being divided on mentions of minority policy issues, they are instead united by a feeling that policy debate does not win local elections. Indeed, a number mentioned that not only is it difficult for local candidates to get media coverage, but it is particularly difficult for local candidates to garner coverage on *policy* issues. One white candidate mentioned several policy issues that she tried to emphasize in her campaign but said most did not resonate. When asked why, she said that there were national issues that attracted more attention. She also pointed out that during that particular campaign, her party was faring poorly, so "the story was that we were tanking." Consistent with the literature on horse-race journalism, coverage of strategy, tactics, and leaders seems to take priority over coverage of substantive policy issues, and this seems to affect all candidates equally. Indeed, as Chapter 2 pointed out, there is little difference in the *amount* of policy issue coverage that white or visible minority candidates receive, even though the type of policy issue emphasized varies depending on candidate race.

To the extent that the media do focus on candidates' policy interests, it is perhaps not surprising that they might zero in on those issues that are informed by personal stories. Visible minority candidates cannot shed their ethnocultural background. Although they have other interests and motivations, they are informed by their experiences with discrimination, racial profiling, and inequity. In addition, because visible minority candidates' personal narratives are perceived as different and therefore interesting, their coverage is more likely to examine the link between this background and their political engagement. That said, white candidates are equally informed by their personal histories, professional expertise, and early interactions with public figures, and while the media do draw attention to these formative experiences, these stories are typically less frequent and less evocative. Meanwhile stories about visible minority candidates often revolve around themes of hard work and triumph and are grounded in experiences that voters may view as exceptional and to which they may therefore not relate. This is somewhat of a concern given, as one white candidate put it, "Politics is very populist. You have to reflect the populace. They have to be able to relate to you." Almost without exception, visible minority candidates were conscious of this and in their interviews drew attention to the ways that they tried to connect with voters from diverse backgrounds. When you look at their coverage, however, this is not the major takeaway point. Rather, visible minority candidates appear more closely linked to their "own" communities and issues than to others.

By contrast, even when white candidates told me during their interviews that immigration and multiculturalism were among their priorities, these issues rarely figure in their policy coverage. One such candidate explained that "by the nature of my constituency, I got involved in a number of issues and particularly immigration and refugee policy. The influence there was a very ethnically diverse constituency with a lot of newcomers." Of the two dozen articles about this candidate that appeared during the 2008 writ period, half connected her to some policy issue, but only one related to immigration. Similarly, I found five articles about a white candidate who had formerly served in the immigration portfolio and who in our interview signalled this issue as important; three of these articles mentioned a policy issue but none related to immigration.

The conclusion to which I therefore return is that while a number of visible minority candidates acknowledge their interest in so-called minority issues, the overall portrayal is not a mere reflection. Visible minority candidates express interest in other issues, while white candidates told me that they emphasized immigration and multiculturalism policy. These self-presentations are not fully borne out in the media's coverage, however.

Candidate Self-Presentation and Image Management

Few politicians have a direct line to voters and thus must rely on the media to present themselves publicly. Of course, candidates assist in the process by providing professional photographs, distributing slick campaign materials, and arranging structured press conferences, but ultimately the media decide what image the public sees. The media choose the visuals, parse the quotations, and write the headlines. They are responsible for a story's angle, frame, and very existence. Even so, we cannot underestimate the choices that candidates make. All candidates – and indeed, all of us – engage in some element of stage management. We seek to put our best face forward and to conform to socially accepted standards of behaviour. In the image-centric world of politics, this desire is perhaps magnified, with most of my interviewees noting that even a single misstep can have grave consequences. To guard against mistakes, candidates and their staff work to tailor careful messages, hone the candidate's public speaking abilities, and cultivate a style becoming an elected official. In this section, I examine candidates' impression management strategies, the factors that affect these, and the extent to which these choices may influence media coverage.

A number of people with whom I spoke suggested that politics is a sales profession, and candidates have to find ways to appeal to voters. One staffer said, "The way that you focus, how you sell yourself in your literature, and the way you talk to voters is key." Interviewees emphasized that branding is not straightforward, because the characteristics that appeal to one set of voters may alienate another segment of the population. One candidate told me, "I used the youth angle to project a lot of energy and change and a lot of positive attitude, but at the same time, people see that as [indicative of] inexperience, so it's a double-edged sword." Presenting an image that is genuine and consistent seems to be top-of-mind. As one strategist put it, "Some minority candidates play up their minority background. Others say, 'Yeah, I'm in the soccer league here, my son's in the daycare, my wife is on the PTA' ... You have to be comfortable in your skin. You can't pretend to be like the Joneses if you've never met the Joneses." A white staffer seconded this when he said, "You package each candidate differently based on their skill set, based on who they are and what – in terms of biography – they come with."

Political parties often play a role in this branding. One staffer said that it is not happenstance that particular candidates or legislators appear before the media to talk about specific issues. She suggested that if visible minorities appear in the media talking about immigration or multiculturalism, "that's who the party sent out to talk about those issues." She went on to say that her party would not send a young candidate out to talk about seniors' issues and would probably choose someone with a family to talk about children's issues. Another staffer pointed to the Ontario government's communications strategy following a shooting at a community barbecue in Toronto's Danzig neighbourhood in July 2012. The staffer noted that while the minister of children and youth services and the minister of community safety and correctional services have responsibility for this kind of issue, it was rookie MPP Michael Coteau who was at the forefront. Coteau is black and a former Toronto school board trustee. A third staffer suggested that efforts are made to couple candidates at appearances, so that if one candidate were "articulate and fluently bilingual," she would attend an event with a male visible minority candidate who was not. A staffer of Asian origin told me that she would be sent to "Asian events" simply because of her ethnicity. As these examples reveal, it is not just candidates but parties that engage in impression management strategies.

Unsurprisingly, then, the need to project an appealing public image was mentioned by a wide range of candidates from across all parties. However, women and visible minority candidates were much more likely to raise concerns about self-presentation, particularly in relation to their appearance and speech.[13] Recognizing that he might have to overcome stereotypes about his communication abilities, a visible minority candidate told me that whenever he spoke in debates, he would post the videos online "so that people could see and hear that I was able to articulate myself ... The assumption is that someone who is racialized, who is a visible minority, may not have the language skills, may not be articulate, so I wanted to highlight that I have those skills in abundance." This same candidate also emphasized his professional background and ensured he was "very well-dressed and very polished" in an effort to counteract negative perceptions about young visible minorities. Two female candidates with business backgrounds noted that they were cognizant of the need to appear professional "but not too professional." One who ran in a fairly rural riding said she had to "reshape [her] image from being this über-professional policy person to somebody who can relate on the street." She recalled that her staff would say, "Go home and take off that suit. Can you wear a sweater rather than a suit? Can you wear a dress rather than pants?" Her staff would tell her to wear her plain gold wedding band instead of her diamond ring, and she made sure not to wear high heels when campaigning in certain parts of the riding. These choices are partly a response to predictions about the image that will resonate most positively among voters.

A number of factors can affect candidates' choices about self-presentation. Perhaps chief among these is the composition of the candidate's riding. Unsurprisingly, the larger a riding's immigrant and minority population, the more likely candidates were to draw attention to their socio-demographic backgrounds, and it is in these highly diverse ridings that visible minorities are most likely to run. Sometimes, the focus on one's background is an attempt to connect with voters, while in other cases, it is an attempt to distinguish oneself from one's opponents. In an article about her nomination content, Yasmin Ratansi "insisted she had broad support, [she] nevertheless made clear efforts to win the backing of the South Asian community. 'I am the only candidate in this contest who is of South Asian heritage and understands your issues, because they are my issues too,' she said in an interview with the *Weekly Voice*, a community newspaper" (Cowan 2004, A10).

Under certain conditions, white candidates also engaged in strategic socio-demographic presentation. For example, a white MP who represented a highly diverse riding told me that on her website, she was always sure to post photographs with "diversity" in them. Strategic socio-demographic presentation was also evident among white candidates with ethnic minority backgrounds, such as Ukrainian, Polish, Greek, and Italian. One candidate commented that this strategy is "totally helpful for two reasons. One, people saw me as someone who would understand their struggles because of my ethnocultural background. Second, they knew that I understood the importance of celebrating one's ethnic origin in the Canadian context." When I look at the coverage of white candidates who mentioned their ethnic minority heritage as a strategic advantage, however, this element of their backgrounds is never referred to.

In contrast, a visible minority candidate who ran in a relatively diverse riding told me, "I'm not ashamed of anything, and I don't shy away from talking about anything, but I don't necessarily talk about my ethnic or faith background ... I don't want to alienate other people who may not relate to it." Even among visible minority candidates who told me that they intentionally downplay their ethnocultural or religious heritage, I can find a number of references to these characteristics in their coverage. There is not, in other words, a straight-line relationship between self-presentation and media portrayal.

Moreover, visible minority candidates cannot simply sell themselves as ethnic or immigrant candidates because this has the potential to alienate them from white voters, as well as voters from other minority racial and ethnic communities. A visible minority strategist said, "I know of no riding where any one community voting all one way could win if all the other people [voted differently]. It's probably impossible in Canada, so you need to appeal outside of your community and your constituency." A white MP with ethnic minority origins confirmed this sentiment: "We're all different. We all come from different backgrounds. We all look different. People with long last names, people with ethnic or different diversities, people from mixed backgrounds, and you got to work with everybody."

This reality means that candidates need to think carefully about their characteristics and the qualities they present to voters. A visible minority candidate insisted, "During all of the time that I have run in my riding, the last thing that I have ever did is to say who I am, my ethnicity, my religion. That does not play an active role." This particular candidate ran in a riding where about one-quarter of the population identifies as a member of a visible minority group. In light of this, the candidate emphasized, "I present myself as a Canadian, as having the same values as everyone else. If I try to highlight my ethnicity, my religion, these things, then I will lose. I will gain a minority – a strong minority – but I will never make it ... I present, 'I am a Canadian just like you. My values are like yours, I have the same desires as you.'" However, when I asked him whether the media pick up on this message – that he is Canadian just like everyone else – he said no. Another visible minority candidate said the media "did not cover [me] as a credible person who knows her stuff." She noted, "I took public finance. I know exactly what I'm talking about. Do the media care? No. The media say, 'I don't know what this ethnic woman is doing here.'" A candidate who had worked as a model prior to entering politics says she explicitly downplayed this part of her résumé, focusing instead on her advanced education and community involvement. Nonetheless, all but one of her articles mention modelling.

Few visible minority candidates denied their ethnocultural heritage or even shied away from talking about it; a number also readily admitted that they infuse their backgrounds into their communications when it will be advantageous. If anything, visible minority candidates were more open to talking about their backgrounds and their self-presentation than were white candidates. Although white candidates also talked about the importance of appealing to voters, some seemed to have thought less about branding and image management, perhaps because they do not have to. This conclusion is buoyed by findings presented in Chapter 2 and in the section that follows, which suggest that while visible minority candidates may have to prove themselves in order to be seen as credible competitors, this is less true for white candidates. Visible minorities are likely to think more consciously about their backgrounds and how to present themselves because, quite frankly, they have to.

In some cases, visible minority candidates intentionally downplay their socio-demographic characteristics or complement them with references to their involvement in "mainstream" organizations and "Canadian" society. The website of a Calgary-based MP, Devinder Shory, provides an excellent example of this strategy. In his biography, Shory's Indian birthplace and immigration history are highlighted. He writes that "like many new Canadians," his foreign credentials were not recognized when he arrived in the country, so he "loaded linen trucks [and] drove cabs" before becoming a lawyer and "being called to the Alberta bar." Here, we can see that references to Mr. Shory's immigrant experience, which are probably targeted to newcomers in his riding, are then bridged by the mention of his standing in a "mainstream" profession: the law. The biography goes on to mention Shory's work with the YMCA, public library, and other community organizations, in addition to being the recipient of an Outstanding Service Award from the Calgary Filipino Community. Again, we can see the interplay between the minority and mainstream dimensions. The bio concludes, "in his spare time, Devinder enjoys exploring *other cultures* and their ideas. His passions remain politics, law *and giving back to his country, Canada*" (Shory 2012; emphasis added).

In spite of such efforts, mentions of race, immigrant background, and support from minority communities appear in article after article about visible minority candidates, often with little reference to their other dimensions. By contrast, a number of white candidates talked about their upbringing and the ways that they use their own backgrounds as a point of connection with minority voters. In spite of this, few media stories mention the socio-demographics of white candidates. Moreover, skeptics dismiss these inconsistencies and focus instead on the finding that, yes, visible minority candidates sometimes do draw attention to their ethnocultural heritage. What this point overlooks, however, is the ways in which visible minority candidates talk about their backgrounds. Often they do so not to set themselves apart as different – the narrative that typically runs through their news coverage – but instead to show how in spite of their race, they are very much like other Canadians. In their study of members of Congress, Zilber and Niven (2000, 61) came to a similar conclusion, noting that "for most African American members, the discussion of race is about a commitment to inclusion, while in the media it is conveyed as a preference for exclusion."

One strategist with whom I spoke said that the media and other observers focus on visible minority candidates' own references to their background as a "proof point" and ignore all the other ways that they present themselves. This was confirmed by a candidate:

> I talk about my parents coming to Canada and succeeding, but in the context that I talk about it, it's because that's one of the reasons that I'm involved and want to give back ... So I mention it, but beyond that, I don't really talk about my family ... At the same time, often in the media, probably because of my appearance and background, they automatically talk about the immigrant success story. They talk about the first generation. Maybe it's a cultural norm, but it's a common media practice, and it happens often.

Another visible minority candidate with a penchant for flashy dressing said that his wardrobe "ended up getting more attention than saying I've been involved with activism or was heavily involved in human rights. Some of those other things may have been glossed over, and they highlighted the 'well-dressed, good suits.' Some of it was definitely presented by me, but in terms of a focus, I think sometimes the media focused more so on it."

Admittedly, there appears to be a tension in candidates' behaviour between appealing to ethnic or immigrant voters – a plausible core constituency – and presenting themselves as "Canadian" so that they appeal to other voters. One staffer said candidates often modify their self-presentation depending on the context. A candidate confided that she struggles with finding a balance between her "Canadian" and "ethnocultural" identities. She noted that if she downplays her ethnic heritage, her own community will criticize her, but if she emphasizes it too much, other voters will see her only as an ethnic representative, and she will lose credibility. This sort of balancing act is not something that white candidates talked about or with which they seemed to grapple, and it is thus not a factor that really complicates their coverage. Whereas visible minority candidates can expect at least some of their news coverage to focus on their race, minority status, or other socio-demographic features regardless of how they present themselves, white candidates are not subject to the same sort of racialization. To be sure, white candidates' media portrayal is not always a mirror reflection of their self-presentation, but it is much less likely to be influenced by racialized assumptions.

Measuring Candidates' Self-Presentation against their Media Portrayal

The analysis in Chapter 2 showed that visible minority and white candidates' viability coverage is roughly equivalent in the aggregate, but incumbency has an important effect on this pattern. Visible minority challengers receive far less viability coverage than white challengers, while all incumbents – regardless of race – receive approximately equal amounts of viability coverage. This suggests that viability coverage is influenced, at least in part, by a candidate's *actual* viability, that is, by their skills, experience, and qualifications. Past research reveals that visible minorities in fact bring superior qualifications to the electoral arena, including higher levels of education, more professional backgrounds, and longer roots in the community; some suggest that they need to meet this higher bar in order to overcome their perceived racial disadvantage (Biles and Tolley 2008; Black 2000b, 2003, 2008b). If this is the case, then we should actually expect visible minorities to receive significantly more viability coverage than white candidates. This raises two questions. First, are visible minority candidates more viable than white candidates? And second, does their media coverage reflect the skills and qualifications that they bring to the table?

To answer these questions, I constructed an index that ranks the electoral viability of the sixty-eight candidates whose media coverage I examined in Chapter 2. The index includes data on three measures: candidates' electoral outcomes (i.e., elected or defeated), incumbency, and riding competitiveness.[14] The rationale for including electoral outcome in the index is perhaps the most obvious: candidates who win can claim viability, while those who lose cannot.[15] I created a dichotomous variable to indicate whether the candidate won or lost in the 2008 election. Successful candidates were coded as 1 in the index, and defeated candidates were coded as 0. Of the candidates in the sample, 66.2 percent were elected while 33.8 percent were defeated. Although half of the visible minorities in the sample won their electoral races and half were defeated, fully 82.4 percent of the white candidates were elected. As a result, the bulk of the defeated candidates (73.9 percent) are visible minorities, while the bulk of the elected candidates (62.2 percent) are white.

Turning next to incumbency, again the relationship between this variable and candidates' electoral prospects is well established, with incumbents enjoying an electoral advantage in single-member plurality systems; some Canadian estimates suggest that advantage could be as much as 10 percent (Cox and Thies 2000; Eagles 1993, 2004; Jacobson 1990; Johnston and Pattie 1995; Kendall and Rekkas 2012; Krashinsky and Milne 1986). Incumbents were coded as 1 in the index, and challengers were coded as 0. In my sample, 55.9 percent of candidates were incumbents, while 44.1 percent were challengers. Visible minority candidates make up a larger proportion of the challengers in the sample (53.3 percent), while white candidates make up a larger proportion of the incumbents (52.6 percent). This suggests that white candidates have the edge on this front as well, although only marginally.

Finally, the index includes a measure of riding competitiveness – party support stability – that was developed by Marc André Bodet (2013). Party support stability measures a party's performance based on its past and present vote shares in the riding in the previous two elections. This dichotomous measure classifies ridings as either strongholds or battlegrounds; strongholds, even when they are non-competitive or weakly competitive, are still safer than battlegrounds, where candidates and parties can expect a much tougher electoral fight.[16] This distinction is consonant with the way media and voters tend to understand political reality. Indeed, although the measure arguably stems from more sophisticated calculations than most voters or reporters would use, it mimics the logic that people employ when making predictions or inferences about a candidate's chances of winning. The index measure of party support stability is based on data from the 2004 and 2006 elections. To reflect the "boost" that candidates get when they run in their own party's stronghold, these ridings were coded as 1. Ridings that are another party's stronghold or a battleground are both comparatively more difficult for a candidate to win and so they are coded as 0. Among the candidates in the sample, 44.1 percent ran in their own party's stronghold, while 55.9 percent ran in another party's stronghold or in a battleground riding. White candidates were more likely to run in their own party's stronghold (52.9 percent of white candidates, compared to 35.3 percent of visible minority candidates). The visible minority candidates thus faced a tougher electoral context, with the bulk (64.7 percent) running in ridings where their parties had historically been less competitive.

All three measures – electoral outcome, incumbency, and riding competitiveness – were aggregated to create an index measure ranging from 0 to 3, where 0 represents the least viable candidates and 3 represents the most viable candidates.[17] Average viability of the candidates in the sample was 1.66, while the median was 2. Eighteen candidates (26.5 percent) were challengers who ran in another party's stronghold and were ultimately defeated; these candidates scored a 0 on the index. Meanwhile, twenty-four candidates (35.3 percent) were incumbents running in their own party's stronghold and who were elected; these candidates scored a 3 on the index. Among white candidates, 44.1 percent would be considered "most viable" (i.e., scoring a 3), compared to 26.5 percent of visible minority candidates. On average, the white candidates in the sample would be considered more viable than their visible minority counterparts.[18] So, do the most viable candidates receive the most viability coverage? And how does candidate race influence this relationship?

Each candidate's viability score was compared to their viability coverage, which was derived from the manual content analysis described in Chapter 2. Stories with no insider or quality mentions for the candidate were scored as 0, while those with at least one insider or one quality mention were scored as 1. Articles in which the candidate received both types of mentions were scored as 2. Separate analyses were run for the visible minority and white candidates so that the comparison between candidate viability and media coverage could in turn be compared to candidate race. The results are shown in Table 8.

This table shows a moderate positive relationship between candidate viability and media mentions of candidate quality or insider status. The relationship is roughly the same and statistically significant regardless of candidate race. In other words, in the aggregate, the media are reflecting what both visible minority and white candidates bring to the table. What the aggregate results conceal, however, is the relative discounting of unknown visible minority candidates, which can be observed by looking at the viability coverage of the least viable candidates in Table 8. Specifically, while 94.0 percent of stories about the least viable visible minority candidates include no insider or quality mentions, the comparator for white candidates is 51.8 percent. Put differently, while only 6 percent of the least viable visible minority candidates could expect to see some mention of their viability in

TABLE 8

Insider and quality coverage, by candidate viability and race (% stories)

Candidate viability score		No insider or quality mentions	Insider or quality mention	Insider and quality mention
0	All candidates	70.7	26.0	3.3
	Visible minority	94.0	6.0	0.0
	White	51.8	42.2	6.0
1	All candidates	60.6	37.2	2.2
	Visible minority	35.1	63.5	1.4
	White	78.3	18.9	2.8
2	All candidates	32.4	63.4	4.2
	Visible minority	26.2	69.0	4.8
	White	44.3	52.6	3.1
3	All candidates	11.5	83.0	5.5
	Visible minority	13.6	80.0	6.4
	White	10.4	84.6	5.0

NOTE: Kendall's tau–c = 0.371 ($p < .01$).

news coverage, nearly half of the least viable white candidates could expect the same. As visible minority candidates become more viable, however, their coverage improves dramatically and is more or less on par with – and sometimes even better than – that of their white counterparts. In other words, among the least viable candidates, race has a strong impact on insider and quality coverage. These findings and those reported on in Chapter 2 suggest that visible minority candidates must achieve some degree of credibility – either through incumbency, an impending electoral win, or running in a riding where their party has traditionally been competitive – in order to receive some viability coverage. This is less so for white candidates, who appear to be accorded at least some viability coverage even when their objective qualifications perhaps do not support this. This is consistent with US survey analysis by Linda Williams (1989), who found that while white voters are willing to elect qualified black candidates, they are more likely to view white candidates as possessing those qualifications and, specifically, as capable of achieving various policy goals. In other words, the standard imposed on candidates differs depending on their race. Although the media's coverage of candidate viability does, overall, reflect candidates' actual viability, there is evidence that racialized assumptions may influence how the least viable visible minority candidates are covered. The same cannot be said for white candidates. This pattern of having to prove oneself is repeated when other socio-demographic dimensions – namely gender – are examined.

The male and female candidates in the sample achieved roughly equivalent viability scores.[19] Using the procedure outlined above, I compared these viability scores to the candidates' viability coverage. Again, I found a moderate and positive relationship between candidate viability and resulting viability coverage, which holds regardless of candidate gender. However, the least viable female candidates receive far less viability coverage than the least viable male candidates. Specifically, while 46.9 percent of less viable male candidates (i.e., those with viability scores of 0 or 1) received an insider and/or quality mention in their coverage, this number drops to 13.4 percent for similarly situated female candidates; the difference is statistically significant. Among the most viable candidates, however, gender differences in viability coverage are negligible, suggesting that once women have proven themselves, their coverage improves. Consistent with my findings on visible minority candidates, it would appear that prototypical candidates – that is, those who are white or male – are assumed to be viable even if their objective viability suggests otherwise, while less conventional candidates are not automatically associated with electoral viability.

An examination of race and gender in tandem provides additional confirmation of this thesis. More than half (51.1 percent) of less viable white male candidates received an insider and/or quality mention, compared to just 15.8 percent of less viable white female candidates. Among visible minority candidates, I find a similar but even starker pattern, with 43.6 percent of less viable visible minority male candidates receiving some viability coverage, compared to just 4.2 percent of their female counterparts. These differences are all statistically significant. In other words, most male candidates can expect at least some positive viability coverage even when they may not be all that viable. This is much less true for female candidates. Being an unknown or unlikely contender definitely hurts everyone's coverage a little bit, but it hurts women more and visible minority women the most. Once candidates have somewhat of a proven record, their coverage does improve, but aggregate analyses conceal the disparities and leave us with the erroneous impression that viability coverage is simply a reflection of the qualifications that candidates bring to the table. This appears not to be the case; indeed, there is anything but a mirror relationship between candidate self-presentation and resulting media coverage. Rather, mediation is occurring, and candidates' socio-demographic characteristics, including their race and gender, affect those calculations.

Even Playing Field, Different Starting Points

A number of interviewees – both visible minority and white – conceded that the bar is indeed set higher for visible minorities. The sense is that while white candidates start at zero, visible minority candidates start below that and then have to work their way up. This belief is consistent with the above analysis of candidates' viability coverage. Visible minority candidates do not start at the same point as their white counterparts, but once they have proven themselves as incumbents with an electoral victory, the differences in coverage are relatively negligible. As one visible minority candidate put it, "The threshold or standard is higher because you have to first prove that you're not what they thought you were and then you have prove that you are a serious candidate." A female candidate pointed out that "if women need to prove themselves as being qualified and ready and all of that sort of thing, layer onto that what it means to be a visible minority, and the bar is even higher because there are a whole other series of cultural biases and perceptions, linguistic issues that come into play, that would make it even more challenging." This point was confirmed by a visible minority staffer who said visible minority candidates have to work harder to be portrayed positively in the media, and "they have to be mindful that what may not be covered for a non-minority candidate can become a story for you." Another visible minority respondent said, "In Ottawa, on Parliament Hill, if a minority makes a misstep, it becomes a huge story, and their picture is on the front page of the paper. But if the same misstep was made by another person of the same, same education, same background and everything but was white, it would not be a front-page story."

Three visible minority candidates to whom I spoke mentioned family problems that surfaced during their time in politics. All of them suggested that the media's coverage of these issues was driven in part by their race and ethnicity and that the coverage was an attempt to discredit them. A number of interviewees also pointed out that political organizing by ethnic or immigrant communities is portrayed in the media as suspicious and unfair, while the courting of the (white) seniors' vote or endorsements by corporations is seen as unproblematic.

The increased scrutiny is not restricted to the media, but plays out among political elites as well, although often as a defensive strategy based on predictions about potential coverage. For example, one interviewee who had been closely involved in his party's recruitment of ethnic candidates said that when individuals approach him about running, he asks them, "Are you clean? You got luggage? Any skeletons in your closet? Have you ever declared bankruptcy? Have you ever beat up your wife? Has your wife ever beat you up? Have you ever crossed the street or pissed on the wrong side?" He says that as a result of his intense questioning, many "feel violated," but he tells them, "If I don't violate you now, you're going to get violated during the election." A visible minority candidate who has also been involved in candidate recruitment says that while all candidates are subjected to a background check, "All parties at all levels in all provinces probably do more stringent background checks on candidates from ethnic backgrounds." Another interviewee who has been involved in recruitment said that visible minority candidates have to be stronger because they already stand out, so the media will scrutinize them more.

Candidates did point out, however, that once journalists got to know them, their coverage often changed. A visible minority candidate explained,

> When I was first elected, I was not a known commodity. So I think there was a little bit of "Who is this guy? Where did he come from and what's his story?" Then that kind of disappeared ... It's the evolution of the narrative, right? Clearly, in the beginning my narrative was who I am, what I have done, and why I am running, and I think it was fair for the media and the public to want to know that. But that narrative has now evolved because I have much more experience as a public servant, and I'm involved in a lot of policy files.

None of the white candidates with whom I spoke described the need to prove themselves. In contrast, this sentiment was expressed matter-of-factly by most of the visible minority candidates that I interviewed. This difference reaffirms the conclusion that while racialized coverage is subtle, candidate race does affect coverage and this cannot be explained as simply a function of self-presentation. Quite simply, visible minority and white candidates are assessed according to different metrics, and this mediation is reflected in their coverage.

Race Still Matters

Consistent with the findings of the media study presented in Chapters 2 and 3, my interviews with candidates show, in a number of ways, how race still matters. Interestingly, however, a number of candidates with whom I spoke were quite hesitant to talk about the role of race in politics. In contrast, a number of candidates – white, visible minority, male, and female – pointed to sexism in politics and differential media treatment for men and women. I asked some interviewees about the reticence to talk about race, and they offered a number of explanations. A visible minority MP suggested that feminism has given a definition to, and voice against, sexism, but there has been no similar movement for racism. People do not know the parameters, so they are afraid to talk openly about it. Another visible minority MP said that people do not want to talk about race because "Canada has prided itself on being this great country in which there is no racism, and we're not like the US and blah blah blah. No one wants to speak about what is really going on. And if you do, you're targeted." She says that there is "politically correct double-speak" about Canada's purported tolerance, and that when she raised issues related to racism, it was viewed as "poking a finger in the eye of a country that had taken me in and given me these opportunities." In her view, "I did speak the unspoken words ... I did bite the hand that feeds me ... I reached [the position] I reached because Canada had allowed me to do it, and now I'm accusing Canadians of racism." Another visible minority candidate confided, "I would never say publicly some of the stuff that I'm going to tell you because I don't want to come across as a whiner or defensive or bitter ... But I think it's important to know the type of ignorance that exists out there."

A white MP who ran against a visible minority candidate in British Columbia said he was, in fact, shocked by the racism that some voters expressed to him. A number of voters made racial slurs about his opponent, and this particular candidate said the campaign really revealed the tensions and feelings of racial threat that still exist in his community. This sentiment was seconded by another white candidate who said that partisans who would not typically vote for her switched allegiances because they could not bear to support her visible minority opponent: "They would rather vote for the Liberal woman with the Caucasian name."

Of course, white candidates have a race, just as visible minority candidates do. However, for most white candidates, race does not seem to be a complicating factor. Even white candidates who ran in racially diverse ridings tended not to cite race as an issue, except perhaps from an administrative standpoint. For example, a number of white candidates noted that the complexion of their ridings required that they translate documents, assist with immigration questions and casework, recognize religious and cultural days of significance, ensure they have appropriate clothing to attend ethnocultural community events, or learn a few words in the languages that their constituents speak. There are thus imperatives associated with representing a racially diverse riding, but unlike visible minority candidates, white candidates do not seem to perceive their own race as a barrier, even when it is so visibly different from that of the majority of their constituents.

This finding is hardly earth-shattering, but the extent to which issues of voter-candidate racial differentiation seemed not to cross the minds of white candidates was somewhat unexpected. I had assumed that those who ran in ridings with large visible minority populations might consider how being racially "different" from the majority of voters might affect their electoral opportunities. Certainly, this concern was expressed by visible minority candidates who ran in ridings with a large number of voters from outside their own ethnocultural community. Nonetheless, such concerns were not raised by white candidates. More often, white candidates seemed somewhat confused by questions about the impact of the race on their communications and self-presentation. For example, when asked whether constituents had ever expressed any concerns about the fact that their MP's demographic background was so different from that of the majority of the residents in the riding, one respondent paused and then queried, "You mean because I'm white? ... Uh, no. I've never heard that, never considered that." Another white candidate told me that her race is not a factor in her diverse riding because she just presents herself "as the best-qualified person for the job, and [visible minority voters] respect that. They kind of respect power." Other candidates echoed this attitude, noting that they are accepted by voters from other cultural backgrounds because they "work hard" and "build bridges." None suggested that their race has any kind of impact on their electoral prospects. This appeal to meritocracy is consistent with the literature on internalized oppression. Karen Pyke (2010) notes that the "hard work" narrative wrongly presumes that anyone can succeed on the basis of their skills, qualifications, and determination. Such appeals do not recognize unequal starting points or systemic barriers and thus conceal the extent to which so-called objective standards can result in inequitable outcomes.

In contrast to their white counterparts, visible minority candidates almost without exception mentioned concerns about not being viewed as appropriate representatives, the perception that they would not relate well to constituents, the need to balance their ethnocultural and "Canadian" identities, and questions about their ethnic lineage. An interview with a staffer did reveal one possible exception to this statement. He noted that while most visible minority candidates have to think about how to win over voters from other communities, "Olivia [Chow] never had to do that. It was a little bit different for her. No one would ever assume she was just there as a Chinese candidate, partly because she's married to Jack [Layton]." In a separate interview, a visible minority candidate from another party also drew attention to Chow's media coverage, which she suggested has been quite favourable: "I'll be blunt about it. [Chow] is an ethnic candidate married to a white man. Now, if I had married a white man, would my coverage be different? I'm sure it would be." These statements place the issue of racial privilege front and centre because they suggest candidates are treated differently if they appear to be more closely linked to "whiteness." A candidate of mixed-race origin alluded to this as well, suggesting that he has not faced the same barriers or treatment as other visible minorities because he's "only half visible minority in some ways."

By comparison, a candidate of Asian ethnicity who ran against a slate of white competitors noted that at the door, she would "regularly get questions like 'So, what's your background? Where are you from?' I bet you [my opponent] never got that." A visible minority MP said that voters are generally receptive but still "there are numerous incidents where it's incredibly demotivating and frustrating and, at times, that made me want to quit politics." He says veiled ethnic slurs were shouted at him in the House of Commons, and he has received anonymous emails that tell him to "go back" to his country or call him "pathetic" or a "terrorist." This interviewee told me that white candidates are naturally viewed as neutral bridgers, while visible minority candidates are seen as representatives of their own communities. By drawing attention to visible minority candidates' racial origins, connections to their "own" ethnocultural communities, and interest in so-called minority issues – all patterns identified in Chapter 2 – the media only reinforce this perception.

Although the media's portrayal of visible minority candidates is partly based in fact, it is not completely congruent with candidates' self-presentation. Certainly visible minority candidates bring pieces of themselves to their political narrative – as do white candidates – but they present themselves in a less racialized manner than their media portrayals suggest. As we might expect, riding diversity exerts a strong influence on candidates' self-presentation, and both white and visible minority candidates tailor their strategies to the citizens who elect them. Nonetheless, only visible minorities appear to struggle with their *own* racial background and how it might affect their electoral prospects. Visible minority candidates note that they have to balance their various identities and suggest that their motivations are often questioned. My comparison of non-incumbent candidates' viability and their resulting media coverage provides persuasive confirmation of this point, with visible minority challengers receiving significantly less viability coverage than their similarly situated white counterparts. Quite simply, unconventional, unproven candidates need to work harder to be seen as credible contenders. Although the impact of gender and age on political experiences was often referred to by white candidates, few appear to have considered the possible effect of race. This is true even when white candidates run in ridings where the bulk of voters are from demographic backgrounds that are different from their own. My findings thus suggest that race matters in Canadian politics, and it matters most for visible minorities. Racialized assumptions colour the way in which visible minorities are framed and portrayed. These assumptions guide the choices that determine what is newsworthy and what merits mention, and these decisions are not race-blind. This conclusion is underscored in the chapter that follows, which contains insights from a series of interviews with Canadian journalists.

5
Journalists and the Framing of Race

"Many journalists feel that they aren't listened to by management in terms of stories and angles. Angles that are perhaps different are often summarily dismissed because they don't always fit the mold of what some managers think stories should be."

– Greg Freeman, former columnist with the
St. Louis Post-Dispatch

The media play key roles as connectors, as shapers, and as reflectors of the world around us. They select the issues and events to which our attention will be drawn, choose the voices that will be heard, and frame stories in ways that will resonate. In so doing, they prime citizens to think about particular issues and help to set the political agenda. This book argues that these choices are not neutral. Rather, they are influenced by assumptions about race and diversity, and these assumptions have a disproportionate effect on visible minorities in politics. These judgments are driven by institutional pressures, organizational imperatives, and journalists' individual decisions, but also by dominant societal norms and culture, which the media reflect and are embedded within. While these factors were discussed briefly in this book's introduction, this chapter looks more concretely at the conditions that contribute to the media's end product.

This chapter is based on qualitative interviews with thirteen Canadian journalists who spoke with me about news routines, news judgment, diversity in the media, and the coverage of race in politics.[1] All respondents work or had worked in print media at large Canadian dailies or the Canadian Press wire service, covering Canadian politics or current affairs. Although the sample is not representative, it does include some of the most experienced and well-recognized journalists on these beats. Most respondents were reporters, two were columnists, and two were editors. Three of the thirteen respondents have visible minority backgrounds, and the remainder would be considered white, although one of these identified as having an ethnic minority background. One-third of those interviewed were women. Interviews were conducted in two waves, the first mainly in the fall of 2012 and the second in the fall of 2013, with one interview taking place in the summer of 2014; all but two were conducted by telephone. In cases where the interview was conducted in confidence, respondents' names and identifying details have been removed.[2]

Interviews ranged from twenty to fifty minutes, although most were about a half hour in length. The interviews were audio-recorded and, while I did not follow a set format, questions generally centred on how journalists select the stories that they cover and why they cover them the way that they do. I also asked about the role of race in politics and news coverage. Participants were provided a topic guide and were given the option of taking any questions or subjects "off the table," but none choose to do so.[3] All interviews were transcribed, and interview data were analyzed using the same approach described in Chapter 4. The interviews are supplemented by a number of secondary source materials, as well as original data on journalism course curricula and guidelines on diversity and reporting.

The chapter begins with an exploration of journalistic practices. This includes a discussion of news gathering, news judgment, and the role of narrative in news reporting. I argue that these routines take place against a backdrop of institutionalized whiteness. Not only are newsrooms generally quite racially homogeneous, but there is little diversity training and guidelines about reporting on race are imprecise. The journalists with whom I spoke expressed very little concern about this, however, noting that the media are generally fair, and that editors and readers provide the appropriate oversight. These conversations help us to understand the choices that journalists make when deciding whether to cover a story and how to frame it, as well as the considerations that may influence these decisions. Diversity does not appear to be top-of-mind for most journalists. The chapter concludes that this lack of reflection on the salience of race contributes to the patterns of coverage that have been documented in the preceding chapters.

News Gathering and News Routines

Research on the media has tapped extensively into the routines and norms that characterize the newsmaking business. This "occupational ideology"

(Ericson, Baranak, and Chan 1987, 120) centres on objectivity, neutrality, and independence and provides journalists with a set of procedures for determining and reporting on the news. This process includes both the practice of news gathering, whereby information is collected, and actual news-making, in which facts are given meaning through their selection, organization, and interpretation (Gemi, Ulasiuk, and Triandafyllidou 2013).

When asked about their news routines, most interviewees described either a bottom-up or collaborative process for deciding on and assigning story topics. In some cases, they noted that an editor may suggest a story to them, but largely it is up to individual reporters to identify and pursue the key issues within their area of specialization. A reporter who covers politics for an outlet based outside Ottawa described a fairly self-directed process. She said, "I usually just send [my editors] an email, and I say, 'I'm going to be working on this, this, and this. And they say 'okay' ... So if I'm interested in a topic, it has never happened that I have not written on it." A long-time columnist said, "Most days, it's just a conversation, and we talk back and forth. We settle on a topic and perspective and away I go." An assignment editor noted that there are significant events that "have to be covered" while other stories are dictated by "our own background, our own knowledge of a topic, which tells us it's important and should be addressed."

When determining which stories are worth covering, three criteria emerged as most important. First, reporters have to be able to get the information and background they need to write a story, otherwise it will be dropped. This means they need to be able to track down data or convince key participants to speak with them. Having access to good visuals is also important, although more so in a broadcast format. Time, space, and resource considerations are a second criterion. In the end, some news is not covered or covered less extensively than originally planned because there are competing events or issues, space limitations, or difficulty compiling the story before deadline. The final factor journalists consider when deciding which stories to pursue is newsworthiness. One editor noted that "the common metric or criteria for deciding 'Let's do this story and not that story' is 'Will that story capture the interest of a reader?' And that's it."

Eda Gemi, Iryna Ulasiuk, and Anna Triandafyllidou (2013, 268) have identified four criteria that journalists use when determining the newsworthiness of an issue or event: "it is easy to understand; it conveys a clear meaning (good or bad, black or white, rarely is news 'grey'); it usually involves elites (political or other); and it has a sense of surprise/unexpectedness."

Other research suggests that journalists may evaluate the item's timelines, proximity, and interest to the audience, as well as its significance and the extent to which it includes elements of conflict or sensationalism (Shoemaker and Vos 2009). Richard Nisbett and Lee Ross (1980, 45) further suggest that information that is "(a) emotionally interesting, (b) concrete and imagery-provoking, and (c) proximate in a sensory, temporal or spatial way" is most likely to be selected for news coverage. Events involving people about whom the audience is likely to have strong feelings or that take the form of an anecdote or case study are also more likely to be covered (Shoemaker and Vos 2009). Each of these definitions of newsworthiness is germane to reporting on visible minorities in politics because such stories can typically be told from a standpoint of contrast, surprise, and unexpectedness while still being proximate and easy to understand.

In deciding what is newsworthy, most journalists I interviewed noted they have quite a bit of latitude over the kinds of stories that they write. However, a few mentioned that their decisions are influenced by what they think will be of interest to their newspapers. As one put it, "It's not just what I'm interested in, but what will the newspaper find acceptable, interesting, for its pages. So, there's also assumptions there that I have to make [about] what my boss thinks is interesting." This reporter went on to say that because many of the people in positions of leadership in the media sector are older, Canadian-born, and perhaps did not grow up in a context that was as multicultural as today's, they have a different definition of what the "norm" is, and "that probably contributes to added interest in candidates who are not white, Anglo-Saxon, Protestant, or Catholic." Another reporter noted that in the course of his research for an article on a visible minority candidate, he discovered that she was divorced. He originally did not include this detail in his story, but was then encouraged to do so by an editor who said, "Oh no, put that in. That's really interesting."

Moreover, media executives' views, when known, may prompt news-gatherers to look for particular stories, to focus on specific issues, or to avoid other perspectives. David Randall (2000, 17) observes, "Reporters competing to get their stories published anticipate executive values and are prepared (or feel obliged) to adopt practices which are at odds with their private values." One poll of print journalists in Canada found that 56 percent believe owners' views and interests are frequently reflected in the paper's non-editorial news content (Soroka and Fournier 2003). Not only may reporters summarily eliminate stories believed to be incompatible with the real or imagined perspectives of the leadership cadre, but there is also a selection bias in that managers are inclined to hire employees with compatible viewpoints. As a result, even if owners are not involved in news production, their hiring decisions and personal preferences may lead journalists to produce stories that align with the owners' perspectives.

When asked about the process that they follow after they have decided to cover a story, respondents provided explanations that were more or less consistent with the description offered by one of the journalists with whom I spoke:

> Generally, I'm going to sit down and ask myself, "Well, what do I already know about the story?" ... Based on that, "Who can tell me more or challenge the assumptions that I might have?" And then you just start following people, and they'll tell you about their experience. From there, you keep on moving down to further widen you pool of sources.

An editor noted that some of what reporters need to write stories "is in plain sight. Some of it you need to pursue. Some of that is pursuit of paper [documents]. And some of it is pursuit of people who are in a position to trust you to let you know what's really going on and trust that you'll handle it responsibly. And that takes years." Most described an iterative writing process that relies heavily on research and sources, but also intuition and experience. This flexibility creates an environment in which mediation can occur because journalists are able – and indeed required – to make judgments about which stories will be covered and how they will be told.

Objectivity and News Judgment

In my questioning, I asked respondents to reflect on the notion of "objectivity." Several rephrased the question to instead focus on "fairness," with one noting that while complete objectivity is impossible, fairness is attainable. In his view, the job of a journalist is to "provide a perspective that is true or at least 'truthy', and that is a reflection of my own reading and research and reporting and life experience." Another said, "Objectivity is a concept that I've never believed in. I think it's a lousy standard and a useless thing for a journalist to try and aspire to ... The best we can do, and I think it's quite achievable, is we can be fair and accurate ... but that's not synonymous with objectivity." For this journalist, such a standard entails seeking opposing viewpoints, fact-checking, and, where necessary, providing an opportunity for implicated actors to respond to accusations. An editor suggested that reporters collect a range of opinions to ensure that a story is "fair, balanced and true" even though space constraints often mean that not all these opinions can be included, because the process "helps the reporter understand" the issue.

Most noted the need to engage multiple sources, although several did mention a tendency to "go back to the some of the same people each time because they're recognized as the go-to people on it." Another said, "Some of us are really lazy, and I'm as guilty as anybody else on that front." However, she noted that diversifying sources is "more time-consuming, it's difficult, and it's often hard to reach out to people you don't already have a relationship with." She also explained that even if she asked a visible minority member of Parliament to comment on a particular issue, "You will rarely get more than what the party line is on anything." Typically, she said, the MP would refer to the party's official critic for the portfolio. In her interviews with journalists, Emily Drew quotes one who admitted, "It takes effort to go outside of [my] comfort zone. And who am I most comfortable with? ... People like me." Drew goes on to note that "most white journalists in my sample were careful to point out that their professional habits were not intentionally exclusionary. They stressed that bias in news content was the result of pressure in timing and deadlines, more than any conscious choice to exclude people of color" (Drew 2011, 363).

Journalists in my sample similarly referenced these constraints, with one arguing that well-resourced newspapers have a much easier time framing stories about diversity in nuanced ways because their reporters have the time and "luxury" to "go down the rabbit hole and glean information." He described a feature piece that he had written; for his research, he conducted three separate interviews with the subject, accompanied her on the campaign trail, and did a number of telephone interviews with other sources. He worked on the piece for a number of weeks and was able to "stew on it." This journalist pointed out that this process would simply not be possible for "most metro reporters at smaller papers who are doing two stories a day, every single day."

While the respondents placed a high priority on the fairness and accuracy of their journalism, most conceded that they bring parts of who they are to all their reporting. A columnist noted, "Every life story informs everything we do no matter what it is we do. There are elements of my life that affect my work." A reporter agreed, saying, "There's nothing you can do about who you are ... I go to new places, I cover events, I write about things that I think are interesting. And I'm sure every experience that I've lived in my life played into those decisions somehow." However, he noted that although he is a white reporter who has covered a number of "diversity" stories, in the context of his work no one has ever commented on his race or ethnicity. This may be because, as one columnist claimed, "Most people who are involved in or around politics are, frankly, colour-blind." She noted that people who live in the "political fishbowl ... don't really notice that there are fish of any colour other than party colours."

A former reporter who is a visible minority said that while he found the media leadership to be "permeable" and "open to people of different kinds of backgrounds," he found this to be less so among journalists themselves. However, a different columnist said she cannot recall ever hearing a reporter suggest that being a visible minority might be an issue for a candidate or leadership prospect, although she has heard journalists "discuss the fact that an openly gay leadership aspirant or a woman might face a different set of expectations." This interviewee had the sense that while gender still matters in politics – and by extension, to the media – race does not.

Of course, people may simply be less comfortable discussing issues related to race because racial bias tends to be much more implicit. John Miller, a former journalist and now professor emeritus at Ryerson University, told me that reporters get defensive when they are asked about racism because "it's almost like an accusation that they're deliberately setting out to do this ... That's not really the case. Much of what differentiates coverage is in fact unconscious. It's resorting to a stereotype as a shortcut and portraying someone a certain way or asking them questions that they wouldn't ask of, say, a white candidate."

That said, reporters noted that stories are not written in isolation, so even if journalists do bring personal biases to a story, there are checks and balances. Many referred to editors who will challenge their facts, sources, and assumptions. A visible minority reporter said that a lot of times, it is her editors – "white, fifth-generation Canadians" – who point out issues related to diversity that she herself has missed. Others said that if you "burn a source" or obtain a reputation for not being fair, "you wouldn't last very long." This interviewee suggested that achieving fairness is not "that difficult because there are so few stories where you'd have a vested interest or skin in the game. For us, it is a job ... and there's just a professional instinct for fairness, to have that balance in the story, the two sides, the three sides." Consistent with John Miller's observation above (and rather unsurprisingly), most respondents balked at any suggestion that their reporting might be unfair or biased.

Narratives and Assumptions

Political reporters are faced with fast-moving issues, multiple actors, and stories with several dimensions. This creates a challenge given that a key objective is to cut through the complexity to deliver a product that citizens are able to easily digest and understand. The challenge is exacerbated when covering electoral campaigns because the news cycle is even further compressed, press secretaries engage in intense spin, and candidates strive to appeal to a broad swath of voters by presenting themselves as multidimensional. My interviews suggest that in this context, journalists are often drawn to familiar narratives. John Miller told me that what happens in newsrooms is that "somebody is assigned a story, and it fits the pattern of the previous story, so they automatically leap to a conclusion that it's 'this kind' of story. They start limiting their sources ... and produce exactly the same kind of story."

In describing a profile he had written about a visible minority MP, one former journalist admitted that he had fallen back on an "easy trope." We discussed some of the gendered and racialized references in the story, and the interviewee told me, "I talked extensively to [the MP] about her background not only because it was interesting and worth reporting on, but I hope I tried to give it some better shading than a three-hundred-word wire piece or a fifty-second radio piece would do." He admitted that he may not have been successful and, as he pointed out, was still "participating in that social construction." Another reporter said, "I covered Brampton–Springdale because Ruby Dhalla was one of the candidates. She's high-profile, in the media a lot, and she's attractive. There was the issue where she had been parachuted into her riding, so that made it interesting too. And also just the changing demographics in that riding. All of that made it a spicy, sexy story."

Another journalist said that the media tend to "fall back" on safe stories, including the "immigrant narrative" that characterizes reporting on visible minority candidates. She also admitted that "when you see a candidate speaking who isn't white, you assume that they have all of this baggage, and they care about these issues like immigration [or] multiculturalism more than any other candidates." Another referred to a member of Parliament whom he had written about because

> It's just a good story, a classic immigrant story. Came to Canada after getting his law degree in India, couldn't rub two nickels together, couldn't practise law here, scraped his money together, worked as a taxi driver, family all lived in one tiny little apartment. Got his law degree here, worked his way up, and now he's an MP. So that's just a compelling sort of story, an immigrant sort of thing.

John Miller provided a similar take, noting that all reporters "want to tell something interesting about each candidate, what differentiates them." For newcomers, Miller says an underdog frame is often adopted: "This can be a positive or negative but usually is a negative because the reader, who has no other contact with the person, might assume, well, this person has little hope, is a newcomer, and is unfamiliar with the issues."

When asked about the circumstances that would compel them to include information about a politician's socio-demographic background in a story, most respondents said they would do so when it was central to the story. In one columnist's words, "It's relevant if it's relevant and it's gratuitous if it's gratuitous." Speaking as a "white reporter," another said, "I am conscious that if I am going to introduce race as a description in my story, then it needs to be organically tied to that story." None of the journalists with whom I spoke referred to a set of guidelines for determining when race is relevant to a story, although one mentioned the newspaper's policy manual, which stipulates that the race of a subject should only be mentioned if it is pertinent to a story. The manual does not provide any criteria for establishing pertinence.

Indeed, a reporter noted that many visible minorities present themselves as "general election candidates" in that they "torque" or avoid "putting out their background as much as you might expect." Using Rathika Sitsabaiesan as an example, he noted that while she is careful to reach out to Tamil-speaking constituents about related issues, she also "sends signals" to the broader community to indicate "I'm like you." Journalists are left to determine which aspects of the candidate's self-presentation they will emphasize, which they will set aside, and what sort of balance they might achieve between portraying the candidate as a "minority" versus someone who is more "mainstream."

Another columnist spoke about Alice Wong, then the minister of State for seniors who also happens to be of Chinese origin. In this case, he said "there would have to be some reason for me to describe her as Chinese, in essence that she has a unique position because of her Chinese-ness in that particular story." He said that the only time in which he could see her background being relevant would be in reference to her riding, which is heavily ethnically Chinese; respondents broadly agreed with this assertion, noting that race and ethnicity are pertinent in cases where candidates are running in racially diverse ridings. Of course, this assertion of "relevance" is based in part on the assumption that geographically concentrated minority voters may be inclined to support particular kinds of candidates, an assumption that does not appear to come into play when the candidate is white and running in a riding with large numbers of white voters. In some cases the criteria for determining "relevance" are quite contested.

For example, one interviewee said journalists seem to struggle less with issues related to race and more with those related to sexual orientation. He referred to newsroom discussions that occurred when a prominent Conservative denounced Russia's anti-gay laws: "[He] is gay. And everybody in Ottawa knows that ... But do we say in a story, 'The gay [member of Parliament] denounced the anti-gay law?'" It was decided that the MP's sexual orientation would not be mentioned because his position is not one "uniquely held by gay people ... So the fact that he's gay is irrelevant to his policy position because it's one that is held by people of all sexual orientations." Meanwhile, another reporter reflected on Maria Mourani, an MP who was expelled by the Bloc Québécois after she criticized the Quebec Charter of Values. This reporter judged that Mourani's Lebanese background "would be relevant. That's probably why she felt as strongly as she did about [the Values Charter] because she feels some kinship to those who might be affected by the charter." However, just as "the gay MP's" perspective is not one "uniquely held by gay people," neither is Mourani's perspective uniquely held by those with minority backgrounds. This divergence of opinion on how to treat such cases underscores the murkiness of a criterion like "relevance." It also highlights the different ways that journalists think about and report on socio-demographic characteristics; race, sexual orientation, and gender are not all treated the same.

Diversity Training and Curricula

In my interview with John Miller, he noted that journalists did not, and still do not, have many specific tools to help them cover diversity fairly and accurately. He said that in the early 1990s, he tried "for several years to get the newspaper industry interested in diversifying coverage and ... there was absolutely no interest." As a result, Miller decided to develop a course on covering diversity, which was first offered at Ryerson in 1997. The course was mandatory for all third-year journalism students, and it provided instruction on how to overcome stereotypes, delay framing stories, and apply the same news judgment to all people, regardless of their race or other sociodemographic characteristics. The course was abruptly cancelled in 2006 in response to "quite a bit of student resistance and resistance from other faculty." When I asked Miller why the course was discontinued, he said there were many reasons – sometimes contradictory – voiced by both white and visible minority students. Among the objections, however, was a rejection of the premise of inherent bias. In Miller's view, people like to believe that "we're fair ... and capable of treating everybody the same. We resent it when somebody suggests that we're not, even if it's not called racism. Even if it's called racially differentiated coverage. We really take that personally." Referring to the news media's reluctance to evaluate its own performance, the Kent Commission concluded, "The press, which assumes a license to criticize every other institution, is the least open of any to criticism of its own performance. It controls the principal channel through which criticism can be expressed and heard" (Canada 1981, 175). There are, indeed, strong reactions to initiatives aimed at improving the media's coverage of race and, perhaps unsurprisingly, few targeted strategies for addressing this.

Moreover, there is still very little diversity training available to or required of journalism students. This conclusion is based on a review of the curricula in the country's forty-nine journalism programs, which are offered in universities, colleges, and through joint university-college initiatives. Programs vary in length from eight months to four years and can terminate in an undergraduate or graduate degree or a college diploma. For this analysis, course requirements were determined by examining course calendars and program websites and, when necessary, contacting departmental officials. The main focus was the extent to which programs incorporate some facet of diversity training into their course curriculum. Of particular interest were courses related to immigration, race, multiculturalism, and other forms of demographic diversity. The results are shown in Table 9.

TABLE 9

Diversity curriculum in Canadian journalism schools

	n	%
Programs with diversity courses	21	43
Diversity mentioned in course title	6	12
Diversity mentioned only in course description	15	31
Programs without diversity courses	28	57
Total	49	100

Of the country's forty-nine journalism programs, twenty-one (43 percent) offer a course that includes some mention of "diversity" in its title or course description; this may be a reference to "immigration," "race," "multiculturalism," or "diversity." In eight programs (16 percent), these courses are required to graduate. In only six programs (12 percent) are there course titles that explicitly include the words "diversity," "immigration," "race," or "multiculturalism;" these are courses in which diversity can be assumed to be a central focus rather than merely a supplement (e.g., "Gender, Diversity and the Journalist," "Media and Diversity," "Diversity Reporting," "Covering Immigration and Transnational Issues," "Race, Ethnicity and Technology," "Changing Multicultural Mosaic in the GTA"). Only two programs – one at Mohawk College and a second joint program at University of Toronto and Centennial College – make an explicit diversity course mandatory. Fifteen programs (31 percent) have course titles that suggest a broad societal focus (e.g., "Journalism and Society," "Journalism and Social Change," "Social Issues in Journalism," "International Journalism," "Urban Politics and Society for Journalists," "Global Citizenship"), but the course description includes a reference to, or module on, cultural diversity. Among these are also two programs that require students to complete a course requirement in a cognate discipline, and these may have a focus on cultural diversity.

Of course, issues related to diversity may be addressed through informal workshops or as supplementary topics in other courses, but these are not systematically integrated into the curriculum (Lindgren 2013). Some schools, such as Carleton University, require students to demonstrate proficiency in a language other than English, but this seems to be as much about preparing students to work as foreign correspondents as it is about cultural competency. In short, less than half of Canada's journalism schools provide their students with any opportunity to take a diversity-related course, and in only 16 percent of programs is such a course required. In the United States, by contrast, Rodney Benson (2005, 8) notes that courses on media and multiculturalism are "virtually mandatory in most university journalism and communication programs."

None of the journalists with whom I spoke could recall receiving any specific diversity training. One noted that he is interested in immigration and thus covers it frequently, but "no one taught me how to do that. I just went and did it on my own." Another was skeptical about what such training would look like and, essentially, "what kind of shortfalls such training would seek to address."

Guidelines for Reporting on Race and Diversity

Outside of the classroom, both the Canadian Newspaper Association (1995) and the Canadian Association of Journalists (2011) have authored statements on the media and diversity.[4] In addition, provincial and regional press councils, to which most newspapers belong, have policies on the portrayal of diversity (MediaSmarts 2012a). Many outlets also publish guidelines for their reporters to follow. For example, the *Globe and Mail's* "Editorial Code of Conduct" specifies in its section on photography that journalists and editors must "avoid stereotyping by race, gender, age, religion, ethnicity, geography, sexual orientation, disability, physical appearance or social status" (*Globe and Mail* 2013). No guidelines are given as to what constitutes "stereotyping."

The *Toronto Star's* "Newsroom Policy and Journalistic Standards Guide" specifies in a section on "Racial References" that "no reference, direct or indirect should be made to a person's race, colour or religion unless it is pertinent to the story." The guide says that race is relevant when giving the description of a missing person or a criminal suspect at large, as well as in cases where a crime or action may have been racially motivated. Apart from these somewhat self-evident examples, nothing more is said about the situations in which race may or may not be relevant to a story. However, the manual's preamble notes, "No code of conduct can cover every eventuality ... Common sense, good judgment and the journalist's own moral compass must be brought to bear to any set of guidelines" (*Toronto Star* 2011). Reflecting on the paper's coverage of diversity, Kathy English, the paper's public editor, admits that "on most days, the *Star* falls short" (English 2014). She says that reflecting Toronto's diversity means that "our journalists need to seek out visible minority sources for comment on all the broad issues that affect our entire community – not just the issues that affect their specific communities. We should not accept easy stereotypes and tokenism. And just as importantly, we must understand how a disproportionate level of negative coverage of visible minorities can skew perceptions of reality" (English 2014). The *Star's* own assessment of its coverage suggests that common sense does not, on its own, obliterate racialized coverage.

The absence of firm guidelines about "pertinence" and "stereotyping" is problematic because, as Drew (2011, 361) points out in her study of the media's coverage of racial issues, journalists are not always attuned to how particular language or visuals will be interpreted, particularly as these relate to minority communities. She quotes one reporter who asked, "How was I to know that a pregnant Black woman's picture could be perceived as degrading?" The photo, which ran on the newspaper's front page as part of a series on the "racial divide" in the United States, caused a protest and calls for advertisers to boycott. The reporter said that "at the time ... he was not able to understand the concerns about how the image re-played a singular version of Black families but in retrospect, he told Drew, "its offensiveness was abundantly clear" (Drew 2011, 371).

The Canadian Press Stylebook, to which a number of news organizations adhere, warns that the "potential for offence lurks in every news story" (McCarten 2013, 19). It suggests that "reporting should reflect the ethnic diversity of the country in a natural way, free of explicit or unconscious racism" (22). Echoing the standard invoked by several journalists with whom I spoke, the stylebook counsels journalists to "identify a person by race, colour, national origin or immigration status only when it is truly pertinent" (22). It continues, "Race and ethnicity are pertinent when it motivates an incident or when it helps explain the emotions of those in confrontation. Thus, references to race or ethnic background are relevant in reports of racial controversy, immigration difficulties, language discussions, and so on" (22).

In distinguishing the contexts in which a subject's racial background might be mentioned, the stylebook goes on to note that "race is pertinent in reporting an accomplishment unusual in a particular race: for example, if a Canadian of Chinese origin is named to the Canadian Football Hall of Fame" (McCarten 2013, 22). Statistically, yes, there are very few Canadian footballers of Chinese origin, but it is nonetheless deeply problematic to assert that some achievements may be atypical of certain *races.*[5] A logical corollary would be the antiquated notion that particular races are more naturally athletic or that one gender is better at math or science. That reporters might use the criterion of "racially unusual accomplishment" to guide their news judgment smacks of the racial stereotyping and essentialism that the Canadian Press's standard is actually aimed at overcoming.

I asked the editor of the stylebook, James McCarten, to reflect on this. After some thought, he said that "'unusual' is probably not the right word there." Nonetheless, he notes that when something is "historically relevant" or a "first," it merits mention because "journalism often times is all about firsts. Something that is happening for the tenth time is nowhere as newsworthy as something that is happening for the first time." Later on in our conversation, McCarten said that it is difficult to "legislate" when race might be relevant to a story because "you have to take a certain amount of licence, you have to put a certain amount of faith in a reporter's ability to tell a story well, and it falls to the reporter – to the individual storyteller – to know 'when is this relevant and when is it not.'" He argues that the onus is on journalists to "make value judgments" about when a particular piece of information is central to a story.

It is noteworthy that the stylebook's section on sexism counsels journalists to "Treat the sexes equally and without stereotyping ... The test always is: Would this information be used if the subject were a man?" (McCarten 2013, 23). There is no mention of this "reverse test" in the section on race and ethnicity (e.g., "Would this information be used if the subject were white?"), nor does the stylebook suggest that gender is pertinent in reporting an accomplishment unusual for members of a particular sex. An earlier edition of the stylebook in fact directed that reporters should "never suggest surprise that a woman has talent" (Tasko 2006, 22). Such a standard is not clearly outlined in the section on race and ethnicity.

The differential treatment of race is exemplified even in the stylebook's section titles, with the passage on gender reporting called "Sexism" while the parallel section on "Race and Ethnicity" is noticeably not labelled "racism."[6] When I asked James McCarten about the reasons for this discrepancy, he said, "Sexism perhaps has to be approached a little bit differently in terms of the advice we're providing because we're maybe more likely to slip into it ... whereas we're far less likely in this day and age to make the mistake of accidentally slipping into racism. It's not that it's impossible, but I would ... suggest that the sexism trap is a more likely one for us to fall into." He argues that while there is language around race and racism that is "verboten," this is less so when it comes to sexism. In his view, the presentation of these two sections of the stylebook is a reflection "of societal attitudes." Although there are plans to revise the stylebook in advance of the Canadian Press's hundredth anniversary in 2017, McCarten does not anticipate changes to these two sections. He explained that they "are not really top of mind," nor does he see them "as overly problematic." In his view, "The principles that are in play there are all very sound; I don't think there is anything there that cries out for changing."

Unlike the broadcasting sector, which is regulated by the Canadian Broadcast Standards Council, the newspaper industry is largely self-regulated.[7] There are no requirements to uphold principles related to racially inclusive reporting, nor are there any mandatory monitoring or binding mechanisms to ensure compliance (MediaSmarts 2012b).[8] As one interviewee put it, "Journalists are not 'professionals.' We don't have a college of journalism. We're not admitted to the journalism bar. We're not expelled from journalism for status unbecoming our profession. We're just people doing our job. And we'll do that job in different ways." As James McCarten put it when I spoke with him, "We have to hope that people are going to be able to use their best judgment and make a decision that is informed and intelligent ... Really, at the end of the day, it comes back to common sense."

Although it is true that not every possibility can be codified, the absence of clear guidelines means the inclusion of demographic information may be inconsistent, context-specific, and subject to a journalist's own perceptions, choices, and intuitions about newsworthiness and pertinence. Definitions of "common sense" or "relevance" are not neutral. Indeed, these notions are situated in a context in which whiteness is viewed as the norm, foreignness is seen as exotic, and minorities are outliers in politics, as well as in newsrooms. As I discuss below, "mainstream" perspectives are privileged in a way that is so prevalent and institutionalized it almost goes unnoticed.

Diversity in the Newsroom

Most reporters, editors, and news executives in Canada are white (Media-Smarts 2012b). There are very few programs for increasing staff diversity, and most outlets express very little concern for doing so. In their survey of Canadian newsrooms, John Miller and Caron Court found that the proportion of editors who were strongly committed to improving the diversity of their ranks had actually decreased from 26 percent in 1994 to 13 percent in 2004. The authors note that "in explaining the lack of representativeness, a large number of editors said, 'Minorities just don't apply here,'" even though a majority agreed that journalism schools are graduating more minority journalists (Miller and Court 2004). Moreover, only one newspaper they surveyed reported taking any active measures to recruit minority candidates, and no news agencies have any formal leadership training programs for visible minorities (Miller and Court 2004).

News executives may, in fact, be in denial about the barriers that minority reporters face, with editors who responded to Miller and Court's survey almost unanimously rejecting the suggestion that their newsroom's tradition and culture might impede the hiring and retention of minorities. Moreover, while 46 percent of editors in 1994 believed they needed more knowledge about race and ethnocultural relations to effectively manage their newsrooms, ten years later only 16 percent agreed (Miller and Court 2004). This confidence is not congruent with the lack of diversity in newsrooms. Editors seem to be glossing over the obstacles that stand in the paths of minority journalists and greater heterogeneity in the news business. Discussing the dearth of journalists of colour, one commentator, a visible minority, summed it up as "a lot of talk, and no commitment to change ... That's the story of diversity in Canadian journalism. It is not going to improve until more editors make peace with the fact that, as the gatekeepers of the profession, it is their job to do the heavy lifting" (Domise 2015b).

That said, scholars disagree about the effect of journalists' demographic backgrounds on actual news content. Some research has found that a reporter's race or gender can influence the presentation of the news (Gidengil and Everitt 2003a; Mills 1997; van Zoonen 1998), while others find no such effect (Rakow and Kranich 1991; Ross 2001; Weaver 1997; Zilber and Niven 2000). To the extent that I noticed differences among the white and visible minority journalists I spoke with, it had to do with the extent to which they appeared to have reflected on or considered the role of race in their reporting. Visible minority journalists tended to more easily recognize that racial considerations sometimes influence news gathering and production, but even they felt that coverage is still generally fair. White journalists were somewhat more reluctant to admit that race might influence how a story is told, although certainly some of those with whom I spoke – especially those with considerable experience – were able to recall instances when racial assumptions may have affected their reporting.

Even if there is not a "straight-line" correlation between newsroom diversity and news content, "the degree to which news managers can communicate their vision regarding diversity to the newsroom, and the degree to which journalists and other employees buy into that vision, heavily influences whether news coverage will include the full diversity of the communities journalists serve" (Pease, Smith, and Subervi 2001, 9). The media offer a representation of our values, our norms, and our priorities. When diversity is absent from the newsroom, a symbolic message is sent about what matters and what does not.

In discussing diversity in the media, several respondents with whom I spoke admitted that newsrooms are not very diverse. A visible minority reporter said diversity was "seriously lacking." Another said, "If you look at most newsrooms in Canada, they don't always reflect the population." However, this journalist – who identified himself as an ethnic minority – did note that newsrooms have changed over the years:

> I was an exotic fauna when I arrived. There weren't a lot of people with vowels at the ends of the names when I first walked into a newsroom. So, it's changed and not just multiculturally but culturally as well. There is a lot more demand ... Now it's not unheard-of to try and have an Arabic speaker on your staff and someone who speaks Spanish ... I think we're all looking for people who can help us when news breaks, not just in Canada, but around the world.

A visible minority reporter told me about a letter she received from a reader who was upset about a story she had written about a plane crash. The letter began, "For starters, what type of name is that? Are you male or female?"

Some interviewees suggested that an absence of diversity in the newsroom does limit the way that stories about immigration and multiculturalism are told. One reporter said that "there isn't anyone to (a) flag those stories or (b) who has the connections to people." She went on to say that more homogeneous newsrooms "don't have an entry point into those communities." A visible minority reporter said that her background sometimes "puts people at ease." She says that when she interviews other minorities, they can be "more open because they're not as intimidated ... And maybe if they've been hurt before by reporters who are Caucasian, they feel like they can give me a chance." Nonetheless, this reporter stressed that all journalists are capable of producing quality stories about diverse communities: "You don't require the badge of being a woman or being Muslim or being the child of immigrants to report on these communities effectively."

When asked whether journalists with minority backgrounds are pigeon-holed into covering so-called diversity issues, a white columnist recalled a Ghanian-born colleague who arrived at his newspaper in 1989 and was assigned to the "multiculturalism beat because he was the only black reporter in the newsroom. And it was a terrible thing to do ... 'You're a cultural minority. Go cover the cultural minority.' It's stupid." He noted, however, that the paper "has moved far, far from that." A visible minority reporter referred to a colleague with a Chinese background who "bristles when they try to assign her stories about the Chinese community" and observed that a Punjabi-speaking colleague is "kind of pigeonholed with those stories."

Nonetheless, an editor with whom I spoke said that he had personally not seen any evidence of minority reporters being confined to particular stories. In his words, "If you're a good reporter, you're a good reporter. Only a foolish editorial supervisor would turn down a good story." That said, when Dan David, a CBC journalist of Mohawk descent, resisted his employer's demand to concentrate his reporting on Aboriginal issues – something he found limiting – he was told that his contract would lapse (Roth 1996). Other studies also point to the difficulties facing journalists with minority backgrounds. As Cecil Foster, a black journalist, puts it, "I have been working in mainstream media in Canada for about 12 years and I am still an outsider ... You get a sense of being invisible, of your presence being tolerated, but not expected" (quoted in MediaSmarts 2012b).

Institutionalized Whiteness

The invisibility to which Foster draws attention underpins the racialization of news coverage as well as the institutionalization of whiteness in the mainstream media. "Institutionalized whiteness" is about the ways in which particular perspectives, norms, and standards of behaviour are privileged and pervade the public sphere, organizations, and social interactions. When I speak of "whiteness," I am not talking specifically about a race, but rather about an ideology. Richard Dyer (1988, 44) suggests that "white is not anything really, not an identity, not a particularizing quality, because it is everything." White is viewed as standard, as "normal," as the property against which those of other backgrounds are judged. Ross Perigoe and Mahmoud Eid (2014, 51) pick up on this point: "This power is 'invisible,' for it cloaks itself as not being a category at all, yet it controls definitions of societal norms." Stuart Hall (1990, 14) notes, "The 'white eye' is always outside the frame – but seeing and positioning everything within it."

In a media context, this metaphor of the "white eye" underscores the demographic dominance of whiteness, the organizational practices that privilege "mainstream" behaviours and ideologies, and the narratives that position "non-white" as atypical and difference as newsworthy. Institutionalized whiteness was not named but nonetheless recognized by the Kerner Commission, which was appointed in 1967 to examine civil unrest in several American cities. The commission noted in its report that the "media report and write from the standpoint of a white man's world ... This may be understandable, but it is not excusable in an institution that has the mission to inform and educate the whole of our society" (National Advisory Commission on Civil Disorders 1968, 366). Because of the dominance of whiteness, few notice its presence nor how it contributes to racialized coverage. Indeed, the power of the "white eye" lies in its positioning as unproblematic. As Frances Henry and Carol Tator (2002, 9) point out, "White people perceive themselves as colourless and therefore without privileges and subjectivities."

In drawing attention to the power of whiteness, however, I am not ascribing individual intent nor attributing blame to "racist" journalists. Focusing on singular actors reinforces the power of whiteness because it denies the ways in which whiteness pervades our culture, structures, and everyday experiences. This pervasiveness is why I did not note considerable differences between white and visible minority journalists. Institutionalized whiteness washes over these distinctions, because the "white eye" is impersonal; it is about the "institutional practices, routinized behaviours, and normative values [that] work in concert to structure the ways in which media institutions ... privilege particular interpretations" (Jiwani 2006, 30). These interpretations include mythologies about Canadians' tolerance and inclusivity, the reduction of racism to individual acts rather than systemic problems, and the weaving of narratives about exotic outsiders, hard-working immigrants, disloyal foreigners, and parochial interlopers into the coverage of minorities in politics. Not only do these assumptions often go unspoken, but discussions about race and the media are virtually silenced. In one study of the coverage of racial issues in the United States, a Latino journalist told the researcher, "White people's inability to talk openly about matters of race is a professional handicap, keeping them from ever getting to the heart or root of half the issues" (quoted in Drew 2011, 363).

Indeed, a number of the journalists with whom I spoke noted forcefully that race is not an issue in their reporting and that it does not change how they tell a story in any substantive way. More than one maintained that the media are "colour blind." Although this may be true, by pretending that we do not "see colour" (or by refusing to do so), we ignore the myriad ways that race continues to matter: the fact that visible minorities are woefully underrepresented in politics in most positions of power, that they experience discrimination (both explicit and hidden), and that they often appear in the pages of our newspapers in stereotyped stories and images. This is not about singling out individual racists (although that is needed too), but instead about the power, privilege, and institutionalization of whiteness. Falling back on some mythical notion of race-blindness does not emancipate us from the power of race; indeed it only serves to reinforce existing racial inequalities.

In a 2015 speech, New Brunswick MP John Williamson drew attention to the tension between Canada's employment insurance scheme – which provides relief to umemployed workers – and our simultaneous reliance on temporary foreign workers to fill job shortages. He said in his speech that "it makes no sense to pay 'whities' to stay home while we bring in brown people to work in these jobs." Many media commentators – mostly white – came to Williamson's defence, arguing that while the remarks were inelegant and maybe even racist, Williamson himself is most certainly not a racist (Ivison 2015; Selley 2015). Reflecting on the incident, Andray Domise, a Toronto media commentator and former municipal council candidate argued:

> There are few reactions more typical of Canadian media than a collection of white people reaching consensus on who or what qualifies as racist ... An argument over whether or not John Williamson is racist is beside the point. The point is we should know better, or at least try to do better. We've just had a spate of media-driven conversations on the impact that both overt and subtle racism is having on Canada's communities of colour ... Yet once again, when confronted with exactly the kind of racism that exemplifies Canada's approach to people of colour, knee-jerk defensiveness and a lack of media self-awareness provide it with cover. (Domise 2015a)

Only by acknowledging the persistence of race will journalists be able to think reflexively and critically about how news practices, limited newsroom diversity, relatively homogenous source lists, and implicit racialized assumptions influence news judgment and reporting. The notion of "colour-blindness" is a myth that contributes to a profound silence about race and racism. A far more apt metaphor would be one that acknowledges our deafness. Not only are we reluctant to talk about race, but most of us are also unwilling to listen to stories about its institutionalization and effects, the ways in which it influences economic, social, and political life, and the doggedness with which it persists.

As a result of this deafness, racialized news coverage continues unimpeded and is positioned as though it is reasonable, unproblematic, and completely detached from any sense of racial hierarchy. The effects of racial mediation are indeed maximized when images and content that are grounded in racialized assumptions are presented unquestioningly as natural and common-sense. This invisibility is what gives racial mediation and racialized media coverage its power. Although none of the journalists with whom I spoke expressed blatantly racist attitudes, many – and indeed most of us – are complicit in the production of racialized coverage because we do not acknowledge how deeply ingrained racial assumptions and institutionalized whiteness affect news coverage. Our silence gives voice to racial mediation.

Conclusion

"You can't be what you can't see."

— Marie Wilson, the White House Project

"Papering over the issue of race makes for bad social theory, bad research, and bad public policy."

— Douglas S. Massey, sociologist

"If we want to fix this, the first step is to admit something is wrong. Start by saying it to yourself, but say it out loud: 'Canada has a race problem.'"

— Scott Gilmore, *Maclean's*

In the midst of the research for this book, I learned that Lincoln Alexander had passed away. Alexander had been a member of Parliament, cabinet minister and lieutenant governor of Ontario. He was also black. In a tribute, his former colleague Perrin Beatty (2012, A10) noted that Alexander "did not want to build his career around race, but he understood that he would be judged as an example, both within the black community and outside. Canada had started to dismantle some of the barriers that minorities face, but it was not blind to colour; race was always there, whether spoken or not." Lincoln Alexander was elected in the riding of Hamilton West in 1968, and while the barriers that Beatty mentions have to some extent been broken down, Canada remains "not blind to colour." Race is always here, whether acknowledged or not.

Although we have come some way from a history in which white immigrants were prioritized for admission into our country, minority Canadians were disenfranchised, and Anglo-Saxon men occupied the corridors of power, we have not yet achieved full equality. This task seems even more daunting when one considers the steps that have been taken to address racial imbalance. The Charter of Rights and Freedoms prohibits discrimination on the basis of race, as does federal, provincial, and territorial human rights legislation. Workplaces have programs to identify and recruit qualified visible minority applicants, as employers increasingly recognize the value of a diverse workplace. Anti-racism and diversity training are offered in several organizations, including government bureaucracies. School curricula have been rewritten to highlight the contributions of Aboriginal people, immigrants, and minorities to our country. Apologies and redress have been offered in an effort to repair historical injustices. Visible minorities are increasingly well educated, fluent in Canada's official languages, and express a strong desire to contribute to the country's political, economic, and social life. And yet, our elite and executive ranks remain predominantly white; visible minorities are underrepresented in our elected bodies by a factor of about one-half. Many visible minorities still report overt and implicit discrimination, which highlights the extent to which they remain outsiders even once they manage to work their way in. This reality is reflected in and also reinforced by racially differentiated media coverage.

What Have We Learned?

That race matters is perhaps the single most important finding of this book. Yes, there is little evidence of blatant racism, and the media do "get it right" more often than they get it wrong, but news coverage is in no way race-neutral. Coverage is racially differentiated, and racialization is unevenly applied in that it affects visible minorities more so than any others. Because whiteness is viewed as a neutral standard, anything that deviates from this is considered newsworthy. This results in skewed story selection, racialized framing, and coverage that distinguishes the white norm from the racialized other. These choices are not accidental, natural, or neutral. Instead they are based on assumptions about race, diversity, and whiteness. As a result, race mediates the ways in which politics are covered, with racially differentiated coverage emerging as one consequence.

Racialized framing sets visible minority candidates apart as different and foreign. Visible minority candidates are portrayed as products of their socio-demographic backgrounds, as individuals who have less interest in the policy issues that matter to Canadians and who place a disproportionate focus on the interests of their "own" communities. This portrayal can delegitimize and devalue visible minorities' contributions, both real and potential. Although all candidates receive some personal media coverage – coverage that discusses their family histories or interests – stories about visible minority candidates are much more likely to focus on this kind of biographical trivia than stories about white candidates. Such coverage may help to humanize candidates, but visible minority candidates may not benefit in the same way that white candidates do. This is because coverage of a white candidate's background is generally normalizing ("I'm just like you! I understand your needs and concerns"), while the coverage of visible minority candidates' backgrounds typically sets them apart in that it focuses on how they are *different* from the white norm.

Even ostensibly positive coverage can have negative consequences, with visible minorities' success stories viewed as indicative of systemic fairness and equality. This view conceals the extent to which minorities are still viewed as accessories to the political process. Reflecting on criticisms launched at Harinder Takhar when he encouraged South Asian Canadians to support his bid for the Ontario Liberal leadership, Haroon Siddiqui (2013, A23), a *Toronto Star* columnist, asked:

> Why is it worse than corralling, say, fellow farmers, fellow bankers, fellow Rotarians or fellow Torontonians to your political cause? Why is it bad to organize Sikh delegates for a voluntary political activity but good to organize an entire taxpayer-funded public school system based on faith? It is a lingering racist narrative of Canadian politics that anything "ethnic" is bad. This is doubly hypocritical: we decry "ethnic politics," yet praise our ethnic pluralism.

There is a double standard, with visible minorities' "foreignness" viewed as noteworthy, while the background of other Canadians is deemed to be neutral. Visible minorities' electoral strategies are narrow and potentially divisive, while other Canadians are bridgers and brilliant tacticians, praised for their efforts to involve immigrants and minorities in the political process.

Some may argue that it is unrealistic to expect the media to completely disregard race in their coverage of Canadian politics. I agree. Race is relevant. It is embedded in our institutions, our assumptions, and our every interaction. It cannot and should not be ignored. The converse of racialized coverage is not, however, the complete absence of race from coverage. Race should be covered, but the modes and methods for doing so must change. The notion that it is natural to draw attention only to visible minorities' racial backgrounds is deeply problematic and serves only to further normalize whiteness and reproduce racial disparities.

Not only is the focus of visible minority candidates' coverage different, but so too is its form. Visible minorities' coverage is less prominent, more negative, and more filtered than that of their white counterparts. We are less likely to see visible minorities quoted in stories and more likely to see articles that include their photographs. When paraphrases of candidates' policy positions appear in a story, these are more likely to focus on white candidates than visible minority candidates. These structural features reinforce the framing of visible minority candidates as principally a product of their socio-demographic backgrounds and as less serious, less central contenders.

Of course, not all coverage is racialized, and there are instances in which candidates' portrayal is not noticeably differentiated by race. For example, both white and visible minority candidates appear in the pages of our newspapers in roughly equal proportions. The positioning of candidates' policy interests, while different for white and visible minority candidates, is not squarely divided according to racialized stereotypes. And while there are differences in the portrayal of political viability, in the aggregate white and visible minority candidates receive equivalent insider and quality coverage. It should also be noted that while the racialized patterns identified in this study are systematic and statistically significant, differences in coverage between white and visible minority subjects are often quite small, a point that was discussed in Chapter 2. This does not diminish the power or potential of racialized coverage – indeed, it may simply be evidence of the insidiousness of racialization and the difficulties associated with detecting it – but it does give some hope about the scope of the problem and our ability to address it. It is also the case that language about race and diversity is often careful and considered, and in a number of stories racial aspects are completely set aside, thus putting the focus on more politically salient issues and characteristics. This fact suggests that there has been some evolution from historical patterns of prejudice and "symbolic annihilation," but race continues to matter. We are in a period of transition, perhaps, but the pace is slow, and racial considerations continue to mediate our politics.

Theorizing the Media's Coverage of Race in Politics

In offering a theory of racial mediation, this book makes an original contribution to research on race, media, and politics. Racial mediation suggests that racial considerations influence news reporting, that these are not simply a product of context or candidates' self-presentation, and that we have not yet entered a postracial world. Cultural norms, journalistic practices, and institutionalized assumptions about whiteness and diversity all work together to ensure that race still matters. This has also been documented in the American literature on minorities and politics, which has found evidence of racially differentiated coverage among white and minority candidates (McIlwain and Caliendo 2011; Schaffner and Gadson 2004; Schwartz 2011; Terkildsen and Damore 1999; Zilber and Niven 2000). This book contributes new empirical data while providing a basis for theorizing the relationships among race, the media, and politics.

Consistent with the literature on modern racism, racialized coverage is often nuanced and implicit, a finding that pushes us to think through our definition and operationalization of racialization. As Chapter 3 showed, these nuances are particularly evident in the coverage of visible minority women, where subtle racialized and gendered assumptions underpin the portrayal of these candidates. A number of my conclusions dovetail with research on gendered mediation, which has typically focused on white women, but it is clear that there are important differences when we look specifically at visible minority women. These include an emphasis on the "exotic," framing that either questions or idealizes minority women's loyalty and servitude, and a tendency to minimize these candidates' qualifications and successes while drawing significant attention to their mistakes. These narratives are subtle and were largely undetected when the research design centred on quantitative coding. This subtlety underscores the importance of pursuing multiple lines of investigation while also paying attention to both explicit and implicit types of coverage. Finding ways to persuasively identify implicit racialized coverage is particularly crucial when we consider the effects of such coverage. Importantly, implicit racialized coverage is potentially more damaging than blatant racism, not only because implicit appeals have been found to most effectively engage racial priming (Mendelberg 2001), but also because the subtlety of this kind of coverage makes it easier for critics to suggest that news coverage is fair and does not differentiate on the basis of the subject's race. In so doing, the potentially damaging consequences of racial mediation are overlooked.

One of the most telling disparities identified in this study is the finding that visible minority candidates must first prove themselves in order to be accorded coverage that is on par with that of their white counterparts. This finding came through in my analysis of media coverage, my comparison of the portrayal of non-incumbent candidates' viability, and in my interviews with candidates, staffers, and even journalists. Time and again, the evidence suggests that visible minority candidates are subjected to a different set of assessment criteria, that they must achieve a higher standard to be taken seriously, and that they are, in effect, unfit until proven otherwise. White candidates, even when inexperienced, are portrayed as more natural polit-icians than visible minority candidates, or at least more likely contenders. As a result, they receive more favourable news coverage even when they have not yet proven their mettle. Fowler and Lawless (2009) noted something similar in their own examination of the media's coverage of American gu-bernatorial contests. They found that non-incumbent and inexperienced candidates were more often the target of gendered media coverage because their unknown quality led journalists to rely on familiar narratives when framing stories. My own study contributes an additional layer to our under-standing of viability coverage because it goes beyond gender and forces us to see that while the playing field may appear roughly even, the starting point for visible minority candidates can be dramatically different.

This notion of innate political fitness extends to the coverage of white candidates who run in ridings with high numbers of visible minority voters. Although some news coverage remarks on the differences between these white representatives and their electors, the majority does not. Instead, white candidates are presented as cultural bridgers who are able to successfully engage ethnic communities, while visible minority candidates are framed as inward-looking and parochial, viable largely in diverse ridings, and inter-ested only in the needs of their co-ethnic counterparts. When they are por-trayed otherwise, visible minorities' socio-demographic backgrounds still remain front and centre, with their ability to connect to voters outside of their own ethnocultural communities noted as a distinct asset. This ability is neither expected nor apparently natural.

This book offers a multi-dimensional exploration of mediation in that it looks not just at media outputs, but also media inputs. In the first place, it includes an examination of candidates' self-presentation. This analysis sug-gests that the media's portrayal of visible minority candidates is not always congruent with those candidates' recollections of their messaging, policy interests, and self-presentations. Nearly all candidates engage in some form of strategic self-presentation, but in my interviews with them, visible minority candidates put forward a less racialized – or at least more nuanced – image than their media coverage presents. This is particularly true for candidates who ran in less racially diverse constituencies, who tended to downplay their racialized status in a way that was not evident in their news coverage. This is the first Canadian study to document visible minority and white candidates' accounts of their electoral, communication, and image management strategies and to assess how candidate race affects self-presentation and resulting media portrayals. The findings will help advance the growing literature on political marketing and communication.

Apart from candidate inputs, this book also provides insights into a second type of media input, namely, the work, routines, and decisions of journalists themselves. This focus is not always present in studies of media portrayals, a gap that leaves us less able to understand the challenges that journalists face and the reasons that they select and frame news items in the ways that they do. Although racism is far from endemic in mainstream Canadian newsrooms, the media – like other organizations and, indeed, society – are steeped in a culture of institutionalized whiteness. By including the voices of journalists within these pages, this book helps move us beyond a "blame the media" frame to identify the multitude of factors that contribute to racialized coverage. The problem is not an individual one, but rather institutional, cultural, and systemic.

This book contributes to the conversation on race, pushing us to move beyond attitudes of denial, silence, and half-measures and instead open our eyes to the ways in which race matters and how it manifests itself in our politics, the media, and broader society. In addition, it complicates the discussion by examining how a wide swath of research on politics has downplayed or ignored the impact that race has on political opportunities, experiences, and outcomes. Understanding the impact of race means we cannot simply "add colour and stir." Rather, we need new theoretical frameworks and new empirical approaches to flesh out how intersecting identities affect individuals and our institutions. Such research needs to go beyond an examination of race and gender and extend to factors like ability, sexual orientation, age, class, and Aboriginality. Research designs that combine qualitative and quantitative analyses will help us pull apart the effects of these complex and interlocking factors, while the inclusion of diverse voices will help broaden our perspective. Stories are important, and real voices help give life to the data, statistics, and findings that scholars generate.

Future Research Directions

In spite of its scope, this study does leave some questions unanswered, and these provide fruitful avenues for future research. First, research should be expanded beyond the English-language daily print media. This study did not look at the French- or foreign-language media, and only a small number of stories were drawn from Quebec newspapers. Given the institutionalization of the patterns found in this study, expanding the scope beyond the English-language media might not reveal dramatically different results. Nonetheless, in the absence of data, such a conclusion is merely speculative. We should also examine other platforms, including social media, community newspapers, and the ethnic media. All of these are forums in which the patterns I have identified may be altered or reproduced, and it is important to understand how the media source may affect the coverage of race in politics.

Second, the research should extend beyond visible minorities. Studies confirm that Aboriginal peoples are also subjected to racialized framing, but often with different imagery and stereotypes (Fleras 2011; Henry and Tator 2002). Stories about model minorities, dutiful Canadians, and Bollywood princesses are replaced by tropes about noble savages, fearless warriors, and plight and poverty. Understanding how these narratives are interwoven into the news coverage of Aboriginal politicians is important. While there are currently only seven members of Parliament with Aboriginal origins, we have seen Aboriginal peoples flex their political muscle with the Idle No More movement and organizing around missing and murdered Aboriginal women. When Winnipeg elected Brian Bowman as its mayor in the fall of 2014, a number of media outlets drew attention to his Métis heritage, even though he did not readily promote it in his campaign literature or on his website (Friesen 2014; Thomson 2014; Tolley 2014). This suggests that we would be likely to find similar patterns of racialization if we were to also look at the coverage of Aboriginal people in politics.

The empirical strategy would need to be adapted, however, if the focus of study were to shift to Aboriginal candidates. Although the literature on modern racism remains relevant, the theoretical framework would need to capture the unique experiences of Aboriginal peoples, who are not only a racialized minority but also a national minority with constitutional status, autonomy, and, in many cases, self-governance, and a history that includes not just racism but also cultural genocide as a result of the legacy of the residential schools system. Engaging in a careful study of Aboriginals in politics demands a different theoretical framework, one that more carefully discusses colonialism, indigeneity, nationalism, and cultural genocide. The research would also have to employ a much less quantitative approach than was adopted in Chapter 2. There is a small-numbers problem in that so few Aboriginal candidates have run or been elected outside of band organizations. Consequently, statistical analysis is less compelling, and the focus should be much more qualitative and discursive.

Third, research should extend beyond campaign-period coverage to look at portrayals of politics in non-electoral contexts. For example, the horse-race coverage that is so frequent in the media's reporting on campaigns might shift away from a focus on strategies, poll results, and vote choice and towards more substantive issue-based discussions once a government has been formed. This shift may in fact benefit visible minorities because it could draw attention away from their socio-demographics and difference, and toward the work that they are doing on behalf of their constituents. Moreover, having proven their "worth," elected visible minorities may no longer be subject to coverage that positions them as unlikely contenders or long shots. Conversely, outside the highly scrutinized campaign period, the media may be less careful in their reporting and we may, as a result, see more racially differentiated coverage. The effect of electoral context is thus unclear; further research is needed.

Fourth, this study could and should be replicated at other levels of government, where we may find different patterns of candidate coverage. Municipally, the absence of political parties and lower reliance on marketing and communications professionals, especially in smaller centres, could alter the ways that candidates present themselves. Meanwhile, the comparative accessibility of municipal councillors and mayors could result in different kinds of media portrayals. At the provincial level, responsibility for such "mainstream" policy areas as health care and education, where the presence of immigrants and minorities can dramatically alter service needs, would present an interesting case study for examining the racialization of policy issue coverage. We should also think about the coverage of various groups outside of Parliament, legislatures, and councils, whether as voters, protesters, or engaged citizens.

Finally, we need more precise measures of candidate self-presentation. Although the interviews used in this study help us identify the ways in which candidates present themselves, these are first-person accounts. Candidates could have been selective in what they told me, or incorrectly remembered their tactics and strategies. Although interviewees were, by my estimation, generally frank and candid, we need to think critically about subjective self-reports. The viability index that was constructed in Chapter 4 is an example of a more objective measure, which should be supplemented by an examination of candidates' campaign literature, press releases, advertisements, and debate statements (see, for example, Gidengil and Everitt 2003a; Koop and Marland 2012). This will not only improve our measures of self-presentation, but help us compare candidates' image management strategies across media, temporal period, and audience.

But So What? Does Media Coverage Even Matter?

In multiple ways, this book has demonstrated that race influences political news coverage, but this finding begs the question: Does media coverage even matter? In Chapter 1, I drew attention to some of what we already know about media effects. Certainly, this area of research is contested, but most of the literature on media effects comes to a similar conclusion: media coverage matters. The media are citizens' primary link to politics, and we know that voters' assessments of policy issues can be altered depending on how they are framed in the media. We also know that racialized frames can activate race as a salient criterion and that racial priming effects can be strongest when they are implicit and centre on subjects about which voters have little first-hand information. In an era of tight electoral races and close vote margins, even small differences can have lasting consequences.

In my interviews with candidates and staffers, I asked whether media coverage mattered. A former cabinet minister replied, "The media are very important in terms of the outcome of the campaign. A lot of people just believe whatever they read in the media, so they can either promote or defeat you ... The media can have a huge impact on the success or the failure of somebody's campaign." A strategist and former candidate said that even though people think for themselves, there is "no question" the media have an impact. She commented that with media coverage, "A narrative goes up, and that narrative can be spin, but usually it's based on experiences, and those are cumulative. So, over the course of the campaign, these stories become the narrative ... So absolutely, huge effect. Huge."

Interviewees also hoped that the media might play an important role in candidate recruitment. A visible minority candidate with a fairly strong media profile noted that as a result of this coverage, "Young children – black children, Muslim children, Sikh children, Hindu children, anyone who is some sort of minority – can relate to you and think, 'Hey, you made it. We can make it too.' So that's sort of a positive." On the more negative side, some interviewees said that media coverage may turn off potential candidates. They mentioned individuals who were "gun-shy" because they did not want their lives to be subjected to such intense public scrutiny.

Although it is difficult to draw a causal relationship between media framing and electoral outcomes, it is through the media that we learn much of what we know about politics. We thus need to consider how racialized coverage affects the quality of the information environment, particularly when that coverage is systemically and disproportionately directed at visible minority candidates. Even if the instances are somewhat rare, or the effects are quite subtle, racialization puts visible minorities at a disadvantage. More-over, in highlighting candidates' socio-demographic features, immigrant backgrounds, perceived inexperience, and links to their "own communities," such coverage turns our attention away from the political and towards the personal. Electoral campaigns are increasingly not about policy issues, the public sphere, or even about voters. Instead, we fixate on individual actors, gaffes, the horse race, and personal narratives, which are tied together in metaphorical language about "us and them," "good and bad," "winners and losers," and "insiders and outsiders." As Karrin Anderson (2011, 331) notes, "Media frames are consequential because they shape the ways in which people understand and participate in a democracy. When voters are side-lined ... or seduced by ... metaphors, they become passive observers of the political system rather than engaged participants."

Who Is to Blame?

This book has pinpointed the shortcomings of media coverage, the institutionalization of whiteness in newsrooms, the lack of training and discussion about reporting on diversity, and the ways in which the media have failed in their responsibility to employ analogous news judgment when reporting on and framing candidates, regardless of their race. All of this could be taken as evidence that the media are solely to blame. Nothing, in fact, could be further from the truth. The political system is just that – a system – with interwoven parts, processes, and players, of which the media are just one.

Rarely is any problem or outcome the work of a single element: political parties, the public, and candidates themselves all contribute to media outputs.

POLITICAL PARTIES

In Canadian politics, parties are one of the key players, particularly at the federal and provincial levels. Parties provide leadership, organizational and fundraising capacity, and policy expertise, as well as an important link between voters and candidates. During elections, these functions increase in importance, and much of the campaign is oriented around parties, from the leaders' debates to the focus on party polling numbers, to discussions about party tactics and advertising. Local candidates are often sidelined not just by the media, but also by the parties themselves.

This message came out loud and clear in my interviews with candidates. One long-time visible minority MP observed:

> National campaigns tell [candidates] to preferably talk about nothing ... They don't want their candidates in the media talking about what they will do for their community. They want a homogeneous message ... The candidates who do try to tailor their messages to their constituents often run counter to their own personal and political fortunes because the leadership will see that as being a rebel or maverick and marginalize you within your own political party.

The notion of parties silencing candidates is not restricted to a single party. A staffer from a different party said that when a candidate does talk to the media, the goal is "message box, message box, message box. Sticking to what the party tells you to say and sticking to those bullets." A first-time candidate from another party similarly recalled, "We weren't allowed necessarily to talk to the media and, you know, we were kind of restricted in what we were able to do and not able to do ... The national campaign preferred it that way, as well, that we would just stay away from the media."

Parties' efforts to minimize local candidates' interactions with the media have several implications. First, if candidates are not talking about local issues, then the media will turn their attention elsewhere, a situation that is probably exacerbated by the leader-centric campaigns that now characterize electoral politics. The result is that neither local candidates nor local issues are covered. Second, if an incident does attract media attention, local candidates who have maintained a low profile are unlikely to have honed their media relations skills or developed relationships with journalists. They may thus emerge behind the story or respond ineffectively. The media – and the central party – control the narrative, often at local candidates' peril.

Interviewees also told me that political parties can exacerbate racial differentiation. A white candidate who ran against a visible minority told me that opposing parties sometimes try to use race as a wedge. He said that his opponent's party "was sending people into my office at the end of the night [and] they were obviously trying to [audio-]record me. They would say something very racist, and they would try to get me to agree with them. This happened on four or five occasions in the campaign office ... [They were] trying to bait me into saying something they could construe as racist." In such a scenario, we should fully expect to see racialized media coverage because race itself underpins the conflict. Visible minority candidates and staffers, meanwhile, reported being sent to "ethnic" events or press conferences about so-called minority issues not necessarily because of their expertise but because of their backgrounds.

Parties can thus contribute to racialized patterns of coverage. They may pigeonhole visible minority candidates into stereotypical minority roles or limit their ability to speak to broader issues. Visible minorities who run in the most racially diverse ridings may be particularly disadvantaged as parties seek to highlight not just their efforts to attract so-called ethnic voters but also their inclusivity through an often ceremonial parading of their diverse candidates. In other ridings, parties may attempt to exploit perceived racial divides in an effort to strategically one-up their opponents, a tactic that tends to invite the "gotcha" journalism that often dominates election coverage.

THE PUBLIC

In laying blame, we cannot overlook the role of the public. We as citizens consume this kind of media coverage. We as voters support this brand of politics, albeit often grudgingly, but few among us do much to address racial inequities, instead spouting rhetoric about Canada's multiculturalism and inclusivity. Visible minority candidates with whom I spoke suggested that while most voters are quite receptive, race is still a distinguishing factor, as are gender and age. In one candidate's words, "The first thing people see is the fact that I'm a person of colour, a woman and young. I'm still seen as different." Another visible minority candidate said, "I don't want you to think that racism is dominant and prevalent ... Okay, it exists, and a small minority express it, but many won't say it to my face. They'll say it to my canvassers, but they won't say it to my face. So, it's there. It's visible, it's not insignificant." A number of interviewees emphasized that racism is not confined to white voters; some visible minorities said that they experienced prejudice from other minorities, particularly those who identified with religious or cultural traditions different from their own. One visible minority candidate said that she faces criticism from within her own community by members who question her choice of hairstyle and decision not to wear "traditional" dress. This candidate's experiences reinforce that the media alone are not responsible; bias and prejudice can emanate from anywhere, including from within minority communities.

A number of interviewees suggested that we do not see better media coverage because we simply do not demand better. Even those who succeeded in their campaigns cautioned against complacency. One candidate said, "The success is not evidence that we've become more accepting of young candidates or minority candidates. It's just that I specifically was somewhat lucky or talented or whatever it was ... Sometimes success stories almost make us naïve about some of the real issues."

These "real issues" stem from a privileging of whiteness, the downplaying of racial inequality, and a propensity to see disadvantage not as institutional or systemic but as a function of individual misdeeds. Cultural norms and values are highly resistant to change, particularly when only a handful of citizens rise up to demand change. We cannot expect media coverage to be less racialized than the society it reflects.

CANDIDATES

Finally, we need to consider the role that candidates play in generating the patterns of coverage to which this study has drawn attention. Although we should be cautious about blaming the victim, a number of interviewees put the onus squarely on candidates themselves. According to one, "A lot of members of Parliament want to blame the media for everything, but if you do your homework and you work hard, there's not much the media can do but report that. There are some MPs who have left a lot of bare ass hanging out, and the media report that."

One interviewee who has managed several campaigns and also ran as a self-confessed "sacrificial lamb" said that people will never be fully happy with their coverage but then continued, "Did we get coverage on our goofy press conference? Probably not. And there's probably a reason for that. But the more proactive you are, if you're doing something original, if you're doing something newsworthy, you will get coverage. People who complain are people who failed at doing that." A visible minority candidate said, "If you want to be a candidate, you have to get your message out. That's your job. It's not the media's job." This was echoed by another visible minority legislator who said, "I always remind myself that [the media] have a job to do, and their job is to get a story. Their job is to make sure they get to the bottom of a particular story ... They're not just going to take my talking points and run with them. Why should they?"

Not only did interviewees draw attention to the ways in which they contribute to simplistic media coverage, but some also engaged in the kind of racialized and gendered commentary that this study has critiqued. For example, near the end of our conversation, a white male MP was discussing the inroads made by the NDP in the Greater Toronto Area in the 2011 election. He described the campaign of then MP Rathika Sitsabaiesan: "Well, Rathika ran. Six months before, you looked at her, it's like she's a schoolgirl from back in the farm country. But then the makeup gets done, the Tamils all of a sudden come out, and we all got whomped." The racialized and gendered language is striking, particularly given the extent to which interviewees generally avoided overtly criticizing their political opponents, often even choosing not to mention them by name. A second white interviewee, a former MP, said that "many, many [minority candidates] who put their names forward aren't remotely qualified. And I actually feel that they're quite emboldened – the word 'audacious' is a bit strong – but very, very confident about their abilities when, frankly, I don't think that it's always warranted." As evidence, the interviewee claimed that these potential candidates simply do not have the credentials and their English "isn't perfect." Racialized and gendered commentary does not just come from the media, in other words.

Candidates often displayed a sense of resignation. A number suggested that the patterns of coverage that this project has brought to light are simply a part of politics. A white candidate said, for example:

> If you don't like the questions, then don't go into politics. I mean, c'mon. You can make some things off-limits, like your children, maybe whatever is going on in your personal life and marriage or not marriage or if you're divorced or gay or whatever, but that's what this is all about. It's important. [Voters] need to trust you

because they're going to vote for you, and they want to know. So if you think you can run and hide, forget it ... There shouldn't be any whining about this.

A visible minority candidate who expressed some dissatisfaction with her coverage nonetheless also seemed to accept this part of public life: "When you enter into public service, nothing is private anymore ... You are going to get attacked, so you have to develop thick skin for that ... When you enter into politics, your private life is no longer yours." This sentiment was echoed by another visible minority candidate who said, "Once you commit yourself to public life, you're basically committing to live in a fishbowl. And you have to be aware of that, and if you don't have thick skin or didn't have thick skin before, well, you better develop it pretty quick." A third visible minority candidate said, "In the media, when I am criticized, this is fine with me. It's an understandable thing that will happen. For others, who cannot withstand criticism, which the vast majority are, they will not choose the road of politics."

The lack of desire for change is perhaps as revealing about the state of Canadian politics as it is about media coverage. The ambivalence does nothing to improve the state of political reporting, nor the experiences of visible minorities in politics. Systemic change requires a desire to see it realized, and the "that's just politics" syndrome is one of the most powerful obstacles to achieving change.

Deracializing Political News Coverage

Although the complete erasure of race from news reporting is unrealistic – and arguably undesirable – we can achieve a less racially differentiated news environment, one that draws attention to race in a serious, sensitive, and meaningful way, by thinking about the assumptions that guide news judgment. This requires greater reflexivity about the notion of relevance, and the ways in which racial thinking may influence this. It also requires a de-escalation of the 24-7 news cycle that privileges breaking news and quick hits, often at the expense of considered news judgment. Indeed, in responding to complaints that it had included excessive references to "Somali" drug dealers when reporting on Mayor Rob Ford's alleged crack video, the *Toronto Star* emphasized that it was a "first story," "written on deadline" and "in great haste," that was subsequently revised to remove more than half of the Somali references (English 2013). This apology draws attention to the demands that journalists face and how the speed at which they are expected to produce stories can impair news judgment and result in more racialized coverage. But what would less racially differentiated coverage look like?

As a starting point, stories that draw attention to the socio-demographic characteristics of visible minority candidates should at a bare minimum also mention the backgrounds of white candidates. This recommendation may strike some as ridiculous – why would a story need to mention that someone is *white*? – but that puzzlement only underscores the extent to which "whiteness" and "diversity" are viewed differently. After all, if we subscribe to the principle of fair and balanced coverage, why should race only be mentioned when the subject is not white? Were we to apply analogous news judgment, then it should be self-evident that in a story in which a visible minority's race is mentioned, so too should the race of any white person. Doing so would challenge the assumption that whiteness is neutral and that only deviations from this standard merit mention.

Stepping beyond this, journalists should work to integrate diversity issues into "mainstream" stories about Canadian politics. This will avoid visible minorities being relegated to coverage about "famous firsts," "model minorities," "cultural curiosities," and "ethnic politicking." The visible minority candidates with whom I spoke often referred to their economic policy interests, but they rarely appear in coverage of these issues. This is perhaps because they are not viewed as credible commentators on such issues, but also a function of journalists' propensity to turn to the usual suspects for quotations and story input. The corollary of this tendency is that white candidates do not typically appear in stories about ostensibly minority issues, unless the article is about ethnic vote-getting and campaign strategy, or the candidate in question is also the minister responsible for immigration, citizenship, and multiculturalism. The effect is to narrow the range of voices that speak to particular policy issues, while giving the impression that visible minority candidates care more about "their own" than about the big picture.

Journalists should also give some consideration to the ways in which assumptions and stereotypes influence their interpretation of the reality around them. To be clear: a reliance on information shortcuts is necessary in a complex world, and this inclination is not confined to journalists. However, the achievement of fair, balanced, and reflective coverage demands that reporters take steps to mitigate their reliance on faulty heuristics. This would help them avoid coming too quickly to an evaluation of the problem, misinterpreting events, or reaching a wrong conclusion as a result of incorrect assumptions. Just as *The Canadian Press Stylebook* counsels journalists to ask, "Would this information be used if the subject were a man?" so too should they ask, "Would this information be considered relevant if the subject were white?" This test needs to be applied at each step of the newsmaking process.[1] In addition, journalists need to ask questions about the extent to which racial considerations may have influenced story topic, narrative arc, language and metaphor use, image and source selection, as well as the placement, tone, and prominence of an article. Already, journalists give consideration to the fairness, balance, and credibility of their reporting. They must also include a frank assessment of the extent to which subtle, implicit, or hidden racial assumptions may influence their news judgment. They must confront the ways in which considerations about race mediate their reporting.

These changes in practice will require a reshaping of news norms, which currently place a premium on conflict and novelty and thus encourage stories that set visible minorities off as different, problematic, or outside the mainstream. Such a change may also promote a focus on more substantive engagement and a turn away from facile storylines, although certainly the contraction of the media landscape, economic pressures, and space constraints may act as a counterweight. At the very least, traditional story frames must be revisited and journalists need to question the narratives that have dominated the coverage of visible minorities in politics to date. More fundamentally, the media must work to challenge cultural assumptions that individualize disparity, discount institutional and systemic explanations, and regard the status quo as acceptable and unproblematic. In this way, they will go beyond framing diversity as merely "a cultural tile in Canada's multicultural mosaic" (Fleras 2012, 133). Absent this, the media cannot claim to be fulfilling their function as a neutral conduit through which we learn about the world around us.

Although diversifying newsrooms and the executive ranks of Canada's news media has often been suggested as a panacea, the extent to which such measures will rectify racial bias is unclear. Certainly, there is nothing to be lost when organizations work to include diverse perspectives within their ranks. However, to believe that hiring targets or diversity training will magically undo centuries of institutionalized whiteness is naïve at best. Racial mediation is not an individual act, but rather a function of organizational cultures and institutional practices; these include standard news routines and definitions of newsworthiness as well as a business model that prioritizes efficiency and demands a focus on the unusual, the unexpected, and the novel. All of this works against the achievement of coverage that is less racialized. These institutional pressures were made clear in my interviews with journalists, where I noticed very few differences between those with white and visible minority backgrounds, particularly when it came to describing their news gathering, sourcing, and story framing practices. The problem is structural, and structural change rarely happens quickly.

Structural lethargy has stymied progress towards greater equality, but so too has our general reticence to acknowledge that race influences our decision making, interpersonal relationships, and everyday life. The journalists with whom I spoke largely rejected the idea that race has any effect on their reporting, and candidates and staffers were hesitant to talk about the role of race in politics. Most would acknowledge that there are racial disparities in society, but there was a sense that these sorts of things happen "out there," rather than in our own workplaces and professional relationships. This perspective is not unique to the individuals with whom I spoke. In the preface to his book on racism in Canada, Augie Fleras (2014, x) writes, "Racism is brushed off as a relic of the past, relatively muted and randomly expressed, isolated to a few lunatic fringes or articulated by the sadly misinformed, and banned from public domains." However, as Sarah Milstein (2013; emphasis in original) notes, "Everyone is born with a racial bias ... so even if you do not identify as a racist, racism is baked into you. And then it's reinforced by our culture. No point in feeling guilty because you're a human *and* the product of a racist society. But, by all means, feel bad about yourself if you choose not to identify and work against your racial bias."

We need to acknowledge that politics, like our society, is not race-blind. Those who claim they do not see race may think that this assertion demonstrates their racial acceptance. What it really does is set aside all the ways that race does in fact matter and thus perpetuates the racial disparities enumerated in this book. As Debra Thompson (2008, 542) puts it, "Privilege often does not recognize privilege as such – it is instead interpreted as normalcy. The notion of race neutrality promotes the idea that this normalcy is available to everyone regardless of race when evidence dictates that it surely is not." Race affects the choices that political parties make, the strategies that campaigns adopt, and the ways that the public views candidates for office. Most of the visible minority candidates with whom I spoke noted they are subjected to questions about their racial background, suspicions about their motives, and a sense that they need to meet a higher bar than their white counterparts. Race is infused into all these interactions and outcomes. Although research on Canadian politics often begins with the premise that race doesn't matter, this book undermines that assumption by presenting powerful evidence on the impact of race on media representations. These representations do not exist in isolation: they are a reflection of our culture, our politics, and our democracy.

For those of us born without a visible minority background, this book raises troubling questions about our complacency and reluctance to confront or even acknowledge the extent to which we are complicit in structuring and maintaining a political system in which individuals are not always judged by the content of their character but instead by the colour of their skin. There are also important questions about the legitimacy of our voices, and the ways in which our participation in the conversation may reassert, rather than redefine, our own privilege. Referring to an essay written by Peggy McIntosh entitled "White Privilege: Unpacking the Invisible Knapsack," Jessie-Lane Metz (2013), a woman of colour, notes in a blog post that:

> [McIntosh] casually appropriated the collective pain of Black people and rolled out excruciating examples of our experiences in an itemized list. Her article, largely in bullet-point form, highlights a number of ways in which Black people are treated differently from white people on a daily basis. The beneficiaries of this article are largely white. Peggy herself benefitted from becoming a central voice in anti-racist activism, and still charges $10 for a copy of her article, after doing nothing more than stealing our pain, putting it in her words, and becoming an expert in a struggle that is not her own ...White people get to read it without having to feel the pain of racism; they get to see how lucky they are to have such privilege, get to assume this article is unproblematic and pivotal in their own personal growth, and also feel a sense of self-satisfaction if they haven't personally entertained all of the racist thoughts and actions in the article.

Metz's post resonated with me because it pinpoints the discomfort I have felt since beginning this project. In particular, it made me question my choice to pursue this research and to share the stories of people engaged in a struggle that I have not personally experienced. My standpoint as a white woman was clear when I was talking to visible minority candidates, some of whom showed obvious (and understandable) discomfort about revealing the impact of race on their political experiences. My standpoint was equally evident when I interviewed white men who stumbled over their words in an effort to use language that wouldn't be perceived as sexist or racist, or when I talked with other white women who adopted the language of "we."

I cannot shed who I am, but I have tried to share the stories of these individuals in their own words, as plainly and sensitively as possible. For immigrants, people of colour, and those who engage in anti-racism work, the book's conclusion that race matters will not come as a surprise. Visible minorities feel its effects everyday. I write about their stories in the hope that their voices will help each of us to see, to overcome the silence, and to work towards a world in which we don't just *say* race doesn't matter, but we actually make that happen.

APPENDIX
... Coding Scheme for Content Analysis

Coders were given detailed instructions to assist them in identifying and making decisions about each variable. Detailed coding instructions are available on request from the author. The following variables were included in the coding scheme:

- Coder ID
- Item ID
- Candidate's name
- Publication in which article appeared
- Page number on which article appeared
- Date of publication
- Number of words in article
- Article includes a photo of the candidate
- Article type (news, column, editorial)
- Region in which newspaper is published (British Columbia, Prairies, Ontario, Quebec, Atlantic, national)
- Province in which the candidate ran
- Percentage visible minority population in candidate's riding
- Gender of candidate
- Party of candidate
- Race of candidate (e.g., white, South Asian, Chinese, black, West Asian, Arab, Japanese)
- Candidate is a visible minority
- Candidate was elected
- Candidate is an incumbent
- Article mentions candidate is a visible minority
- Article mentions candidate is white

- Article mentions candidate identifies with a non-Judeo-Christian religion
- Article mentions candidate speaks a minority (non-official) language
- Article mentions candidate speaks a majority (official) language
- Article mentions candidate is an immigrant or foreign-born
- Article mentions candidate is Canadian-born
- Article mentions candidate's parent(s) are immigrants or foreign-born
- Article mentions candidate's parents are Canadian-born
- Article mentions the minority composition of the candidate's riding (e.g., visible minority, non-English/non-French, non-Judeo-Christian, immigrant)
- Article mentions the mainstream/majority composition of the candidate's riding (e.g., white, French/English, Judeo-Christian, non-immigrant)
- Article mentions candidate's support from minority communities
- Article mentions candidate's support from mainstream/majority communities
- Article portrays candidate as a political insider
- Article portrays candidate as a novelty
- Article portrays candidate as being of high quality
- Article mentions a political or election-related poll or survey in the headline, sub-headline, or first three paragraphs
- Article mentions a political or election-related poll or survey in the rest of the story
- Article uses a game frame in the headline, sub-headline, or first three paragraphs
- Article connects the candidate to a policy issue
- Article connects the candidate to a crime/justice issue
- Article connects the candidate to a social welfare issue (e.g., social assistance, social housing, homelessness, poverty, pensions, low incomes)
- Article connects the candidate to an immigration or multiculturalism issue
- Article connects the candidate to some other policy issue [identify with appropriate code]

  - Aboriginal issues
  - Agriculture, forestry, fishing, mining
  - Cities and infrastructure

- Defence and security
- Democratic reform
- Economy
- Education
- Employment and labour
- Energy, electricity, hydro, gas
- Environment
- Families, seniors, or youth
- Foreign affairs
- Gay and lesbian rights
- Government
- Health
- Intergovernmental relations
- Trade and industry
- Transportation
- Other

- Article is mostly about the candidate
- Article includes a direct quotation from the candidate
- Article includes a quotation about the candidate
- Article includes a paraphrase of something the candidate has said
- Tone of the candidate's coverage in the article (i.e., positive, negative, neutral)

Notes

INTRODUCTION

1 The study by Jeffrey Reitz and Rupa Banerjee has been the source of some debate. Some researchers have critiqued both the authors' contextualization and their interpretation of the results, expressing concern in particular over the ways in which Reitz and Banerjee have operationalized "Canadian identity" and concepts related to "social integration" (Palmer 2006; Wood and Wortley 2010). While these critiques may have merit, they are not relevant to the authors' conclusions on visible minority voting rates. Here, their findings are unambiguous: visible minority Canadians are less likely than white Canadians to say they have voted in the last federal election. This pattern is particularly acute among second-generation Canadians.

2 When referring to both reporters and editors, I use the umbrella term "journalists."

3 While Miller and Court's (2004) survey had a modest response rate (38 percent), their findings may actually overestimate the number of minorities in Canadian newsrooms given that the survey was most likely to have been completed by the most diverse workplaces. Indeed, in a companion article, Miller (2006, 8) notes that "most non-participating papers refused to return subsequent phone calls and emails. Those who did gave various reasons. One editor said filling out the questionnaire is 'a no-win situation,' because the paper had very few minority journalists. Another said, 'I feel uncomfortable even talking about this.'"

CHAPTER 1: UNDERSTANDING RACIAL MEDIATION

1 Carole Pateman and Charles Mills are the authors of *The Sexual Contract* (Pateman 1988) and *The Racial Contract* (Mills 1997). *Contract and Domination* is, in essence, a conversation between Pateman and Mills in which they argue that the sexual and racial contracts should be brought together to address the domination brought about by patriarchy and white supremacy.

2 Jennifer Schwartz (2011, 381) employs three similar frames in her study. She describes them as a personal frame "emphasizing personal or professional background"; a strategy frame "emphasizing campaign strategy or horserace position in polls"; and an issue frame "emphasizing position or action on policy issues."

CHAPTER 2: RACIALIZED MEDIA COVERAGE IN CANADIAN POLITICS

1 The newspapers included in the study were the *Globe and Mail, National Post, Vancouver Sun, Vancouver Province, Victoria Times-Colonist, Calgary Herald, Edmonton Journal, Saskatoon Star Phoenix, Regina Leader-Post, Winnipeg Free Press, Windsor Star, Toronto Star, Ottawa Citizen, Montreal Gazette, Saint John Telegraph-Journal, Halifax Chronicle Herald/Sunday Herald, St. John's Telegram,* and *Charlottetown Guardian.*

2 Candidates who ran in ridings in Quebec were excluded because only English-language newspapers were included in the analysis. This left 1,178 candidates in 233 ridings outside of Quebec, a number of whom ran for minor parties. Focusing only on those who ran for the Conservatives, Liberals, and New Democrats left me with 698 candidates. I selected a stratified sample comprising 9.7 percent of these candidates.

3 All stories were scanned to ensure the subject was in fact a candidate in the 2008 federal election. Occasionally, I came across stories about individuals who shared the same name as a particular candidate. For example, an economist at the University of Manitoba who is quoted frequently in the *Winnipeg Free Press* rather inconveniently shares his name with John McCallum, also an economist and the Liberal MP for Markham–Unionville. The stories about McCallum the professor were excluded from the sample.

4 A list of the coded variables can be found in the appendix; the full set of coding instructions is available from the author. To construct the coding scheme, I examined a number of coding schemes developed for other projects and drew from the existing literature. I revised the scheme several times before sharing it with the coding team.

5 Coders were hired through Carleton University's career centre. A job posting yielded nearly a hundred applications. The three successful applicants were all master's students; one in political science, one in international relations, and one in journalism and communications. As part of their training, coders were asked to review the coding scheme before gathering for in-person training. After the coders practised on a sample of articles drawn from the 2011 election, I revised the coding scheme to clarify concepts and decision rules. Following this, the coders were asked to independently code twenty-five articles from the 2006 election over a two-day period. This portion of the training used a test-standard approach, whereby coders' coding decisions were compared to my own. All discrepancies were discussed and additional revisions were made to the coding scheme.

6 Intercoder reliability was checked using PRAM, a Program for Reliability Assessment with Multiple Coders (Neuendorf 2002). PRAM calculates average pairwise agreement and a number of other measures of intercoder reliability. Given the parameters of this study, the two most appropriate measures of intercoder reliability are Krippendorff's alpha and Fleiss's kappa. I analyzed intercoder reliability using both statistics and achieved equivalent results. For simplicity, I report here only on

Fleiss's kappa, but can provide more detailed information on all reliability tests on request. Fleiss' kappa (κ) is a measure of intercoder agreement that can be used with nominal data, is suitable for multi-coder situations, and assumes that coders did not necessarily all code the same items (Fleiss 1981). When using Fleiss's kappa, a statistic ranging from 0.60 to 0.74 indicates intermediate to good agreement, while anything over 0.75 indicates excellent agreement. Results below 0.40 are regarded as poor agreement (Fleiss 1981; see also Landis and Koch 1977). Following the pilot coding, two variables were dropped because even after additional training and discussion, intercoder reliability did not exceed 0.30. These dropped variables pertained to mentions of a candidate's outsider status and mentions of a candidate's low quality, which were relatively uncommon and generally quite implicit. Excluding these two variables, average pairwise agreement in the pilot coding was 97 percent, while Fleiss's kappa averaged 0.88. This was deemed to be an acceptable level of intercoder reliability, and coders were given the remaining articles to code.

7   Average pairwise agreement across the variables coded by the coders was 98 percent, with a range of 82.9 percent to 100 percent. Meanwhile, Fleiss's kappa averaged 0.87, with a range of 0.50 to 1.00. Average intercoder reliability for this study is thus near perfect. Nonetheless, some variables did achieve more moderate levels of agreement. Unsurprisingly, these are the more subjective variables, which are open to interpretation and thus more difficult to code reliably. They include mentions of a candidate's novelty ($\kappa = 0.50$) and quality ($\kappa = 0.67$), and the overall tone of the candidate's coverage ($\kappa = 0.58$). Although intercoder reliability for these variables is below the average and some caution should be exercised when interpreting the results, the range still falls within acceptable levels and, overall, coders did achieve high levels of reliability. We can thus use these data with some confidence and assume that the results are replicable and were not achieved simply by chance.

8   The coders worked at different speeds, most articles took less than ten minutes to code. A total of 275 hours were spent coding the articles in the sample.

9   Although concerns are sometimes raised about the reliability of media studies based on human coding, with some suggesting that scholars find racism in media studies because they, in essence, go looking for it (e.g., Hier 2009), my own comparison of manual and computer-based approaches suggests that the results of this study hold up quite well. Indeed, human coders sometimes provided more conservative estimates of racialized media coverage than their computerized counterparts (see Tolley 2015).

10 Most quotations are drawn from the coverage of the 2008 election, but I have included some from outside the campaign period for two reasons. First, I wanted to ensure that all quotations were as illustrative as possible, and sometimes the best examples were from the inter-electoral period. Second, by including quotations from coverage outside of my media sample – often about candidates whom I did not interview for this project – I am better able to protect the confidentiality of those I did interview. The identities of the interview respondents are more difficult to deduce from the broader selection of examples.

11   To test the difference between the observed and hypothesized proportions for each variable, Pearson's chi-square test is used in most cases. The only exception is when 50 percent or more cells have expected frequencies of less than 5; in such cases, Fisher's exact test is used (Hogg and Tanis 2009). If the chi-square was significant, phi or Cramer's V was also calculated to measure the strength of association between the two variables; phi is the appropriate measure of association for 2×2 nominal tables, while Cramer's V is used for larger nominal tables or when one of the variables is ordinal. Only relationships that achieved conventionally accepted standards of statistical significance are reported; details are available from the author.

12   One of the manuscript's anonymous reviewers wisely pointed out that newspapers sometimes do not place editorial content on their front pages, opting instead for a fully visual presentation. This is important because it would affect interpretations of the *absolute* amount of front-page coverage received by candidates. However, it does not alter comparisons of the *relative* amount of coverage received by visible minority and white candidates, which is the primary objective of this analysis. That is, the lack of editorial content on the front page equally affects all candidates, regardless of race. It is also worth noting that I initially considered a more fine-grained measure of story placement that would account for both section and page number. However, as Charlton McIlwain and Stephen Caliendo (2011, 107) note, section location is somewhat meaningless given how long sections can be, as well as organizational conventions that may place stories about politics in section A at one paper, but a story about a local candidate in the "City" section at another paper. Profiles of candidates will also often appear in a "Lifestyle" or similar section. For this reason, I adopted McIlwain and Caliendo's view that the "most meaningful difference ... is singular: Does the story appear on the front page or not?" (108).

13   Coders recorded any quotation from or about a candidate, regardless of its theme or content, while paraphrases were noted only when they dealt specifically with candidates' policy positions or interests.

14   The number of ridings increased to 338 following the 2012 redistribution of federal electoral districts. At the time of writing, census data for these ridings had not yet been compiled, so the data given here are based on the 2003 representation order and the 2006 census.

15   The characterization of visible minority candidates as cultural bonders may be changing, however. Take, for example, a story from the 2011 election that refers to Conservative candidate Parm Gill, who unseated Liberal Ruby Dhalla in Brampton–Springdale. The story notes, "Like [Dhalla], [Gill is] a westernized member of the [Indo-Canadian] community. Like her he's a crossover candidate, with strong appeal to other voters. If the Conservative tide rises in 905, this is one of the seats" (MacDonald 2011, A23). Interestingly, this bridging narrative is couched in language that assumes Gill would largely have appeal in the immigrant community; it is primarily because of his "westernization" that is he is able to "cross over."

16   Initially, coders were asked to look for other markers of candidate quality, such as professional background and educational credentials. However, in coder training,

it became evident that an acceptable level of intercoder reliability would be difficult to achieve on these dimensions because the definition of what constitutes a "quality" profession or education is highly subjective. By narrowing the focus to attributes like prominence, profile, and length of residence in the community, more acceptable levels of intercoder reliability were achieved. While the measure of quality that was ultimately employed may be somewhat restricted, it is more reliable than would have been the case had a broader definition been employed.

17 This story is also significant among those in my sample in that it is written by Marina Jimenez, a reporter with a Hispanic background, but includes some of the most explicit – and numerous – examples of racialization. Similarly, the literature on women in politics finds that a reporter's gender has only a marginal impact on how he or she covers politics (Goodyear-Grant 2013). It is likely that strong news norms, which encourage a focus on the exception, push reporters – regardless of their race – to highlight the novelty of a visible minority candidate.

18 Note that some stories include both insider and quality mentions, so the reported figures are not mutually exclusive.

19 Although all the ministers responsible for these policy files at the time of the 2008 election were men, none of them were included in my sample, so cabinet positions are not driving the association between male candidate policy coverage and stereotypically male policy areas.

20 The coding instructions defined health issues as those related to hospitals, illness, disease, medical treatment, wait times, health care professionals, and pharmaceuticals. Education issues related to tuition, universities, and schools, such as mentions of all-day kindergarten, for example. Families and seniors issues included generic mentions of families, seniors, youth, and women, as well as specific mentions of domestic violence, child care, teen pregnancy, abortion, adoption, and reproduction.

21 Of course, some suggest that all parties have been doing this for years. As an NDP strategist revealed in an interview with me, "If they say they don't do it, they're lying!"

22 The approach taken in this study is more rigorous than that taken in some others. As an illustration, early on in my research, I contacted the authors of a series of studies on race and gender bias in the American news media and asked if they would share some information about their coding scheme. In an email response, one of the authors recalled:

> "We tended to be pretty loose about these things, so, for any given research project, it's entirely possible that we never actually recorded a rigorous set of coding rules, but instead relied on a somewhat vague set of general principles. Our approach to coding was often a lot like Justice Stewart's famous quote about defining obscenity: we didn't necessarily know how to precisely define what we were looking for, but we knew it when we saw it."

His co-author confirmed this:

"Our data were assembled by a team of students actually reading each article in the sample. We did not use a strict set of key words to trigger the racial issue or importance measures. Instead, we gave students a starter set of articles highlighting the dimensions of interest, and we built from there ... Above all, we tried to give the students a good set of boundaries toward allowing them to use their common sense in categorizing the issue."

These authors do not report any intercoder reliability statistics, which raises some questions about the objectivity and portability of the findings.

CHAPTER 3: PORTRAYALS OF VISIBLE MINORITY WOMEN IN POLITICAL NEWS COVERAGE

1 This sort of narrative is also found in a *National Post* editorial about Liberal MP Hedy Fry that observes, "Were Hedy Fry a member of the Tory government, the Liberals and the bulk of the media would by now have labeled her a 'wing nut,' and pressured the Tories to expel her from caucus. But because she is a Liberal – and perhaps, too, *because she is an MP of colour* – Ms. Fry gets a free pass to continue spewing her claptrap" (*National Post* 2009, A14; emphasis added).

2 Following the 2011 election, of the 308 MPs elected, 76 were women; among these were 15 visible minority women, 2 Aboriginal women, and 59 white women. Visible minority women thus made up 4.9 percent of the House of Commons, while white women made up 19.1 percent. Although reliable data are not available from the 2011 National Household Survey, the 2006 census counted 2.6 million visible minority women in Canada, which is approximately 8.3 percent of the country's total population. White women, meanwhile, made up 42.6 percent of the Canadian population. In proportionate terms, visible minority women's presence in the House of Commons was thus 0.59 of their presence in the general population, or just over half of what is needed to achieve perfect electoral proportionality. By comparison, white women's presence in the House of Commons was 0.45 of their presence in the general population, or just under half of what is needed to achieve perfect proportionality.

3 For current members, articles were retrieved up to January 15, 2013.

4 I am grateful to Megan Gaucher, who helped compile this sample.

5 Abigail Iserhienrhien's (2014) master's thesis examines the news coverage of female MPs in Canada's 41st Parliament and found that visible minority women actually received more coverage than their white counterparts, although this was partly driven by the number of stories devoted to Olivia Chow.

6 The coverage of Sana Hassainia, at the time an NDP MP, included some discussion of breastfeeding and her role as a mother after she was apparently barred from a vote in the House of Commons because she was accompanied by her newborn son. Only one of the articles I examined referred to Hassainia's Tunisian heritage. This was in an interview and, interestingly, Hassainia herself mentioned it. This raises questions about self-presentation, which is addressed in Chapter 4, and also suggests that the coupling of gendered and racialized framing is not absolute.

CHAPTER 4: CANDIDATE SELF-PRESENTATION AND MEDIA PORTRAYAL

1   Three potential interviewees explicitly refused to participate, while at least fifteen simply didn't respond, even after multiple contacts by email, telephone, and social media.

2   One respondent also mentioned skepticism of information gathering, in general. Before the interview, he asked for a letter from my advisor attesting to my identity as a researcher. At the beginning of the interview, he then confided that he had asked for confirmation of my legitimacy because he has on more than one occasion "sent an intern or student to 'interview' another MP or cabinet minister and then turned around and used that information against them." In this context, one can see why researchers may have difficulty procuring interviews with public officials.

3   Visible minority respondents had a range of backgrounds, including South Asian, Chinese, Black, Arab, and Southeast Asian.

4   The distribution of interviewees across parties is partly a reflection of the sampling strategy, which included targeting white candidates who had been elected in highly diverse ridings. In 2008 and earlier, the bulk of these candidates were affiliated with the Liberal Party. Liberal Party members were also somewhat more likely to agree to be interviewed. The relative overrepresentation of Liberals among respondents is not really cause for concern, however, given that I did not notice significant party effects either in the content analysis or during the interviews themselves. Although there are some differences with respect to interviewees' approaches to diversity – notably Conservative respondents tend to frame discussions of race and ethnicity using somewhat more of a strategic frame – I would not say that there is considerable variation.

5   Shortly after I began conducting interviews in March 2011, a federal election was called for May. Given that most potential subjects were running and thus otherwise engaged, I delayed the remainder of the interviews. Interviews recommenced in October 2011.

6   In the security and intelligence literature, the "mosaic effect" is a scenario in which information, seemingly benign or unrelated when considered in isolation, can be pieced together to develop a more complete picture. Applied in the context of this project, one can imagine a reasonably informed observer using his or her knowledge of current events or of the named subjects to deduce the identities of unnamed subjects.

7   Queen's University's General Research and Ethics Board approved this selective release of information. In accordance with their policies, at the conclusion of the interview, participants were told more about the nature of the project, including my interest in race. All were given the opportunity to opt out of the study at this point, although none chose to do so.

8   I am grateful to Varun Uberoi, who made a number of suggestions for improving my recruitment script.

9   As it turns out, my initial concerns about racial priming effects were probably misplaced. The propensity to raise race as an issue did not seem to vary between those who were contacted using the initial, more generic script and those who were contacted using the more specific script. Visible minority women as well as white and

visible minority candidates who ran in ethnoculturally diverse ridings were the most likely to draw attention to race and so-called minority issues, regardless of how they were recruited.

10 One Conservative Party strategist with whom I spoke noted this gap explicitly: "What limited minority representation [the current government] has, has really not important positions. Many of them have no positions ... Now they can walk around and fake it to their constituents, that they're really, really important, that they happen to be the PS [parliamentary secretary] for sport or whatever, but really nobody cares. The Liberals did have the Herb Dhaliwals, the Ujjal Dosanjhs, the Raymond Chans, that were at the cabinet table. They were serious players, they had impact."

11 Several months after this particular interview, news emerged that Finance Minister Jim Flaherty was suffering from health problems. One columnist did observe that "you have to feel for the scrappy little Irishman" (Maher 2013, A8).

12 It is difficult to generalize from a small number of interviews, but I did note that policy issues seemed to be more front and centre for New Democratic candidates than for others. All the NDP candidates with whom I spoke expressed a strong commitment to issues related to social justice and equity, including health care, women's issues, universal child care, labour and employment policy, and immigration and refugee reform. Although these kinds of issues (and others) were raised by candidates from the other two parties, policy seemed to be a bit of a side note – perhaps even a distraction – rather than a primary motivator. Of course, as the NDP's electoral fortunes change, one wonders whether the party will shift its focus away from policy and toward strategy and government formation.

13 One exception was a white male candidate whose riding includes a number of conservative and evangelical Christian voters. His party's support for same-sex marriage was a sore spot for some in this community, so he told me he purposefully highlighted his wife and marital status in his campaign literature.

14 Data for the index were obtained from several sources. The principal sources were (1) candidate profiles compiled by CBC as part of its Canada Votes feature; (2) PARLINFO, a website maintained by the Parliament of Canada; (3) newspaper reports and online searches of secondary sources; and (4) data from Elections Canada. Data on riding competitiveness are derived from a measure of party support stability developed by Marc André Bodet, who generously provided the data I needed. The scale achieves a Cronbach's alpha of 0.713, suggesting that it is moderately reliable. I had initially intended to include other measures, such as campaign spending and office-holding at other levels of government, that David Coletto (2010) suggests will boost the electoral performance of non-incumbent candidates, but their presence only decreased the reliability of the index. As a result, they have been excluded.

15 David Campbell and Christina Wolbrecht (2006) use electoral outcome as a measure candidates' viability in their study of female legislators in the United States, but include both those candidates who won and those who came within 10 percentage points of the victor. They do not provide any justification for this break point, so I elected to use a won-lost measure.

16   Battlegrounds are ridings that are neither weakly competitive strongholds nor non-competitive strongholds. Non-competitive strongholds are those in which one party received a majority of votes (i.e., more than 50 percent) in the previous two elections. To identify weakly competitive strongholds, meanwhile, Bodet uses an equation that takes into account a party's vote shares in the previous two elections. For a full description and calculations, see Bodet (2013).

17   Arguably, the items in the index do not exert equal influence on a candidate's viability. Future research should investigate more fully the relative impact of each of these factors; to simplify analysis at this stage, the items are simply weighted equally.

18   The mean viability of white candidates is 1.9412 (SD = 1.1266), while the mean viability of visible minority candidates is 1.3824 (SD = 1.25565). There is a statistically significant relationship between candidate viability and race (chi-square = 66.494; $p < 0.01$; df = 3; phi = 0.260).

19   Male candidates have a mean viability score of 1.6818 (SD = 1.21565), while female candidates have a mean viability score of 1.6250 (SD = 1.24455). There is no statistically significant relationship between candidate viability and gender among the candidates in the sample.

CHAPTER 5: JOURNALISTS AND THE FRAMING OF RACE

1   The term "journalist" captures reporters, columnists, and editors.

2   Two interviews were not conducted in confidence. One was with John Miller, a former journalist and now a professor emeritus at Ryerson University, who agreed to speak with me only if the conversation was "on the record." The second was with James McCarten, the editor of *The Canadian Press Stylebook*. Given his position and the nature of our conversation, there was no reasonable way for me to protect his identity while still sharing details from the interview, and so I asked for permission to use his name, which he granted.

3   It is worth mentioning that the journalists with whom I spoke seemed somewhat taken aback by the interview procedures that are normally required as part of a standard ethics clearance for research with human subjects. Given that nearly all media or news interviews are conducted "on the record," and subjects are rarely given the option of "striking topics" or "withdrawing answers," these protocols came as quite a surprise to most respondents. One responded on being informed of his rights, "Well, that's awfully kind!"

4   The Canadian Newspaper Association (1995) states that a "newspaper should strive to paint a representative picture of its diverse communities, to encourage the expression of disparate views and to be accessible and accountable to the readers it serves, whether rich or poor, weak or powerful, minority or majority." Meanwhile, ethics guidelines developed by the Canadian Association of Journalists (2011) state:

> "News organizations – including newspapers, websites, magazines, radio and television – provide forums for the free interchange of information and opinion. As such, we seek to include views from all segments of

the population. We also encourage our organizations to make room for the interests of all: minorities and majorities, those with power and those without it, holders of disparate and conflicting views. We avoid stereotypes, and don't refer to a person's race, colour, religion, sexual orientation, gender self-identification or physical ability unless it is pertinent to the story."

5   The belief that there are significant or enduring differences between races and that these can help explain social, economic, or political phenomena illustrates what Frank Reeves (1983) refers to as a "weak racism." This form of racial thinking does not include moral evaluation of inferiority and superiority nor any prescription for action, but does assume races exist, they are different, and these differences have consequences. It is also, notably, still racism.

6   The *Toronto Star*'s (2011) "Newsroom Policy and Journalistic Standards Guide" similarly includes a section on "Racial References" alongside one on "Sexism." The section on sexism states, "Men and women should be treated equally in the *Star*." The section on race does not include any advice about the equal treatment of races.

7   The broadcasting industry is regulated through a legislative framework that includes the Canadian Broadcasting Act (1991). The act requires that television and radio broadcasters "serve the needs and interests, and reflect the circumstances and aspirations, of Canadian men, women and children, including equal rights, the linguistic duality and multicultural and multiracial nature of Canadian society and the special place of Aboriginal peoples within that society" (section 3.1(d)(iii). The act is administered by the Canadian Radio-television and Telecommunications Commission (see Canadian Association of Broadcasters 2004; MediaSmarts 2012a).

8   A number of newspapers have a public editor or ombudsperson who addresses public complaints; many outlets offer corrections or apologies as a result of these interventions. Provincial and regional press councils also have mechanisms to review alleged breaches of journalistic standards or ethics. The tribunals are quasi-judicial, they select which cases they will hear, and there is no appeals process. The councils typically hear cases related to explicit ideological or personal bias in coverage, although some have dealt with diversity issues, such as a newspaper identifying the race of a particular individual.

CONCLUSION

1   New Canadian Media plans to produce a diversity style guide, although it aims primarily to standardize the spelling and definition of cultural terms used by the media. This is an important step but does not address the more prickly – and arguably contentious - issue of news judgment.

Works Cited

Abu-Laban, Yasmeen. 2001. "Challenging the Gendered Vertical Mosaic: Immigrants, Ethnic Minorities, Gender and Political Participation." In *Citizen Politics: Research and Theory in Canadian Political Behaviour*, ed. Joanna Everitt and Brenda O'Neill, 268-82. Don Mills, ON: Oxford University Press.

Aday, Sean, and James Devitt. 2001. "Style over Substance: Newspaper Coverage of Elizabeth Dole's Presidential Bid." *Harvard International Journal of Press/Politics* 6 (2): 52–73. http://dx.doi.org/10.1177/108118001129172134.

Allen, Stuart. 2004. *News Culture*. 2nd ed. Berkshire: Open University Press.

Alphonso, Caroline. 2012. "Onus on Health Canada to Fix Drug Policy." *Globe and Mail*, July 25, A5.

Anderson, Karrin Vasby. 2011. "'Rhymes with Blunt': Pornification and US Political Culture." *Rhetoric and Public Affairs* 14 (2): 327–68. http://dx.doi.org/10.1353/rap.2010.0228.

Andrew, Caroline, John Biles, Myer Siemiatycki, and Erin Tolley, eds. 2008. *Electing a Diverse Canada: The Electoral Representation of Immigrants, Minorities and Women*. Vancouver: UBC Press.

Audette, Trish. 2008. "Riding Profile: Edmonton Strathcona." *Edmonton Journal*, October 10, A4.

Axner, Marya. 2012. "Healing from the Effects of Internalized Oppression." In *The Community Tool Box*, ed. Bill Berkowitz. Lawrence: University of Kansas. http://ctb.ku.edu/en/table-of-contents/culture/cultural-competence/healing-from-interalized-oppression/main (accessed May 25, 2015).

Banducci, Susan A., Jeffrey A. Karp, Michael Thrasher, and Colin Rallings. 2008. "Ballot Photographs as Cues in Low-Information Elections." *Political Psychology* 29 (6): 903–17. http://dx.doi.org/10.1111/j.1467-9221.2008.00672.x.

Barber, Marsha, and Ann Rauhala. 2005. "The Canadian News Directors Study: Demographics and Political Leanings of Television Decision-Makers." *Canadian Journal of Communication* 30 (2): 281–92.

Bardeesy, Karim. 2011. "'Why Don't You Wear a Sari?'" *Globe and Mail*, August 20, F3.

Barrett, Jessica. 2014. "No 'Rainbow Families': Ethnic Donor Stipulation at Fertility Centre 'Floors' Local Woman." *Calgary Herald*, 25 July.

Bashevkin, Sylvia. 2009. *Women, Power, Politics*. Don Mills, ON: Oxford University Press.

Bass, A.Z. 1969. "Refining the 'Gatekeeper' Concept: A UN Radio Case Study." *Journalism Quarterly* 46 (1): 69–72. http://dx.doi.org/10.1177/107769906904600110.

Bastedo, Heather, Wayne Chu, and Jane Hilderman. 2012. *Occupiers and Legislators: A Snapshot of Political Media Coverage.* Samara Democracy Reports. Toronto: Samara.

Baumann, Shyon, and Loretta Ho. 2014. "Cultural Schemas for Racial Identity in Canadian Television Advertising." *Canadian Review of Sociology* 51 (2): 152–69. http://dx.doi.org/10.1111/cars.12040.

Beatty, Perrin. 2012. "Alexander Served to Make Things Better." *Ottawa Citizen,* October 26, A10.

Beeby, Dean. 2014. "Canadian Heroes Poll Shows our Top 10 Favourite People, but Not the Conservatives." *Huffington Post,* June 15.

Bejarano, Christina. 2013. *The Latina Advantage: Gender, Race, and Political Success.* Austin: University of Texas Press.

Benson, Rodney. 2005. "American Journalism and the Politics of Diversity." *Media Culture and Society* 27 (1): 5–20. http://dx.doi.org/10.1177/0163443705047031.

Benzie, Robert. 2013. "It's Herstory in the Making." *Toronto Star,* July 24, A6.

Bermingham, John. 2008. "Choice between Harper and Layton, Says NDP Operative." *Vancouver Province,* October 14, A6.

Biles, John, and Erin Tolley. 2008. "Our Unrepresentative but Somewhat Successful Capital: Electoral Representation in Ottawa." In *Electing a Diverse Canada: The Electoral Representation of Immigrants, Minorities and Women,* ed. Caroline Andrew, John Biles, Myer Siemiatycki, and Erin Tolley, 111–35. Vancouver: UBC Press.

Bird, Karen. 2008a. "Many Faces, Few Places: The Political Under-Representation of Ethnic Minorities and Women in the City of Hamilton." In *Electing a Diverse Canada: The Electoral Representation of Immigrants, Minorities and Women,* ed. Caroline Andrew, John Biles, Myer Siemiatycki, and Erin Tolley, 136–55. Vancouver: UBC Press.

–. 2008b. "Patterns of Substantive Representation among Visible Minority MPs: Evidence from Canada's House of Commons." Paper presented at the Annual Meeting of the Midwest Political Science Association, Chicago, April 3.

–. 2011. "The Local Diversity Gap: Assessing the Scope and Causes of Visible Minority Under-Representation in Municipal Elections." Paper presented at "The Political Immigrant: A Comparative Portrait," Montreal, November 18–19.

Black, Debra, and Laurie Monsebraaten. 2004. "No Breakthrough for Women: McDonaugh, Bradshaw Elected in Maritimes; Advocacy Group Alleges Systemic Discrimination." *Toronto Star,* June 29, A10.

Black, Jerome H. 2000a. "Entering the Political Elite in Canada: The Case of Minority Women as Parliamentary Candidates and MPs." *Canadian Review of Sociology and Anthropology* 37 (2): 143–66. http://dx.doi.org/10.1111/j.1755-618X.2000.tb01262.x.

–. 2000b. "Ethnoracial Minorities in the Canadian House of Commons: The Case of the 36th Parliament." *Canadian Ethnic Studies* 32 (2): 105–14.

–. 2001. "Representation in the Parliament of Canada: The Case of Ethnoracial Minorities." In *Citizen Politics: Research and Theory in Canadian Political Behaviour,* ed. Joanna Everitt and Brenda O'Neill, 355–72. Don Mills, ON: Oxford University Press.

–. 2003. "Differences That Matter: Minority Women MPs, 1993-2000." In *Women and Electoral Politics in Canada*, ed. Manon Tremblay and Linda Trimble, 59–74. Don Mills, ON: Oxford University Press.

–. 2008a. "The 2006 Federal Election and Visible Minority Candidates: More of the Same?" *Canadian Parliamentary Review* 30 (3): 30–36.

–. 2008b. "Ethnoracial Minorities in the 38th Parliament: Patterns of Change and Continuity." In *Electing a Diverse Canada: The Electoral Representation of Immigrants, Minorities and Women*, ed. Caroline Andrew, John Biles, Myer Siemiatycki, and Erin Tolley, 299–354. Vancouver: UBC Press.

–. 2011. "Visible Minority Candidates and MPs: An Update Based on the 2008 Federal Election." *Canadian Parliamentary Review* 34 (1): 30–34.

–. 2013. "Racial Diversity in the 2011 Federal Election: Visible Minority Candidates and MPs." *Canadian Parliamentary Review* 36 (3): 21–26.

Black, Jerome H., and Lynda Erickson. 2006. "Ethno-racial Origins of Candidates and Electoral Performance: Evidence from Canada." *Party Politics* 12 (4): 541–61. http://dx.doi.org/10.1177/1354068806064733.

Black, Jerome H., and Bruce Hicks. 2006. "Visible Minority Candidates in the 2004 Election." *Canadian Parliamentary Review* 29 (2): 26–31.

–. 2008. "Electoral Politics and Immigration in Canada: How Does Immigration Matter?" *Journal of International Migration and Integration* 9 (3): 241–67. http://dx.doi.org/10.1007/s12134-008-0069-5.

Black, Jerome H., and Aleem S. Lakhani. 1997. "Ethnoracial Diversity in the House of Commons: An Analysis of Numerical Representation in the 35th Parliament." *Canadian Ethnic Studies* 29: 1–21.

Blatchford, Christie. 2009. "I Ask My Dear Obie, Who Are the Victims? I Ruby Dhalla? Brian Mulroney?" *Globe and Mail*, May 13, A3.

Bleich, Erik, Irene Bloemraad, and Els de Graauw. 2015. "Migrants, Minorities, and the Media: Information, Representations, and Participation in the Public Sphere." *Journal of Ethnic and Migration Studies* 41 (6): 857–73.

Block, Sheila, and Grace-Edward Galabuzi. 2011. *Canada's Colour Coded Labour Market*. Ottawa: Canadian Centre for Policy Alternatives. https://www.policyalternatives.ca.

Bodet, Marc André. 2013. "Strongholds and Battlegrounds: Measuring Party Support Stability in Canada." *Canadian Journal of Political Science* 46 (3): 575–96. http://dx.doi.org/10.1017/S000842391300067X.

Bouchard, Gerard, and Charles Taylor. 2008. *Building the Future: A Time for Reconciliation*. Quebec City: Consultation Commission on Accommodation Practices Related to Cultural Differences.

Braden, Maria. 1996. *Women Politicians and the Media*. Lexington: University of Kentucky Press.

Brean, Joseph. 2011. "MP's Photo Altered to Remove Cleavage; Commons Website." *National Post*, September 23, A8.

Caliendo, Stephen M., and Charlton D. McIlwain. 2006. "Minority Candidates, Media Framing and Racial Cues in the 2004 Elections." *Harvard International Journal of Press/Politics* 11 (4): 45–69. http://dx.doi.org/10.1177/1081180X06293551.

Campbell, Christopher P. 1995. *Race, Myth and the News*. Thousand Oaks, CA: Sage. http://dx.doi.org/10.4135/9781483327211.

Campbell, David E., and Christina Wolbrecht. 2006. "See Jane Run: Women Politicians As Role Models for Adolescents." *Journal of Politics* 68 (2): 233–47. http://dx.doi.org/10.1111/j.1468-2508.2006.00402.x.

Campion-Smith, Bruce. 2008. "Minister Moves On Trustees: Zeal to Manage Message Sees Journalists Shunned, Bureaucrats, Cabinet Ministers Routinely Muzzled." *Toronto Star*, May 26, A1.

–. 2012. "Harper Kicks Off India Visit." *Toronto Star*, November 5, A4.

Canada. 1981. *Royal Commission on Newspapers*. Ottawa: Minister of Supply and Services.

Canadian Association of Broadcasters. 2004. *Reflecting Canadians: Best Practices for Cultural Diversity in Private Television*. Ottawa: Task Force for Cultural Diversity on Television.

Canadian Association of Journalists. 2011. "Ethics Guidelines." http://www.caj.ca/?p=1776 (accessed July 22, 2012).

Canadian Newspaper Association. 1995. "Statement of Principles." http://www.newspaperscanada.ca/about-newspapers/statement-principles (accessed July 22, 2012).

Canadian Press. 2011. "Liberals Launch Bid to Recapture Ethnic Vote." CTV News, June 30, http://www.ctvnews.ca/liberals-launch-bid-to-recapture-ethnic-vote-1.664094 (accessed 10 October 2013).

Canon, David. 1999. *Race, Redistricting and Representation: The Unintended Consequences of Black Majority Districts*. Chicago: University of Chicago Press.

Carroll, Susan J., and Ronnee Schreiber. 1997. "Media Coverage of Women in the 103rd Congress." In *Women, Media and Politics*, ed. Pippa Norris, 131–48. New York: Oxford University Press.

Carstarphen, Meta G. 2009. "Uncovering Race in 2009: Media, Politics and the Reporter's Eye." *Journal of Civil Rights and Economic Development* 24 (2): 403–20.

Chaudhary, Anju G. 1980. "Press Portrayal of Black Officials." *Journalism Quarterly* 57 (4): 636–41. http://dx.doi.org/10.1177/107769908005700413.

Cheek, Julianne. 2004. "At the Margins? Discourse Analysis and Qualitative Research." *Qualitative Health Research* 14 (8): 1140–50. http://dx.doi.org/10.1177/1049732304266820.

Chibnall, Steve. 1977. *Law-and-Order News: An Analysis of Crime Reporting in the British Press*. London: Tavistock.

Chong, Michael. 2004. "Canada without Hyphens." *Globe and Mail*, November 23, A25.

Chui, Tina, and Hélène Maheux. 2011. "Visible Minority Women." Catalogue 89–503-X. Ottawa: Statistics Canada. http://www.statcan.gc.ca/pub/89-503-x/2010001/article/11527-eng.pdf.

Chung, Andrew. 2006. "When a Kiss Isn't Just a Kiss." *Toronto Star*, January 29, A7.

–. 2008. "Liberals Leaning on Trudeau Again; Party Hopes Name Will Translate into Victory against Bloc Incumbent." *Toronto Star*, September 25, A22.

Citrin, Jack, Donald P. Green, and David O. Sears. 1990. "White Reactions to Black Candidates: When Does Race Matter?" *Public Opinion Quarterly* 54 (1): 74–96. http://dx.doi.org/10.1086/269185.

Clark, Campbell. 2002. "Cabinet Takes Aim at Casting Same-Sex Policy." *Globe and Mail,* August 1, A1.

–. 2007. "PM Faces Tough Choices Replacing Female Ministers." *Globe and Mail,* August 9, A1.

Clark, Campbell, and Kim Lunman. 2003. "48 Liberals Line Up against Same-Sex." *Globe and Mail,* August 8, A1.

Cohen, B.C. 1963. *The Press and Foreign Policy.* Princeton, NJ: Princeton University Press.

Cohn, Martin Regg. 2000. "Anti-smuggling Pitch Falls on Deaf Ears; Caplan's Talk about Snakeheads Ignored in China." *Toronto Star,* April 28, A1.

–. 2013. "The Party's Unseemly Kingmaker." *Toronto Star,* January 15, A6.

Cole, Desmond. 2015. "The Skin I'm In." *Toronto Life* (May). http://www.torontolife.com/ informer/features/2015/04/21/skin-im-ive-interrogated-police-50-times-im-black/ (accessed May 26, 2015).

Coletto, David. 2010. "Candidate Quality Matters: Political Experience Leads to Better Results." *Hill Times,* October 18, A20.

Collins, Patricia Hill. 1998. *Fighting Words: Black Women and the Search for Justice.* Minneapolis: University of Minnesota.

Contenta, Sandro. 1993. "Metro Boasts Contenders for Next Cabinet." *Toronto Star,* September 27, A14.

Cosh, Colby. 2009. "Tale of the Tape." *National Post,* January 6, A10.

Coutts, Matthew. 2008. "Winnipeg Feels the Pull from East and West." *National Post,* October 9, A6.

Cowan, James. 2004. "In Don Valley East, It's Ethnicity over Issues." *National Post,* March 31, A10.

Cox, Gary W., and M.F. Thies. 2000. "How Much Does Money Matter? 'Buying' Votes in Japan, 1967–1990." *Comparative Political Studies* 33 (1): 37–57. http://dx.doi.org/10 .1177/0010414000033001002.

Crawford, Trish. 2011. "Gosal Defeats Liberal Incumbent." *Toronto Star,* May 3, U8.

Crenshaw, Kimberle. 1989. "Demarginalizing the Intersections of Race and Sex: A Black Feminist Critique of Antidiscrimination Doctrine, Feminist Theory and Antiracist Politics." *University of Chicago Legal Forum.* Special Issue on Feminism in the Law: Theory, Practice and Criticism: 139–67.

–. 1991. "Mapping the Margins: Intersectionality, Identity Politics, and Violence against Women of Color." *Stanford Law Review* 43 (6): 1241–99. http://dx.doi.org/10.2307/ 1229039.

CRIC. 2004. "New Canada Revisited." Unpublished polling data. Centre for Research and Information on Canada, Ottawa.

Cukier, Wendy, Pinoo Bindhani, Sarah Amato, Shelley Smarz, and Amonrat Saekung. 2014. *DiversityLeads: Women and Visible Minorities in Senior Leadership Positions: A Profile of the Greater Toronto Area.* Toronto: Diversity Institute.

Cukier, Wendy, Margaret Yap, John Miller, and Pinoo Bindhani. 2010. *DiverseCity Counts 2: A Snapshot of Diverse Leadership in the GTA.* Toronto: Diversity Institute.

Curry, Bill. 2002. "Ottawa Eyes Quick End to Gay Debate: Liberals to Consult with Public on Marriage Laws amid Ferment of Competing Solutions." *National Post,* August 8, A1.

Cutler, Fred. 2002. "The Simplest Shortcut of All: Sociodemographic Characteristics and Electoral Choice." *Journal of Politics* 64 (2): 466–90. http://dx.doi.org/10.1111/1468-2508.00135.

Davies, Nick. 2009. *Flat Earth News*. New York: Vintage.

Davis, Howard H. 1985. "Discourse and Media Influence." In *Discourse and Communication: New Approaches to the Analysis of Mass Media Discourse and Communication*, ed. Teun A. Van Dijk, 44–59. Boston: Walter de Gruyter. http://dx.doi.org/10.1515/9783110852141.44.

Dawson, Anne. 2003. "'I Sincerely Apologize.'" *National Post*, April 8, A11.

–. 2005. "Off to the Races: Non-confidence Motion Passes, Negative Campaigning Begins." *National Post*, November 29, A1.

Delacourt, Susan. 2009a. "Dhalla Seeks Federal Ethics Investigation." *Toronto Star*, May 7, A1.

–. 2009b. "End of Dhalla's Political Career? Controversies Taken Together Have Become a Narrative That Could Be Difficult to Shake." *Toronto Star*, May 9, A19.

Delacourt, Susan, and Dale Brazao. 2009. "Nanny Trouble." *Toronto Star*, May 6, A1.

Delacourt, Susan, and Edward Greenspon. 1993. "Liberal Cabinet to Have Lean Look; Chrétien Will Also Appoint 'Outer Circle' of Junior Ministers." *Globe and Mail*, November 4, A1.

Dhamoon, Rita. 2009. *Identity/Difference Politics*. Vancouver: UBC Press.

Diebel, Linda. 2008. "In Ottawa, a Week of Heavy Jockeying." *Toronto Star*, August 30, A1.

–. 2011a. "Jason Kenney: The Man Who Would Be Kingmaker." *Toronto Star*, February 18.

–. 2011b. "Olivia Chow for NDP Leader?" *Toronto Star*, August 29, A1.

Ditchburn, Jennifer. 2006. "Conservatives Aiming for Breakthrough with Ethnic Voters." *Canadian Press Newswire*, August 9.

Dolan, Kathleen. 1998. "Voting for Women in the Year of the Woman." *American Journal of Political Science* 42 (1): 272–93. http://dx.doi.org/10.2307/2991756.

–. 2005. "Do Women Candidates Play to Gender Stereotypes? Do Men Candidates Play to Women? Candidate Sex and Issue Priorities on Campaign Websites." *Political Research Quarterly* 58 (1): 31–44. http://dx.doi.org/10.1177/106591290505800103.

Domise, Andray. 2015a. "A Belief We Refuse to Name." *Torontoist*, March 11. http://torontoist.com/2015/03/a-belief-we-refuse-to-name/ (accessed May 24, 2015).

–. 2015b. "Dear White Editors: Invite Someone Out for a Coffee." *Canadaland*, March 12. http://canadalandshow.com/article/dear-white-editors-invite-someone-out-coffee (accessed May 24, 2015).

Donohue, George A., Clarice N. Olien, and Phillip J. Tichenor. 1989. "Structure and Constraints on Community Newspaper Gatekeepers." *Journalism Quarterly* 66 (4): 807–45. http://dx.doi.org/10.1177/107769908906600405.

Donohue, George A., Phillip J. Tichenor, and Clarice N. Olien. 1972. "Gatekeeping: Mass Media Systems and Information Control." In *Current Perspectives in Mass Communication Research*, ed. F.G. Kline and P. Tichenor, 41–70. Beverly Hills, CA: Sage.

Donsbach, Wolfgang and Bettina Klett. 1993. "Subjective Objectivity: How Journalists in Four Countries Define a Key Term of their Profession." *The Gazette* 51 (1): 53-83.

Doyle, John. 2009. "On Camera, Everyone Can See You Squirm." *Globe and Mail,* May 13, R3.

Drew, Emily M. 2011. "'Coming to Terms with Our Own Racism': Journalists Grapple with the Racialization of Their News." *Critical Studies in Media Communication* 28 (4): 353–73. http://dx.doi.org/10.1080/15295036.2010.514936.

Dyer, Richard. 1988. "White." *Screen* 29 (4): 44–65. http://dx.doi.org/10.1093/screen/29.4.44.

Eagles, Munroe. 1993. "Money and Votes in Canada: Campaign Spending and Parliamentary Election Outcomes, 1984 and 1988." *Canadian Public Policy* 19 (4): 432–49. http://dx.doi.org/10.2307/3551388.

–. 2004. "The Effectiveness of Local Campaign Spending in the 1993 and 1997 Federal Elections in Canada." *Canadian Journal of Political Science* 37 (1): 117–36. http://dx.doi.org/10.1017/S0008423904040065.

Eagly, Alice H., and Antonio Mladinic. 1989. "Gender Stereotypes and Attitudes toward Women and Men." *Personality and Social Psychology Bulletin* 15 (4): 543–58. http://dx.doi.org/10.1177/0146167289154008.

Elshtain, Jean Bethke. 1993. *Public Man, Private Woman: Women in Social and Political Thought.* 2nd ed. Princeton, NJ: Princeton University Press.

English, Kathy. 2013. "Star Overdid 'Somali' References in Ford Story." *Toronto Star,* May 25, IN6.

–. 2014. "Diversity is Right Course." *Toronto Star.* June 21. IN6.

Entman, Robert. 1993. "Framing: Toward a Clarification of a Fractured Paradigm." *Journal of Communication* 43 (4): 51–58. http://dx.doi.org/10.1111/j.1460-2466.1993.tb01304.x.

–. 2004. *Projections of Power: Framing News, Public Opinion, and US Foreign Policy.* Chicago: University of Chicago Press.

Entman, Robert, and Andrew Rojecki. 2000. *The Black Image in the White Mind: Media and Race in America.* Chicago: University of Chicago Press.

Ericson, Richard, Patricia Baranak, and Janet Chan. 1987. *Visualizing Deviance: A Study of News Organization.* Toronto: University of Toronto Press.

Equal Voice. 2015. *The Essential Guide to Being Elected: Increasing Women's Representation.* Ottawa: Carleton University.

Fairclough, Norman. 2003. *Analysing Discourse: Textual Analysis for Social Research.* New York: Routledge.

Farhi, Paul. 2012. "Women Aren't Principal News Sources on Women's Issues, 4th Estate Analysis Reveals." *Washington Post,* June 25, http://articles.washingtonpost.com/2012-06-25/lifestyle/35461338_1_4th-estate-women-sources (accessed 16 December 2012).

Farnsworth, Stephen J., Blake Andrew, Stuart Soroka, and Antonia Maioni. 2007. "The Media: All Horse Race, All the Time." *Policy Options* 28 (4): 62–68.

Fekete, Jason. 2011. "Auditor-General Rips into Harper's Summit Spending; Ministerial Abuse over Project Funds Lambasted as Well." *Calgary Herald,* October 6, A17.

Ferenc, Leslie. 2008. "Mississauga East-Cooksville (2006 Liberal Albina Guarnieri Won by 9,204 Votes)." *Toronto Star,* October 9, M7.

Fiske, Susan T. 1998. "Stereotyping, Prejudice, and Discrimination." In *The Handbook of Social Psychology*, ed. Daniel T. Gilbert, Susan T. Fiske, and Gardner Lindzey, 357–414. New York: McGraw-Hill.

Fiske, Susan T., and Shelley E. Taylor. 1991. *Social Cognition*. 2nd ed. New York: McGraw-Hill.

Flanagan, Tom. 2011. "The Emerging Conservative Coalition." *Policy Options* 32 (6): 104–8.

Fleiss, Joseph L. 1981. *Statistical Methods for Rates and Proportions*. New York: Wiley.

Fleras, Augie. 2011. *The Media Gaze: Representations of Diversities in Canada*. Vancouver: UBC Press.

–. 2012. *Unequal Relations: An Introduction to Race, Ethnic and Aboriginal Dynamics in Canada*. Don Mills, ON: Pearson.

–. 2014. *Racisms in a Multicultural Canada: Paradoxes, Politics, and Resistance*. Waterloo, ON: Wilfrid Laurier University Press.

Fleras, Augie, and Jean Kunz. 2001. *Media and Minorities: Diversity in Multicultural Canada*. Toronto: Thomson.

Folarin, Babtunde. 2002. *Theories of Mass Communication: An Introductory Text*. Abeokuta, Nigeria: Link Publications.

Foot, Richard, Sheldon Alberts, and Stewart Bell. 2001. "BC Mayors Want Fry to Fully Recant: Complaints of Racism Rare in Canada, Figures Show." *National Post*, March 27, A4.

Fountaine, Susan, and Judy McGregor. 2002. "Reconstructing Gender for the 21st Century: News Media Framing of Political Women in New Zealand." Paper presented at the Annual Conference of the Australian New Zealand Communication Association, Brisbane, July 10-12. http://webenrol.massey.ac.nz/massey/fms/Colleges/College%20of%20Business/NZCWL/pdfs/JMcGregorSFountainePaper.pdf (accessed July 20, 2012).

Fowler, Linda L., and Jennifer L. Lawless. 2009. "Looking for Sex in all the Wrong Places: Press Coverage and the Electoral Fortunes of Gubernatorial Candidates." *Perspectives on Politics* 7 (3): 519-36.

Fox, Richard L., and Jennifer L. Lawless. 2004. "Entering the Arena? Gender and the Decision to Run for Office." *American Journal of Political Science* 48 (2): 264–80. http://dx.doi.org/10.1111/j.0092-5853.2004.00069.x.

Frederick, Angela. 2013. "Bringing Narrative In: Race-Gender Storytelling, Political Ambition, and Women's Paths to Public Office." *Journal of Women, Politics and Policy* 34 (2): 113–37. http://dx.doi.org/10.1080/1554477X.2013.776379.

Frederick, Kristofer A., and Judson L. Jeffries. 2009. "A Study in African American Candidates for High-Profile Statewide Office." *Journal of Black Studies* 39 (5): 689–718. http://dx.doi.org/10.1177/0021934707299641.

Friesen, Joe. 2014. "City's First Native Mayor Seen As Bridge Builder." *Globe and Mail*, November 8, A4.

Gans, Herbert J. 1979. *Deciding What's News: A Study of CBS Evening News, NBC Nightly News, Newsweek and Time*. Evanston, IL: Northwestern University Press.

Gardner, Dan. 2007. "Veil Controversy Cuts to the Heart of Social Debate." *Victoria Times-Colonist*, September 13, A14.

Gay, Claudine, and Katherine Tate. 1998. "Doubly Bound: The Impact of Gender and Race on the Politics of Black Women." *Political Psychology* 19 (1): 169–84. http://dx.doi.org/10.1111/0162-895X.00098.

Gemi, Eda, Iryna Ulasiuk, and Anna Triandafyllidou. 2013. "Migrants and Media Newsmaking Practices." *Journalism Practice* 7 (3): 266–81. http://dx.doi.org/10.1080/17512786.2012.740248.

Gerein, Keith. 2012. "Smith Defends Besieged Candidate." *Calgary Herald*. April 21, A5.

Gershon, Sarah Allen. 2009. "Gendered Appeals Online: A Study of Female Candidates' Websites." Paper presented at the Annual Meeting of the American Political Science Association, Toronto, September 3–6.

–. 2012. "Media Coverage of Minority Congresswomen and Voter Evaluations: Evidence from an Online Experimental Study." *Political Research Quarterly* 20 (10): 1–13.

Gerson, Jen. 2014. "The Lady Wore Red." *National Post*, May 30, A5.

Gidengil, Elisabeth, André Blais, Neil Nevitte, and Richard Nadeau. 2004. *Citizens*. Vancouver: UBC Press.

Gidengil, Elisabeth, and Joanna Everitt. 1999. "Metaphors and Misrepresentation: Gendered Mediation in News Coverage of the 1993 Canadian Leaders' Debates." *Press/Politics* 4 (1): 48–65.

–. 2000. "Filtering the Female: Gender Mediation in Television Coverage of the 1993 Leaders' Debates." *Women and Politics* 21 (4): 105–31. http://dx.doi.org/10.1300/J014v21n04_04.

–. 2003a. "Conventional Coverage/Unconventional Politics: Gender and Media Coverage of Canadian Leaders' Debates, 1993, 1997, 2000." *Canadian Journal of Political Science* 36 (3): 559–77. http://dx.doi.org/10.1017/S0008423903778767.

–. 2003b. "Tough Talk: How Television News Covers Male and Female Leaders of Canadian Political Parties." In *Women and Electoral Politics in Canada*, ed. Manon Tremblay and Linda Trimble, 194–210. Toronto: Oxford University Press.

Gidengil, Elisabeth, Neil Nevitte, André Blais, Joanna Everitt, and Patrick Fournier. 2012. *Dominance and Decline: Making Sense of Recent Canadian Elections*. Toronto: University of Toronto Press.

Gieber, Walter. 1956. "Across the Desk: A Study of 16 Telegraph Editors." *Journalism Quarterly* 33 (4): 423–32. http://dx.doi.org/10.1177/107769905603300401.

Gilens, Martin. 1996. "Race and Poverty in America: Public Misperceptions and the American News Media." *Public Opinion Quarterly* 60 (4): 515–41. http://dx.doi.org/10.1086/297771.

–. 2003. "How the Poor Became Black: The Racialization of American Poverty in the Mass Media." In *Race and the Politics of Welfare Reform*, ed. Sanford F. Schram, Joe Soss, and Richard C. Fording, 101–30. Ann Arbor: University of Michigan Press.

Gilmartin, Patricia. 2001. "Still the Angel in the Household: Political Cartoons of Elizabeth Dole's Presidential Campaign." *Women and Politics* 22 (4): 51–67. http://dx.doi.org/10.1300/J014v22n04_03.

Gilmore, Scott. 2015. "Canada's Race Problem? It's Even Worse Than America's." *Maclean's*, January 15. http://www.macleans.ca/news/canada/out-of-sight-out-of-mind-2/ (accessed June 20, 2015).

Gilovich, Thomas, Dale Griffin, and Daniel Kahneman, eds. 2002. *Heuristics and Biases: The Psychology of Intuitive Judgment.* New York: Cambridge University Press. http://dx.doi.org/10.1017/CBO9780511808098.

Gingras, François-Pierre. 1995. "Daily Male Delivery: Women and Politics in the Daily Newspapers." In *Gender and Politics in Contemporary Canada,* ed. François-Pierre Gingras, 191–207. Toronto: Oxford University Press.

Gitlin, Todd. 1980. *The Whole World Is Watching: Mass Media in the Making and Unmaking of the New Left.* Berkeley: University of California Press.

Globe and Mail. 2005. "Arranging for Ignatieff." November 29, A20.

–. 2013. "Editorial Code of Conduct." http://www.theglobeandmail.com (accessed July 8, 2014).

Goar, Carol. 2002. "Nice Pictures, Message Needs Work." *Toronto Star,* August 6, A22.

Goffman, Erving. 1959. *The Presentation of Self in Everyday Life.* New York: Anchor.

Golebiowska, Ewa A. 2001. "Group Stereotypes and Political Evaluation." *American Politics Research* 29 (6): 535–65. http://dx.doi.org/10.1177/1532673X01029006001.

Goodyear-Grant, Elizabeth. 2007. "Politicians, Journalists and Their Audiences: Gendered Aspects of Televised Election News in Canada." PhD diss., McGill University.

–. 2009. "Crafting a Public Image: Women MPs and the Dynamics of Media Coverage." In *Opening Doors Wider,* ed. Sylvia Bashevkin, 147–66. Vancouver: UBC Press.

–. 2013. *Gendered News: Media Coverage and Electoral Politics in Canada.* Vancouver: UBC Press.

Gorrie, Peter. 2006. "Cracks in Liberal Bedrock; Immigrant Vote No Longer a Sure Thing." *Toronto Star,* January 19, A1.

Greenspon, Edward. 1995. "Robillard Expected to Get Seat in Cabinet; Shuffle Is Part of Referendum Fight." *Globe and Mail,* February 18, A1.

Grewal, San. 2011. "A Shift among Sikhs from Red to Blue." *Toronto Star,* April 8, GT2.

Gunter, Lorne. 2009. "Sensation over Substance." *National Post,* May 13, A18.

Hackett, Robert A. 2001. "The News Media and Civic Equality: Watch Dogs, Mad Dogs, or Lap Dogs?" In *Democratic Equality: What Went Wrong?* ed. Ed Broadbent, 197–212. Toronto: University of Toronto Press.

Hackett, Robert A., and Yuezhi Zhao. 1998. *Sustaining Democracy? Journalism and the Politics of Objectivity.* Toronto: Garamond.

Hall, Stuart. 1990. "The Whites of Their Eyes: Racist Ideologies and the Media." In *The Media Reader,* ed. Manual Alvarado and John O. Thompson, 9–23. London: British Film Institute.

Hancock, Ange-Marie. 2007. "When Multiplication Doesn't Equal Quick Addition: Examining Intersectionality As a Research Paradigm." *Perspectives on Politics* 5 (1): 63–79. http://dx.doi.org/10.1017/S1537592707070065.

Haque, Eva. 2012. *Multiculturalism in a Bilingual Framework: Language, Race, and Belonging in Canada.* Toronto: University of Toronto Press.

Harding, Katherine. 2004. "Party Infighting Plagues Riding." *Globe and Mail,* June 8, A6.

Harell, Allison. 2013. "Revisiting the 'Ethnic' Vote: Liberal Allegiance and Vote Choice among Racialized Minorities." In *Parties, Elections and the Future of Canadian Politics,* ed. Amanda Bittner and Royce Koop, 140–60. Vancouver: UBC Press.

Haynie, Kerry. 2002. "The Color of Their Skin or the Content of Their Behavior? Race and Perceptions of African American Legislators." *Legislative Studies Quarterly* 27 (2): 295–314. http://dx.doi.org/10.3162/036298002X200602.

Heaven, Pamela. 2009. "Richest Canadians on Forbes." *Financial Post,* March 12.

Heldman, Caroline, Susan J. Carroll, and Stephanie Olson. 2005. "'She Brought Only a Skirt': Print Media Coverage of Elizabeth Dole's Bid for the Republican Presidential Nomination." *Political Communication* 22 (3): 315–35. http://dx.doi.org/10.1080/10584600591006564.

Heldman, Caroline, Sarah Oliver, and Meredith Conroy. 2009. "From Ferraro to Palin: Sexism in Media Coverage of Vice-Presidential Candidates." Paper presented at the Annual Meeting of the American Political Science Association, Toronto, September 4. http://dx.doi.org/10.2139/ssrn.1459865.

Henry, Frances, and Carol Tator. 2002. *Discourses of Domination: Racial Bias in the Canadian English-Language Press.* Toronto: University of Toronto Press.

–. 2012. "Interviews with Racialized Faculty Members in Canadian Universities." *Canadian Ethnic Studies* 44 (2): 75–99. http://muse.jhu.edu/login?auth=0&type=summary&url=/journals/canadian_ethnic_studies/v044/44.1.henry01.html.

Henton, Darcy. 2008. "Uppal Hopes Third Time Lucky; Sherwood Park Candidate No Quitter." *Edmonton Journal,* October 8, A4.

Hicks, Bruce M. 2009. "Do Large-N Media Studies Bury the Lead, or Even Miss the Story?" *Canadian Political Science Review* 3 (2): 89–104.

Hier, Sean P. 2009. "Beyond Vernacular Commentary: A Response to Minelle Mahtani." *Canadian Journal of Communication* 35 (1): 173–78.

Hier, Sean P., and Daniel Lett. 2013. "Racism, Media, and Analytical Balance." In *Communication in Question: Competing Perspectives on Controversial Issues in Communication Studies,* ed. Joshua Greenberg and Charlene Elliot, 123–30. Toronto: Nelson.

Hogg, Robert V., and Elliot Tanis. 2009. *Probability and Statistical Inference.* 8th ed. Toronto: Pearson.

Holland, Mark. 2007. "Why Are My Two Best Friends Bains and Alghabra Hyphenated MPs?" *Hill Times,* March 5, A15.

Huddy, Leonie, and Nayda Terkildsen. 1993. "The Consequences of Gender Stereotypes for Women Candidates at Different Levels and Types of Office." *Political Research Quarterly* 46 (3): 503–25. http://dx.doi.org/10.1177/106591299304600304.

Hunter, Justine. 2001. "Fry's Tactic: Shoot First, Ask Questions Later." *National Post,* March 26, A6.

Hutchinson, Brian. 2004. "Chuck Cadman, a.k.a. Other, Sitting Pretty." *National Post,* June 30, A1.

–. 2006. "Hedy Fry Draws a Curious Crowd." *National Post,* May 5, A1.

–. 2010. "Making Canada a Little Less Alluring." *National Post,* October 22, A1.

Ibbitson, John. 2010. "In Ottawa, the Hardest Questions ... " *Globe and Mail,* May 26, A4.

Ibbitson, John, and Joe Friesen. 2010. "The Growing Ties of Immigrants and Conservatives." *Globe and Mail,* October 4, A1.

Iserhienrhien, Abigail Iguosatiele. 2014. "Gender, Race and the Media Representation of Women in the Canadian 41st Parliament: A Critical Discourse Analysis." Master's thesis, Department of Sociology, University of Saskatchewan.

Ivison, John. 2012. "Oda's Legacy Stuck in Limo: Lavish Expenses Obscure Success As Minister." *National Post*, July 4, A1.

–. 2015. "Racist Bozo Eruption Hits Tories." *National Post*, March 10, A5.

Iyengar, Shanto. 1991. *Is Anyone Responsible? How Television Frames Political Issues.* Chicago: University of Chicago Press. http://dx.doi.org/10.7208/chicago/97802263 88533.001.0001.

–. 1996. "Framing Responsibility for Political Issues." *Annals of the American Academy of Political and Social Science* 546 (1): 59–70. http://dx.doi.org/10.1177/000271629654 6001006.

Iyengar, Shanto, and David Kinder. 1987. *News That Matters: Television and American Opinion.* Chicago: University of Chicago Press.

Jacobson, Gary. 1990. "The Effects of Campaign Spending in House Elections: New Evidence for Old Arguments." *American Journal of Political Science* 34 (2): 334–62. http://dx.doi.org/10.2307/2111450.

Jalalzai, Farida. 2006. "Women Candidates and the Media: 1992–2000 Elections." *Politics and Policy* 34 (3): 606–33. http://dx.doi.org/10.1111/j.1747-1346.2006.00030.x.

Jamieson, Kathleen Hall. 1992. *Dirty Politics: Deception, Distraction, and Democracy.* New York: Oxford University Press.

Jedwab, Jack. 2006. "The 'Roots' of Immigrant and Ethnic Voter Participation in Canada." *Electoral Insight* 8 (2): 3–9.

Jeffries, Judson. 2002. "Press Coverage of Black Statewide Candidates: The Case of L. Douglas Wilder of Virginia." *Journal of Black Studies* 32 (6): 673–97. http://dx.doi.org/10.1177/00234702032006003.

Jenkins, Cathy. 2007. "The More Things Change: Women, Politics and the Press in Australia." Working paper. http://ejournalist.com.au/v2n1/cathy.pdf (accessed July 20, 2012).

Jimenez, Marina. 2008. "Immigrants' Loyalty to Liberal Waning." *Globe and Mail*, September 17, A11.

Jiwani, Yasmin. 2006. *Discourses of Denial: Mediations of Race, Gender and Violence.* Vancouver: UBC Press.

Johnson-Cartee, Karen S. 2005. *News Narratives and News Framing: Constructing Political Reality.* Toronto: Rowman and Littlefield.

Johnston, Richard, André Blais, Henry Brady, and Jean Crête. 1992. *Letting the People Decide.* Montreal: McGill-Queen's University Press.

Johnston, Ronald J., and Charles J. Pattie. 1995. "The Image of Spending on Party Constituency Campaigns at British General Elections." *Party Politics* 1 (2): 261–73. http://dx.doi.org/10.1177/1354068895001002005.

Jones, Vernon Clement. 2002. "Cabinet Posting a Benchmark." *Globe and Mail*, June 7, A23.

Kahn, Kim Fridkin. 1992. "Does Being Male Help? An Investigation of the Effects of Candidate Gender and Campaign Coverage on Evaluations of US Senate Candidates." *Journal of Politics* 54 (2): 497–517. http://dx.doi.org/10.2307/2132036.

–. 1994. "Does Gender Make a Difference? An Experimental Examination of Sex Stereotypes and Press Patterns in Statewide Campaigns." *American Journal of Political Science* 38 (1): 162–95. http://dx.doi.org/10.2307/2111340.

Kay, Jonathan. 2007. "National Security vs. Liberal Ethno-politics." *National Post*, February 27, A20.

Kendall, Chad, and Marie Rekkas. 2012. "Incumbency Advantages in the Canadian Parliament." *Canadian Journal of Economics* 45 (4): 1560–85. http://dx.doi.org/10.1111/j.1540-5982.2012.01739.x.

Keung, Nicholas. 2008. "Markham-Unionville (2006 Liberal John McCallum won by 18,616 votes)." *Toronto Star*, October 9, M7.

Khoo, Lisa. 2007. Mixed blessings. Documentary produced for CBC's *The Current*. http://www.cbc.ca/news/background/mixedblessings (accessed January 2, 2012).

Klapper, Joseph. 1960. *The Effects of Mass Communication*. New York: Free Press.

Klaszus, Jeremy. 2008. "Tory Candidate Links Immigrants with Crime, Expresses Regret." *Fast Forward Weekly*, September 25. http://www.ffwdweekly.com/article/news-views/news/tory-under-fire-for-disgraceful-comments-on-immigr/ (accessed September 18, 2012).

Koch, Jeffrey W. 2000. "Do Citizens Apply Gender Stereotypes to Infer Candidates' Ideological Orientations?" *Journal of Politics* 62 (2): 414–29. http://dx.doi.org/10.1111/0022-3816.00019.

Koop, Royce, and Alex Marland. 2012. "Insiders and Outsiders: Presentation of Self on Canadian Parliamentary Websites and Newsletters." *Policy and Internet* 4 (3–4): 112–35. http://dx.doi.org/10.1002/poi3.13.

Krashinsky, Michael, and William J. Milne. 1986. "The Effect of Incumbency on the 1984 Federal and 1985 Ontario Elections." *Canadian Journal of Political Science* 19 (2): 337–43. http://dx.doi.org/10.1017/S0008423900054056.

Krippendorff, Klaus. 2004. *Content Analysis: An Introduction to Its Methodology*. 2nd ed. Thousand Oaks, CA: Sage.

Kvale, Steinar, and Svend Brinkmann. 2009. *InterViews: Learning the Craft of Qualitative Research Interviews*. 2nd ed. Thousand Oaks, CA: Sage.

Kymlicka, Will. "Canadian Pluralism in Comparative Perspective." Pluralism Papers. Ottawa: Global Centre for Pluralism, 2012. http://www.pluralism.ca/images/PDF_docs/pluralism_papers/kymlicka_paper_pp13.pdf.

Lalancette, Mireille, and Catherine Lemarier-Saulnier. 2011. "She's a Bitch, He's a Star: Framing Gender during Leadership Races and Its Outcome on Political Representations in the Media." Paper presented at 61st Annual Conference of the Political Studies Association, London, April 19–21.

Landis, J. Richard, and Gary G. Koch. 1977. "The Measurement of Observer Agreement for Categorical Data." *Biometrics* 33 (1): 159–74. http://dx.doi.org/10.2307/2529310.

Lange, Astrid. 2008. "Media Ownership in Canada." *Toronto Star*, January 16, B5.

Lapp, Miriam. 1999. "Ethnic Group Leaders and the Mobilization of Voter Turnout: Evidence from Five Montreal Communities." *Canadian Ethnic Studies* 31 (2): 17–42.

Lasswell, Harold. 1930. *Psychopathology and Politics*. Chicago: University of Chicago Press.

Lau, Richard R., and David P. Redlawsk. 2001. "Advantages and Disadvantages of Cognitive Heuristics and Political Decision-Making." *American Journal of Political Science* 45 (4): 951–71. http://dx.doi.org/10.2307/2669334.

Leblanc, Daniel. 2007. "Tories Target Specific Ethnic Voters." *Globe and Mail*, October 16, A1.

Lemarier-Saulnier, Catherine, and Thierry Giasson. 2015. "The Iron Lady and the Alpha Male: A Case Study of Gender's Framing During Quebec's Election." Paper presented at the 4th European Conference on Politics and Gender, Uppsala University, Uppsala, Sweden, June 11–13.

Leong, Melissa. 2002. "'Everybody Looks Good' at This Parade." *Toronto Star*, August 4, A1.

Lindgren, April. 2013. "The Diverse City: Can You Read All about It in Ethnic Newspapers?" CERIS Working Paper 95. Toronto: CERIS–Ontario Metropolis Centre.

–. 2014. "Toronto-Area Ethnic Newspapers and Canada's 2011 Federal Election: An Investigation of Content, Focus, and Partisanship." *Canadian Journal of Political Science* 47 (4): 667-96.

Lippmann, Walter. 1922. *Public Opinion*. New York: Harcourt Brace.

Lorde, Audre. 1984. "Age, Race, Class, and Sex: Women Redefining Difference." In *Sister Outsider: Essays and Speeches*, 114–23. Berkeley: Crossing Press.

Lu, Vanessa. 2006. "Toronto Backs Liberals Again." *Toronto Star*, January 24, B1.

Lundell, Åsa Kroon, and Mats Ekström. 2008. "The Complex Visual Gendering of Political Women in the Press." *Journalism Studies* 9 (6): 891–910. http://dx.doi.org/10.1080/14616700802227845.

Lupul, Manoly R. 1983. "Multiculturalism and Canada's White Ethnics." *Canadian Ethnic Studies* 15 (1): 99–107.

MacCharles, Tonda. 2003. "Alliance Motion on Marriage a Trap: PM; Warns of Threat to the Equality Rights of Gays, Lesbians." *Toronto Star*, September 16, A8.

–. 2005. "Familiar Faces Are a Sure Bet for Tory Cabinet." *Toronto Star*, April 11, A8.

–. 2008. "Travelling Tory Woos Ethnic Voters." *Toronto Star*, February 23, A15.

MacDonald, L. Ian. 2011. "The Happy Warrior Tries to Raise a Conservative Tide in Ontario." *Montreal Gazette*, April 13, A23.

Maher, Stephen. 2013. "Busy Flaherty Deserves Some Slack; Weight Gain, Odd Interview Prompted Minister to Explain Health Problem." *Ottawa Citizen*, February 2, A8.

Mahtani, Minelle. 2014. *Mixed Race Amnesia: Resisting the Romanticization of Multiraciality*. Vancouver: UBC Press.

Major, Lesa Hatley, and Renita Coleman. 2008. "The Intersection of Race and Gender in Election Coverage: What Happens When Candidates Don't Fit the Stereotypes?" *Howard Journal of Communications* 19 (4): 315–33. http://dx.doi.org/10.1080/10646170802391722.

Makin, Kirk. 1993. "Election '93, the Day after: 54 Women Will Be Going to Parliament." *Globe and Mail*, October 27, A17.

Malenfant, Éric Caron, André Lebel, and Laurent Martel. 2010. "Projections of the Diversity of the Canadian Population: 2006 to 2031." Catalogue 91-551-X. Ottawa: Statistics Canada. http://www.statcan.gc.ca/pub/91-551-x/91-551-x2010001-eng.pdf (accessed August 2, 2015).

Mallick, Heather. 2001. "It's Been the Week of the Liar: Plus Ça Change." *Globe and Mail*, March 31, F8.

Markusoff, Jason. 2008. "'Conservative' Rivals Go Head-to-Head in City's N.E.; Ethnic Politicking Takes Centre Stage at Campaign Kickoffs." *Calgary Herald,* September 22, A6.

Marland, Alex, Thierry Giasson, and Jennifer Lees-Marshment, eds. 2012. *Political Marketing in Canada.* Vancouver: UBC Press.

Martin, Don. 2001. "How Terrorism Gave Ottawa Its Mojo Back." *National Post,* November 26, A1.

–. 2008b. "Is Grit Fortress Toronto about to Fall?" *Calgary Herald,* September 26, A5.

–. 2009. "Shabby Treatment: The Ruby Dhalla Pile-on Appears to Be an Ugly Combination of Sexism, Prejudice and Pettiness." *National Post,* October 9, A16.

Martin, Sandra. 2011. "Jack Layton's Legacy Won't End Here." *Globe and Mail,* August 23, A8.

–. 2014. "In the Driver's Seat." *Globe and Mail,* March 29, M1.

Marwah, Inder, Triadafilos Triadafilopoulos, and Stephen White. 2013. "Immigration, Citizenship and Canada's New Conservative Party." In *Conservatism in Canada,* ed. James Farney and David Rayside, 95–119. Toronto: University of Toronto Press.

Matthes, Jorg. 2009. "What's in a Frame? A Content Analysis of Media Framing Studies in the World's Leading Communication Journals, 1990–2005." *Journalism and Mass Communication Quarterly* 86 (2): 349–67. http://dx.doi.org/10.1177/10776990090 8600206.

McCarten, James, ed. 2013. *The Canadian Press Stylebook: A Guide for Writers and Editors.* 17th ed. Toronto: Canadian Press.

McCombs, Maxwell, Esteban Lopez-Escobar, and Juan Pablo Llamas. 2000. "Setting the Agenda of Attributes in the 1996 Spanish General Election." *Journal of Communication* 50 (2): 77–92. http://dx.doi.org/10.1111/j.1460-2466.2000.tb02842.x.

McCombs, Maxwell E., and Donald L. Shaw. 1972. "The Agenda-Setting Function of Mass Media." *Public Opinion Quarterly* 36 (2): 176–87. http://dx.doi.org/10.1086/267990.

McDermott, Monika L. 1997. "Voting Cues in Low-Information Elections: Candidate Gender as a Social Information Variable in Contemporary United States Elections." *American Journal of Political Science* 41 (1): 270–83.

–. 1998. "Race and Gender Cues in Low-Information Elections." *Political Research Quarterly* 51 (4): 895–918. http://dx.doi.org/10.1177/106591299805100403.

–. 2005. "Candidate Occupations and Voter Information Shortcuts." *Journal of Politics* 67 (1): 201–19. http://dx.doi.org/10.1111/j.1468-2508.2005.00314.x.

–. 2009. "Religious Stereotypes and Voter Support for Evangelical Candidates." *Political Research Quarterly* 62 (2): 340–54. http://dx.doi.org/10.1177/1065912908320668.

McIlwain, Charlton D., and Stephen M. Caliendo. 2011. *Race Appeal: How Candidates Invoke Race in US Political Campaigns.* Philadelphia: Temple University Press.

McQuail, Denis. 1994. *Mass Communication: An Introduction.* 3rd ed. Thousand Oaks, CA: Sage.

–. 2010. *McQuail's Mass Communication Theory.* Thousand Oaks, CA: Sage.

MediaSmarts. 2012a. "Diversity and Canadian Broadcasting Policy." http://mediasmarts.ca/diversity-media/visible-minorities/diversity-and-canadian-broadcasting-policy (accessed July 22, 2012).

–. 2012b. "Visible Minorities in Newsrooms." http://mediasmarts.ca/diversity-media/visible-minorities/visible-minorities-newsroom (accessed July 22, 2012).

Megyery, Kathy, ed. 1991a. *Ethno-Cultural Groups and Visible Minorities in Canadian Politics: The Question of Access*. Vol. 7 of the Research Studies of the Royal Commission on Electoral Reform and Party Financing. Toronto: Dundurn.

–, ed. 1991b. *Women in Canadian Politics: Toward Equity in Representation*. Vol. 6 of the Research Studies of the Royal Commission on Electoral Reform and Party Financing. Toronto: Dundurn.

Mendelberg, Tali. 2001. *The Race Card: Campaign Strategy, Implicit Messages, and the Norm of Equality*. Princeton, NJ: Princeton University Press.

Mercer, Katie. 2008. "Conservative Rival 'Supports Anti-gay Group,' Grit Claims; Raymond Chan Says Alice Wong Is Fan of an 'Extreme Group.'" *Vancouver Province*, October 1, A8.

Metz, Jessie-Lane. 2013. "Ally-Phobia: On the Trayvon Martin Ruling, White Feminism, and the Worst of Best Intentions." In *The Toast* http://the-toast.net/2013/07/24/ally-phobia-the-worst-of-best-intentions/ (accessed July 24, 2014).

Mickleburgh, Rod. 2006. "Long Shot Runs on Larger-Than-Life Ebullience." *Globe and Mail*, August 28, A7.

Miljan, Lydia, and Barry Cooper. 2003. *Hidden Agendas: How Journalists Influence the News*. Vancouver: UBC Press.

Miller, John. 2006. "Who's Telling the News? Racial Representation among News Gatherers in Canada's Daily Newsrooms." *International Journal of Diversity in Organisations, Communities and Nations* 5: 1–10.

Miller, John, and Caron Court. 2004. *Who's Telling the News? Race and Gender Representation in Canada's Daily Newsrooms*. Toronto: DiversityWatch, Ryerson University School of Journalism.

Mills, Charles. 1997. *The Racial Contract*. Ithaca: Cornell University Press.

Mills, Kate. 1997. "What Difference Do Women Journalists Make?" In *Women, Media and Politics*, ed. Pippa Norris, 41–55. New York: Oxford University Press.

Milstein, Sarah. 2013. "5 Ways White Feminists Can Address Our Own Racism." *Huffington Post*. http://www.huffingtonpost.com/sarah-milstein/5-ways-white-feminists-can-address-our-own-racism_b_3955065.html (accessed July 24, 2014).

Moloney, Paul. 2008. "Scarborough Centre (2006 Liberal John Cannis Won by 11,810 Votes)." *Toronto Star*, October 9, M11.

Murray, Maureen. 1999. "Success Follows Hardship but Mother Paid the Price." *Toronto Star*, December 26, A1.

Nasrallah, Maha, David Carmel, and Nilli Lavie. 2009. "Murder, She Wrote: Enhanced Sensitivity to Negative Word Valence." *Emotion* (American Psychological Association) 9 (5): 609–18. http://dx.doi.org/10.1037/a0016305.

Nath, Nisha. 2011. "Defining Narratives of Identity in Canadian Political Science: Accounting for the Absence of Race." *Canadian Journal of Political Science* 44 (1): 161–93. http://dx.doi.org/10.1017/S0008423910001071.

National Advisory Commission on Civil Disorders. 1968. *Report of the National Advisory Commission on Civil Disorders (Kerner Commission)*. New York: Bantam Books.

National Post. 2001. "Come Together Right, Now." April 11, A19.

–. 2004. "Sikh Actor Is a Model Liberal Candidate Who Offers Health Care Expertise, Too." June 4, A8.

–. 2007. "Liberal Faux-Feminism." February 20, A20.

–. 2009. "Hedy's latest." *National Post*. November 2, A14.

Nelson, Thomas E., Zoe M. Oxley, and Rosalee A. Clawson. 1997. "Toward a Psychology of Framing Effects." *Political Behavior* 19 (3): 221–46. http://dx.doi.org/10.1023/A:1024834831093.

Neuendorf, Kimberly A. 2002. *The Content Analysis Guidebook*. Thousand Oaks, CA: Sage.

Neuman, W. Russell, and Lauren Guggenheim. 2011. "The Evolution of Media Effects Theory: A Six-Stage Model of Cumulative Research." *Communication Theory* 21 (2): 169–96. http://dx.doi.org/10.1111/j.1468-2885.2011.01381.x.

Nisbett, Richard E., and Lee Ross. 1980. *Human Inference: Strategies and Shortcomings of Social Judgment*. New York: Prentice-Hall.

Niven, David, and Jeremy Zilber. 2001. "Do Women and Men in Congress Cultivate Different Images? Evidence from Congressional Websites." *Political Communication* 18 (4): 395–405. http://dx.doi.org/10.1080/10584600152647100.

Noelle-Neumann, Elisabeth. 1973. "Return to the Concept of the Powerful Mass Media." *Studies of Broadcasting* 9: 67–112.

Nova Scotia Advisory Council on the Status of Women. 2014. *Votes for Women: A Political Guidebook*. Halifax: Government of Nova Scotia.

O'Neill, Brenda. 2009. "The Media's Role in Shaping Canadian Civic and Political Engagement." *Canadian Political Science Review* 3 (2): 105–27.

Palmer, Douglas L. 2006. "Where Reitz Is Wrong: Visible Minority Responses to the Ethnic Diversity Survey." Unpublished report. Gatineau: Canadian Heritage.

Palmer, Vaughn. 2013. "How the Liberals Schemed to Woo Ethnic Vote with Quick-Win Apologies." *Vancouver Sun*, February 28, A3.

Pateman, Carole. 1988. *The Sexual Contract*. Stanford, CA: Stanford University Press.

Pateman, Carole, and Charles Mills. 2007. *Contract and Domination*. Cambridge: Polity Press.

Patterson, Thomas. 1993. *Out of Order*. New York: Alfred A. Knopf.

Pease, Edward, Erna Smith, and Federico Subervi. 2001. *The News and Race Models of Excellence Project – Connecting Newsroom Attitudes toward Ethnicity and News Content*. St. Petersburg, FL: Poynter Institute for Media Studies.

Perigoe, Ross, and Mahmoud Eid. 2014. *Mission Invisible: Race, Religion, and News at the Dawn of the 9/11 Era*. Vancouver: UBC Press.

Philpot, Tasha S., and Hanes Walton, Jr. 2007. "One of Our Own: Black Female Candidates and the Voters Who Support Them." *American Journal of Political Science* 51 (1): 49–62. http://dx.doi.org/10.1111/j.1540-5907.2007.00236.x.

Picard, André. 2012. "Health Minister Stands by Ottawa's Role." *Globe and Mail*, August 14, A5.

Postmedia. 2014. "Governance." http://www.postmedia.com/governance-2/ (accessed May 5, 2014).

Pottie-Sherman, Yolande, and Rima Wilkes. 2014. "Good Code Bad Code: Exploring the Immigration-Nation Dialectic through Media Coverage of the Hérouxville 'Code of Life' Document." *Migration Studies* 2 (2): 189-211.

Potvin, Maryse. 2012. "Reasonable Accommodation Crisis: A State of Ethnic Relations in Contemporary Quebec." In *Managing Immigration and Diversity in Canada: A Transatlantic Dialogue in the New Age of Migration*, ed. Dan Rodríguez-García, 249–82. Montreal: McGill-Queen's University Press.

–. 2014. "The Reasonable Accommodations Crisis in Quebec: Racializing Rhetorical Devices in Media and Social Discourse." *International Journal of Canadian Studies* 50: 137-61.

Pritchard, David, and Florian Sauvageau. 1999. *Les journalistes canadiens: Un portrait de fin de siècle*. Québec: Presses de l'Université Laval.

Proudfoot, Shannon. 2008. "Campaign Snapshot." *Calgary Herald*, September 26, A5.

Putnam, Robert D. 2000. *Bowling Alone: The Collapse and Revival of American Community*. New York: Simon and Schuster. http://dx.doi.org/10.1145/358916.361990.

Pyke, Karen D. 2010. "What Is Internalized Racial Oppression and Why Don't We Study It? Acknowledging Racism's Hidden Injuries." *Sociological Perspectives* 53 (4): 551–72. http://dx.doi.org/10.1525/sop.2010.53.4.551.

Quebecor. 2012. "A Communications Giant." http://www.quebecor.com/en/content/communications-giant (accessed January 21, 2012).

–. 2015a. "Board of Directors." http://www.quebecor.com/en/quebecor/board-directors-quebecor-media (accessed May 18, 2015).

–. 2015b. "Management Committee." http://www.quebecor.com/en/quebecor/management-committee (accessed May 18, 2015).

Radwanski, Adam. 2013. "Takhar's Campaign Unabashedly Old School." *Globe and Mail*, January 21, A9.

Rakow, Lana F., and Kimberlie Kranich. 1991. "Women as Sign in Television News." *Journal of Communication* 41 (1): 8–23. http://dx.doi.org/10.1111/j.1460-2466.1991.tb02289.x.

Randall, David. 2000. *The Universal Journalist*. 2nd ed. London: Pluto.

Razack, Sherene, Malinda Smith, and Sunera Thobani, eds. 2010. *States of Race: Critical Race Feminism for the 21st Century*. Toronto: Between the Lines.

Reeves, Frank. 1983. *British Racial Discourse*. Cambridge: Cambridge University Press. http://dx.doi.org/10.1017/CBO9780511898150.

Reeves, Keith. 1997. *Voting Hopes or Fears? White Voters, Black Candidates and Racial Politics in America*. New York: Oxford University Press.

Reitz, Jeffrey, and Rupa Banerjee. 2007. "Racial Inequality, Social Cohesion and Policy Issues in Canada." In *Belonging? Diversity, Recognition and Shared Citizenship in Canada*, ed. Keith Banting, Thomas J. Courchene, and F. Leslie Seidle, 489–527. Montreal: Institute for Research on Public Policy.

Reitz, Jeffrey G., Raymond Breton, Karen Kisiel Dion, and Kenneth L. Dion. 2009. *Multiculturalism and Social Cohesion: Potentials and Challenges of Diversity*. New York: Springer. http://dx.doi.org/10.1007/978-1-4020-9958-8.

Rivlin, Gary. 1992. *Fire on the Prairie: Chicago's Harold Washington and the Politics of Race*. New York: Henry Holt.

Robinson, Gertrude, and Armande Saint-Jean. 1991. "Women Politicians and Their Media Coverage: A Generational Analysis." In *Women in Canadian Politics: Toward Equity in Representation*, ed. Kathy Megyery, 127–69. Toronto: Dundurn Press.

–. 1995. "The Portrayal of Women Politicians in the Media: Political Implications." In *Gender and Politics in Contemporary Canada*, ed. François-Pierre Gingras, 176–90. Toronto: Oxford University Press.

Rogers Media. 2015a. "About Rogers: Our Business." http://about.rogers.com/About/ Our_Business/MediaBrands.aspx (accessed May 18, 2015).

–. 2015b. "Board of Directors." http://www.rogers.com/web/ir/corp-gov/board-directors/ (accessed May 18, 2015).

–. 2015c. "Executive leadership team." http://www.rogers.com/web/ir/overview/senior -leadership (accessed May 18, 2015).

Ross, Karen. 1995. "Gender and Party Politics: How the Press Reported the Labour Leadership Campaign, 1994." *Media Culture and Society* 17 (3): 499–509. http:// dx.doi.org/10.1177/016344395017003009.

–. 2001. "Women at Work: Journalism as En-gendered Practice." *Journalism Studies* 2 (4): 531–44. http://dx.doi.org/10.1080/14616700120086404.

–. 2003. "Women Politicians and the Malestream Media: A Game of Two Sides." Occasional Paper no. 1. Belfast: Centre for Advancement of Women in Politics. http://www.qub.ac.uk/cawp/research/media.PDF.

Roth, Lorna. 1996. "Cultural and Racial Diversity in Canadian Broadcast Journalism – An Excerpt." In *Deadlines and Diversity: Journalism Ethics in a Changing World*, ed. Valerie Alia, Brian Brennan, and Barry Hoffmaster. Halifax: Fernwood.

Russell, Paul. 2011. "Readers eager to discuss, and denounce, homosexuality." *National Post*. October 1. A21.

Sampert, Shannon, and Linda Trimble. 2003. "'Wham, Bam, No Thank You Ma'am': Gender and the Game Frame in National Newspaper Coverage of Election 2000." In *Women and Electoral Politics in Canada*, ed. Manon Tremblay and Linda Trimble, 211–26. Toronto: Oxford University Press.

–. 2010a. "Mediations: Making News about Politics." In *Mediating Canadian Politics*, ed. Shannon Sampert and Linda Trimble, 1–16. Toronto: Pearson.

–, eds. 2010b. *Mediating Canadian Politics*. Toronto: Pearson.

Sanbonmatsu, Kira. 2002. "Gender Stereotypes and Vote Choice." *American Journal of Political Science* 46 (1): 20–34. http://dx.doi.org/10.2307/3088412.

–. 2006. "Do Parties Know that 'Women Win'? Party Leader Beliefs about Women's Electoral Chances." *Politics & Gender* 2: 431–50.

–. 2015. "Electing Women of Colour: The Role of Campaign Trainings." *Journal of Women, Politics & Policy* 36: 137–60.

Sayers, Anthony, and Inayat Jetha. 2002. "Ethnic Minority Politicians in Canada." Paper presented at the Annual Meeting of the Canadian Political Science Association, Toronto, May 29–31.

Schaffner, Brian, and Mark Gadson. 2004. "Reinforcing Stereotypes? Race and Local Television News Coverage of Congress." *Social Science Quarterly* 85 (3): 604–23. http://dx.doi.org/10.1111/j.0038-4941.2004.00235.x.

Schneider, Monica C. 2009. "Gender-Based Strategies on Candidate Websites." Paper presented at the Annual Meeting of the American Political Science Association, Toronto, September 3–6.

Schneider, Monica C., and Angela L. Bos. 2011. "An Exploration of the Content of Stereotypes of Black Politicians." *Political Psychology* 32 (2): 205-33.

Schudson, Michael. 1989. "The Sociology of News Production." *Media Culture and Society* 11 (3): 263-82. http://dx.doi.org/10.1177/016344389011003002.

Schwartz, Jennifer. 2011. "Framing Power: Comparing US Newspaper Visuals of Latino and Non-Latino Candidates." *Howard Journal of Communications* 22 (4): 377-93. http://dx.doi.org/10.1080/10646175.2011.617214.

Selley, Chris. 2015. "Backing Slowly into Disaster." *National Post*, March 11, A9.

Shoemaker, Pamela J. 1991. *Gatekeeping*. Newbury Park, CA: Sage.

Shoemaker, Pamela J., and Tim P. Vos. 2009. *Gatekeeping Theory*. New York: Routledge.

Shory, Devinder. 2012. "About Devinder." http://devindershory.ca/?page_id=2 (accessed December 9, 2012).

Siddiqui, Haroon. 2013. "The Double Standard in Judging Takhar." *Toronto Star*, February 7, A23.

Sigelman, Carol K., Lee Sigelman, Barbara Walkosz, and Michael Nitz. 1995. "Black Candidates, White Voters: Understanding Racial Bias in Political Perceptions." *American Journal of Political Science* 39 (1): 243-65. http://dx.doi.org/10.2307/2111765.

Sigelman, Lee, Carol K. Sigelman, and Christopher Fowler. 1987. "A Bird of a Different Feather? An Experimental Investigation of Physical Attractiveness and the Electability of Female Candidates." *Social Psychology Quarterly* 50 (1): 32-43. http://dx.doi.org/10.2307/2786888.

Simien, Evelyn M., and Rosalee A. Clawson. 2004. "The Intersection of Race and Gender: An Examination of Black Feminist Consciousness, Race Consciousness, and Policy Attitudes." *Social Science Quarterly* 85 (3): 793-810. http://dx.doi.org/10.1111/j.0038-4941.2004.00245.x.

Simpson, Jeffrey. 2008. "BC May Well Play the Role of Heart-Breaker or King-Maker in This Election." *Globe and Mail*, October 1, A21.

Smith, Vivian. 2015. *Outsiders Still: Why Women Journalists Love – and Leave – Their Newspaper Careers*. Toronto: University of Toronto Press.

Smooth, Wendy. 2006a. "African American Women and Electoral Politics: Journeying from the Shadows to the Spotlight." In *Gender and Elections: Shaping the Future of American Politics*, ed. Susan J. Carroll and Richard L. Fox, 117-42. New York: Cambridge University Press.

–. 2006b. "Intersectionality in Electoral Politics: A Mess Worth Making." *Politics and Gender* 2 (3): 400-14. http://dx.doi.org/10.1017/S1743923X06261087.

Smyth, Julie. 2006a. "Broadbent Praised from Afar." *National Post*, November 25, A8.

–. 2006b. "Tory MP's Recipe for a Good Cabinet Mix." *National Post*, December 11, A4.

Son Hing, Leanne S. 2013. "Stigmatization, Neoliberalism and Resilience." In *Social Resilience in the Neoliberal Era*, ed. Peter A. Hall and Michèle Lamont, 158-82. Cambridge: Cambridge University Press.

Sonnenshein, Raphael J. 1994. *Politics in Black and White: Race and Power in Los Angeles*. Princeton, NJ: Princeton University Press.

Soroka, Stuart N. 2002. *Agenda-setting Dynamics in Canada*. Vancouver: UBC Press.

–. 2003. "Media, Public Opinion and Foreign Policy." *Press/Politics* 8 (1): 27–48.

Soroka, Stuart, and Patrick Fournier. 2003. "Newspaper Ownership and the News." *Globe and Mail,* February 12, A17.

Speirs, Rosemary. 2000. "Chrétien's 'Cheerleader' Ruthless and Tough; When the PM Calls, David Smith Is There." *Toronto Star,* April 8, A1.

Sreberny-Mohammadi, Annabelle, and Karen Ross. 1996. "Women MPs and the Media: Representing the Body Politic." *Parliamentary Affairs* 49 (1): 103–15. http://dx.doi.org/10.1093/oxfordjournals.pa.a028661.

Statistics Canada. 2007. *2006 Census Dictionary.* Catalogue 92–566-XWE. Ottawa: Statistics Canada.

Status of Women Canada. 2013. "Gender-Based Analysis Plus." http://www.swc-cfc.gc.ca/gba-acs/course-cours/eng/mod00/mod00_01_01.php (accessed May 18, 2015).

Swain, Carol M. 1995. *Black Face, Black Interest: The Representation of African Americans in Congress.* Cambridge, MA: Harvard University Press.

Taber, Jane. 2003. "You There, Stand Up and Be Counted!" *Globe and Mail,* June 7, A4.

–. 2007. "Fry Doth Protest Too Much, Tory Insider Says." *Globe and Mail,* December 1, A10.

–. 2009. "10 Things You Should Know about Ruby Dhalla." *Globe and Mail,* May 16, F3.

–. 2010. "Women Stepping Up to the Podium, but Falling Down in the Political Arena." *Globe and Mail,* February 27, A8.

–. 2011. "Uppal Takes a Spin at Enabling Harper's Reform Agenda." *Globe and Mail,* November 5.

Taras, David. 1990. *The Newsmakers: The Media's Influence on Canadian Politics.* Scarborough, ON: Nelson.

Tasko, Patti, ed. 2006. *The Canadian Press Stylebook.* 14th ed. Toronto: Canadian Press.

Terkildsen, Nayda, and David F. Damore. 1999. "The Dynamics of Racialized Media Coverage in Congressional Elections." *Journal of Politics* 61 (3): 680–99. http://dx.doi.org/10.2307/2647823.

Thobani, Sunera. 2007. *Exalted Subjects: Studies in the Making of Race and Nation in Canada.* Toronto: University of Toronto Press.

Thomas, Melanee, and Lisa Lambert. 2013. "Private Mom vs. Political Dad? Communications of Parental Status in the 41st Canadian Parliament." Paper presented at the Annual Meeting of the Canadian Political Science Association, Edmonton, AB, June 5.

Thompson, Allan. 1993. "New Metro MPs a Better Mirror of Canada's Increased Ethnic Mix." *Toronto Star,* October 27, A7.

Thompson, Debra. 2008. "Is Race Political?" *Canadian Journal of Political Science* 41 (3): 525–47. http://dx.doi.org/10.1017/S0008423908080827.

–. 2014. "The Comparative Study of Race: Census Politics in Canada, the United States, and Great Britain." In *Comparing Canada: Methods and Perspectives on Canadian Politics,* ed. Martin Papillon, Luc Turgeon, Jennifer Wallner, and Stephen White, 73-94. Vancouver: UBC Press.

Thomson, Graham. 2014. "Walking a Tightrope: Brian Bowman Is Winnipeg's First Métis Mayor, Taking Over a City Roiled by Violence against Aboriginals." *National Post,* November 22, A8.

Timson, Judith. 2009. "Drama on the Rideau: The Truth Is out There." *Globe and Mail,* May 19, L1.

Tolley, Erin. 2003. "Political Processes and the Intersections of Diversity." Unpublished paper. Metropolis Project, Ottawa. http://www.canada.metropolis.net/events/ Diversity/Challenge_Papers/Political_Processes_e.doc (accessed August 2, 2015).

–. 2013. "Partisan Players or Political Pawns? Immigrants, Minorities and Conservatives in Canada." Paper presented at the Annual Meeting of the Atlantic Provinces Political Science Association, Charlottetown, PE, October 5.

–. 2014. "Media and Mayoralty: Race Matters." *Winnipeg Free Press,* October 28, A9.

–. 2015. "Racial Mediation in the Coverage of Candidates' Political Viability: A Comparison of Approaches." *Journal of Ethnic and Migration Studies* 41 (6): 963–84.

Tolley, Erin, and Elizabeth Goodyear-Grant. 2014. "Experimental Evidence on Race and Gender Affinity Effects in Candidate Choice." Paper presented at the Annual Meeting of the Canadian Political Science Association, St. Catharines, ON, May 29 (accessed August 2, 2015).

Toronto Star. 2011. "Newsroom Policy and Journalistic Standards Guide." http://www. thestar.com/opinion/public_editor/2011/12/07/toronto_star_newsroom_policy _and_journalistic_standards_guide.html (accessed July 25, 2014).

Tossutti, Livianna S., and Tom Pierre Najem. 2002. "Minorities and Elections in Canada's Fourth Party System: Macro and Micro Constraints and Opportunities." *Canadian Ethnic Studies* 34 (1): 85–111.

Toulin, Alan. 1999. "Not All Government MPs Like Tax Cuts for High Earners." *National Post,* February 2, A7.

Travers, James. 2002. "PM Sends Message on Ethical Issues." *Toronto Star,* January 16, A21.

Trimble, Linda. 2005. "Who Framed Belinda Stronach? National Newspaper Coverage of the Conservative Party of Canada's 2004 Leadership Race. Paper presented at the Annual Meeting of the Canadian Political Science Association, London, ON, June 4.

–. 2007. "Gender, Political Leadership and Media Visibility: *Globe and Mail* Coverage of Conservative Party of Canada Leadership Contests." *Canadian Journal of Political Science* 40 (4): 976–93. http://dx.doi.org/10.1017/S0008423907071120.

Trimble, Linda, and Natasja Treiberg. 2008. "Xenas and Samurai Swords: News Framing of Male and Female Prime Ministers in Canada and New Zealand." Paper presented at the International Studies Association Annual Conference, San Francisco, March 26.

Tuchman, Gaye. 1978. *Making News: A Study in the Construction of Reality.* New York: Free Press.

Tversky, Amos, and Daniel Kahneman. 1974. "Judgment under Uncertainty: Heuristics and Biases." *Science* 185 (4157): 1124–31. http://dx.doi.org/10.1126/science.185. 4157.1124.

United Nations. 2007. *Report of the Committee on the Elimination of Racial Discrimination.* New York: United Nations.

Unkelbach, Christian, Joseph P. Forgas, and Thomas F. Denson. 2008. "The Turban Effect: The Influence of Muslim Headgear and Induced Affect on Aggressive Responses in the Shooter Bias Paradigm." *Journal of Experimental Social Psychology* 44 (5): 1409–13. http://dx.doi.org/10.1016/j.jesp.2008.04.003.

Vallis, Mary. 2006. "Chinatown May Say 'Chow' to Ianno: Voters Balk at Liberal Gaffes." *National Post,* January 7, A4.

Van Dijk, Teun A. 1991. *Racism and the Press.* New York: Routledge.

Van Gorp, Baldwin. 2010. "Strategies to Take Subjectivity Out of Framing Analysis." In *Doing News Framing Analysis: Empirical and Theoretical Perspectives,* ed. Paul D'Angelo and Jim A. Kuypers, 84–109. New York: Routledge.

van Zoonen, Liesbet. 1998. "One of the Girls? The Changing Gender of Journalism." In *News, Gender and Power,* ed. Cynthia Carter, Gill Branston, and Stuart Allen, 33–46. New York: Routledge.

–. 2006. "The Personal, the Political and the Popular: A Woman's Guide to Celebrity Politics." *Journal of Cultural Studies* 9 (3): 287–301. http://dx.doi.org/10.1177/1367549406066074.

Vancouver Province. 2008. "Cadman Denies Gag." September 26, A14.

Vickers, Jill. 2002. "No Place for 'Race'? Why Pluralist Theory Fails to Explain the Politics of 'Race' in 'New Societies." In *The Challenge of Cultural Pluralism,* ed. Stephen Brooks, 15–38. Westport, CT: Praeger.

Ward, Doug. 2008. "10 Races to Care About." *Vancouver Sun.* September 13. A5.

Ward, Doug, and Tim Lai. 2008. "I'm Protecting the Middle Class, Harper Says; NDP Leader Jack Layton Takes Aim at Former Foreign Affairs Minister David Emerson." *Vancouver Sun,* September 9, A4.

Weaver, David. 1997. "Women as Journalists." In *Women, Media and Politics,* ed. Pippa Norris, 21–40. New York: Oxford University Press.

Wells, Paul. 2001. "How Stock Happens." *National Post,* April 28, B1.

Wente, Margaret. 2009. "The Many Woes of Ruby Dhalla." *Globe and Mail,* May 12, A17.

Werder, Olaf H. 2009. "Media Effects Theories." In *Encyclopedia of Communication Theory,* ed. Stephen W. Littlejohn and Karen A. Foss, 633–36. Thousand Oaks, CA: Sage. http://dx.doi.org/10.4135/9781412959384.n235.

White, David Manning. 1950. "The 'Gate Keeper': A Case Study in the Selection of News." *Journalism Quarterly* 27: 383–90.

Wilkes, Jim. 2008. "Tory Insider Tries Again; A Tight Race for Dechert against Liberal Incumbent in Riding Once Owned by Maverick Carolyn Parrish." *Toronto Star,* October 15, U11.

Williams, Linda. 1989. "White/Black Perceptions of the Electability of Black Political Candidates." *National Political Science Review* 2: 45–64.

Wilson, Ernest J., III, and Lorrie A. Frasure. 2007. "Still at the Margins: The Persistence of Neglect of African American Issues in Political Science, 1986–2003." In *African American Perspectives on Political Science,* ed. Wilbur Rich, 7–23. Philadelphia: Temple University Press.

Wilson, V. Seymour. 1993. "The Tapestry Vision of Canadian Multiculturalism." *Canadian Journal of Political Science* 26 (4): 645–69. http://dx.doi.org/10.1017/S0008423900000421.

Winsor, Hugh. 1999. "The Power Game: Profiting from the Taxing Issue of Family Values." *Globe and Mail,* March 12, A11.

–. 2004. "Redressing BC's Democratic Deficit." *Globe and Mail,* May 17, A4.

Winter, James. 1997. *Democracy's Oxygen: How the Corporations Control the News.* Montreal: Black Rose Books.

Wood, Patricia Burke, and Scot Wortley. 2010. "AlieNation: Racism, Injustice and Other Obstacles to Full Citizenship." CERIS Working Paper 78. Toronto: CERIS–Ontario Metropolis Centre.

Worthington, Peter. 2012. "NDP MP Should Know Country's Basic Facts." *Toronto Sun,* February 15, http://www.torontosun.com/2012/02/15/ndp-mp-should-know-countrys-basic-facts#disqus_thread (accessed September 15, 2012).

Young, Scott. 2008. "The Mosaic Loses to Segregation: Ethnic Minorities Have Little Motivation to Join Mainstream Canada, Preferring the Balkanization They Find." *Vancouver Sun*, February 13, A13.

Yu, Sherry, and Daniel Ahadi. 2010. "Promoting Civic Engagement through Ethnic Media." *PLATFORM: Journal of Media and Communication* 2 (2): 54–71.

Yuen, Nancy Wang. 2009. "The Asian American Vote: The Role of Race in News Media Coverage of the 2008 Democratic Primaries." *Journal of Civil Rights and Economic Development* 24 (2): 421–24.

Zilber, Jeremy, and David Niven. 2000. *Racialized Coverage of Congress: The News in Black and White.* Westport, CT: Praeger.

Index

Printed and bound in Canada by Friesens

Set in Scala and Minion by Artegraphica Design Co. Ltd.

Copy editor: Sarah Wight

Proofreader: Hazel Boydell

Indexer: Christine Jacobs